WASYL NIMENKO

GW01090471

Wasyl Nimenko's fath

eastern Ukraine and his mother was from the west of Ireland O'Dowd clan who commissioned the Yellow Book of Lecan in 1391. Although he spent extensive periods of time in the west of Ireland he was educated in Suffolk at St Joseph's College in Ipswich. He worked as a labourer, kitchen porter, doorman, store man, van driver, waiter, barman, tent erector and as a freezer man in a factory before studying medicine in London.

He studied psychiatry at Oxford and in London but switched to train as a psychotherapist and general practitioner. He worked extensively with the Armed Forces and the homeless and was one of the first medical doctors and psychotherapists in the UK in 1982 to work with survivors of torture as well as with the NYPD in New York after 9/11.

He has written in depth about Carl Jung, the East and Ramana Maharshi. In 1984 he researched stress in women using futuristic computer technology. He researched the use of archaeology in the psychological decompression of wounded soldiers in 2011 and in 2013 described Post Repatriation Stress Disorder. Books he has written include Invisible Bullets, Searching in Secret India, Searching in Secret New Zealand and Australia, Searching in Secret Ukraine and Searching in Secret Orkney. Wasyl has lived in India, New Zealand and Australia but now lives in Gloucestershire in England.

WASYL NIMENKO

SEARCHING IN SECRET ORKNEY

SEARCHING IN SECRET ORKNEY

Published in Great Britain 2015

Copyright © Wasyl Nimenko 2015

The right of Wasyl Nimenko to be identified as the author of this work has been asserted in accordance with the Copyright, Designs and Patents act 1988.

Also by Wasyl Nimenko

INVISIBLE BULLETS

SEARCHING IN SECRET NEW ZEALAND
AND AUSTRALIA

SEARCHING IN SECRET UKRAINE

SEARCHING IN SECRET INDIA

Photographs and other mulitmedia items are available to view free on www.wasylnimenko.org

Religion is for people who are scared of going to hell
Spirituality is for people who have been there.

(Anon)

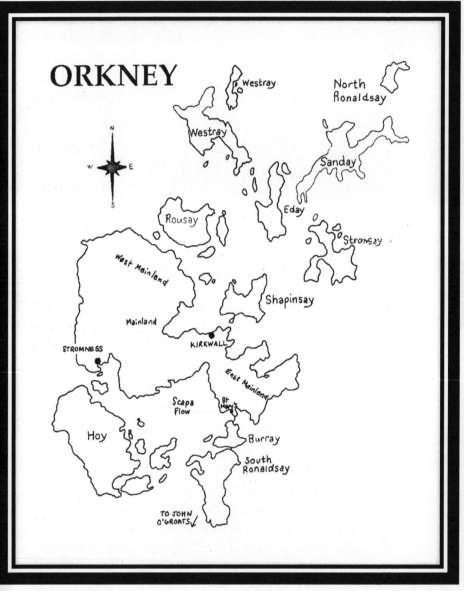

ORKNEY

Chapter 1.

Locum One - Mainland Orkney, South Ronaldsay and Burray Island

We had spent two years travelling ... moving on, sometimes resting sometimes just looking for a place to live. After this we felt the need to settle. Two years in India, Australia and New Zealand had left us in no doubt that Britain was home. We came back in to England and made London our temporary base.

I had worked as a psychotherapist and a single handed GP for fifteen years. But I had given up the idea of permanancey and I was now registered with an agency as a locum GP. I wanted short-term jobs; I didn't want to be locked in by a contract, working full time with other doctors. I decided that I would rather have less job security than be in a job getting ordered around or, worse, getting embroiled in internal politics. Our daughter India had been born four years ago and was now in primary school. This was an ideal time to do locum work.

Within an hour of being home from my first job, I got a phone call from one of the six locum agencies I had enrolled with but hadn't worked with yet.

'It's Jo from BS Locums. Are you available?'

'Just happen to be at the moment. What've you got?'

'Well, would you mind working away from home?'

'I'd rather work closer to home. I've just finished a job in Kent, three hours away.'

'Oh ... this is a little further.'

'How much?'

'North Ronaldsay.'

'Never heard of it. Where is it?

'North of Kirkwall.'

'Haven't heard of that either. Where's that?'

'North Ronaldsay is the most northern part of Orkney.'

'Orkney … now that sounds exciting. When's the job and for how long?'

'It starts in two weeks, with two weeks in South Ronaldsay and two weeks in North Ronaldsay. There's a five-day break in between. The work might be extended for a few more weeks.'

'Hold on while I run this by my wife.' I had been talking aloud and Chrisie had heard everything.

'We can both come up and stay,' she said as she nodded with an enthusiastic smile. 'School won't mind. It would be educational and a holiday for a few weeks.'

'I'll do both, but I'll need to bring my wife and daughter up halfway through,' I said to Jo from BS Locums.

'I'm sure that won't be a problem. We can probably help with their fares. I'll send you an e-mail with the details. All travel costs and accommodation are paid for by the Health Board, and you have a free car with petrol included.' And with this I was psychologically already on my way to Orkney.

'What sort of accommodation is it?'

'In South Ronaldsay you will be staying on Mainland Orkney in a chalet. In North Ronaldsay the GP usually sorts out the accommodation for the Health Board. Or you can sort it out when you are up there.'

'Well, as long as we can stay somewhere which is self-catering, I'll be happy to do the locum.'

'I'll e-mail you the doctor's details, and you can check it out with him. Is it OK to leave it with you?'

'It sounds really good to me.'

'Your flights will be arranged today, and I'll e-mail you

the details and where to go when you get to Kirkwall. If there are any worries at any time, just call me. I hope you have a good trip.'

Later that morning I received my itinerary and the GP's phone number in North Ronaldsay. On the internet I found information about North Ronaldsay and about the local school. Because it was still going to be term time, my daughter India, who was only four, was going to have to spend two weeks away from her own school, and her own school might be happier about releasing her if she was going to be at another school during her usual term time. I gave the headmistress in North Ronaldsay a call and she was very happy to welcome her as a guest pupil for the two weeks. When I asked if I could take anything up there for them, she said that they had everything any other school had, except seeds for trees. I promised to take up as many seeds as I could find before we left.

I wanted to make sure that Chrisie and India would be comfortable being in Orkney whilst I was working, and I wanted to make sure the accommodation was what we would all be happy with, so I made a call to the GP's surgery to find out what was available.

'Are you the GP?' I asked the voice at the other end of the telephone line.

'Yes, I'm the doctor in North Ronaldsay.' I had expected a Scottish person to answer the phone, but, unexpectedly, he had a clipped English accent.

'I'm coming up to do your locum in four weeks time. I'm just ringing to find out about accommodation, as I'm bringing my wife and daughter up with me. My daughter is going to the local school and my wife is studying, so we want somewhere which is self-catering and quiet.'

'Well the locum usually stays with us in the Bird

Observatory.'

'I saw the Bird Observatory on the internet, but we wanted something self-catering, where it would be quiet.'

'There are no self-catering places on the island.'

'We would prefer to rent a cottage if there are any.'

'The only suitable accommodation is at the Bird Observatory. We provide accommodation and food. Your B&B is paid for by the Health Board, but there would be a charge for your wife's B&B.'

'How much will it be for her to stay?' I asked.

'We'll work something out.'

'Can you give me some idea?'

'Don't worry, we'll work something out,' he said. And I left it at that. He was being helpful and I didn't want to push too far.

'Is there a hotel or shop?' I asked.

'There's no hotel; there's a small shop, but it doesn't sell much. It opens twice a week for an hour. We have everything you'll need.'

'And transport?'

'Don't worry, you can use our car.' And with this, and taking him at his word, I agreed that I would see him at the airport in four weeks time. I was a bit uncomfortable about not being independent of the GP because of having to stay in his accommodation. I felt a possible loss of freedom and promised myself to look into this in more detail when I got up there during the first locum post.

Two weeks later I was on the 6.50 a.m. flight from Southampton to Edinburgh with a connecting flight via Inverness to Kirkwall, the capital of the Orkneys. I couldn't see Inverness through the window, either on landing or take-off. Maybe Inverness is a small place, or perhaps I was just sitting on the wrong side of the plane, but before now I had somehow thought that Inverness was a big city. As we left the airport I could see a bright yellow Air Ambulance helicopter, which made me hope that I wouldn't have to deal with any big emergencies and be in need of it. I was confident enough for routine GP work, but big serious stuff still made me nervous … and I still don't like the sight of blood.

Anyway, whilst I was still wondering what happened to Inverness and if I would ever see it, I noticed that I seemed to be holding on rather tightly to the seat in front of me. I think I spotted a couple of the other passengers looking at me pityingly, as if they knew I was a nervous passenger. I was. It had been a very quick half-an-hour flight, but I now noticed there was a nasty cross wind hitting the plane as the pilot tried to get the wheels on the ground on Mainland Orkney. The starboard side was being lifted time and time again, and I wondered if he would have to abort the landing and come in a bit more forcefully. But no, he got the wheels down just before he ran out of concrete … and before I ran out of nerves.

I was waiting in the main airport lounge for my single case to appear when an announcement came over the public address system for me to go to the information desk. I went up to the desk and introduced myself to a young man who had been looking at me since I entered the rather small but modern terminal.

'Got your car,' he said.

'Oh thanks. The agency said they would get me a small car, but I pointed out I was six foot two.'

'Yes, they've got you a bigger one. It's a reasonable size, but it's a bit thirsty. Wants to turn left at every garage.'

'Well, I'm glad the fuel is free,' I said. And within ten minutes, he had whisked me away in his Vauxhall towards his family garage in the centre of Kirkwall. As he drove down to Kirkwall I could see it was very small with a circular bay. There were no tall buildings, and it looked and felt like a small, remote outpost of civilization. There were three small, tough looking fishing boats in the bay, but I couldn't see anything else moving. There was no traffic and no people about. There was a desolate feel about the place, but I carried within me an expectation of a happy life here, which I thought would compensate for it.

When I had finished inspecting the car and signed the hire document, he handed me the keys. I asked, 'Where's the map?'

'What map?' he asked, puzzled.

'The Health Authority said there would be a map for me.'

'Not here. Must be at the Health Authority.'

I felt disorientated and a little anxious. It was winter and mid-afternoon; the sun was beginning to set, and it would soon be dark. I didn't know where my accommodation was, or the hospital, or the Health Authority, and I was meant to be on call in less than three hours at six o'clock.

Eventually, I followed his difficult directions and found myself outside the surgery, which is part of the local hospital complex, and discovered the Heath Authority which was situated across the road from the hospital. The entrance to the surgery consisted of two sets of electrically powered doors. The first opened automatically, but I couldn't work out how to get past the second set of doors. The hinges on the inside indicated that they opened inwards, but there was no electric button in sight. The key to the hire car looked like it was chunky enough to prise the doors open without any damage, but the doors were shut fast. I gave up and went back outside for help.

'Is there some trick to opening these doors?' I was embarrassed and asked a pleasant, smiling, fair haired young Scottish woman in her mid-thirties.

'You just press the button,' she said, but I still couldn't see a button.

'Where is it?' I asked.

'Under here.' And sure enough, hidden under a set of three shelves, there was a small button which I was too tall to see.

I wandered around for a couple of minutes until the same woman appeared through a door and asked, 'Can I help?'

'I'm looking for the office manager, the practice manager?'

'That'll be me.'

'Oh it's you!' and for the second time, I felt a bit foolish in front of this pleasant woman.

'Come with me and I'll give you all you need.' And I followed her to her desk at the back of the practice. 'You'll need these maps.'

'There are six maps here,' I said, after had I counted them. 'Why six?'

'Yes. The Mainland, The West Mainland, the East Mainland, The Southern Isles, one of all the islands just in case, and one of Kirkwall. Oh, and there's one of Stromness Town on the back. You shouldn't be called up that far, but you never know around here.

'I didn't know Kirkwall is a city?'

'Oh yes, we've got a cathedral.' This surprised me, as I couldn't imagine why such a very northerly group of islands would have one.

'Am I covering all of these areas?' I was really surprised at the extent of the patch I was covering. It was a huge area.

'Well, yes, all except the west and north of the mainland.'

'I was told I was covering two practices but not exactly the area they covered.'

'Don't worry, you'll be fine. This is the first time this locum agency has ever covered the out-of-hours shifts. Weekends, the shift starts at six o'clock on Friday evening and finishes at nine o'clock Monday morning. You're the test pilot and basically here to troubleshoot and see if it works.'

'Sounds reasonable. But the agency didn't say I was the first GP to do this.' There were some very dodgy doctors and shenanigans in my last locum in Kent, and although I felt this was going to be a breeze, I wasn't going to be over confident about there not being any trouble ... just in case.

'All the information you need is in the pack,' the young woman said reassuringly, for I was clearly looking aghast at the size of the area. 'Don't worry, you'll get used to it in no time at all. And you'll need this bag of drugs, this bag of disposables and this pad of prescriptions. Oh, and lastly, here are some hints and wrinkles about the medical services. The GPs who've just given up doing this work say it's a quiet job and you probably won't be called out most of the time.'

'Thanks for that. I wasn't sure if I was going to be up all night driving around from one person's house to the next.'

'Definitely not.'

'Where's St Mary's Holm? It's where I'm staying.'

'No bother.' This sounded like a local term I had not come across before. 'You turn right out of here. Follow the road around to the left, then to the right, past the distillery, straight on for six miles, past some road-works where there are temporary traffic lights, and it's just past the post office before a windmill, which you'll see is across the first Churchill Barrier.' This sounded like an impossibly difficult place to find.

'What's the first Barrier?' I asked.

'They're kind of bridges and really called Churchill Barriers. They were built whilst Churchill was Prime Minister. The Italian prisoners of war who built the chapel built these around the same time. They connect the four southern islands. Churchill Barrier No 1 connects the southern tip of Mainland Orkney to Lamb Holm, which is connected to Glimps Holm by Churchill Barrier No 2. Below Glimps Holm is Churchill Barrier No 3, which connects it to Burray, which is connected to South Ronaldsay by Churchill Barrier No 4.'

'So my chalet is before Churchill Barrier No 1?'

'That's it. Richard will take care of you and show you the chapel.'

'Who's Richard and what's with the chapel thing?'

'Wait until you see it. It's one of the island's treasures.'

'Thanks for all your help.' I was mystified, confused, overloaded with information and basically totally lost. I was also very tired, as I had been travelling for over nine hours. It was the feeling of having profound jet lag even though I had not travelled across time zones.

'I'll see you at nine in the morning for you to hand over the maps and any notes you've made about patients, and to restock the drug bag if you use any drugs. Oh, and here's your phone and the emergency pager, and there's a land line at the chalet. And this is the spare phone which uses another network. There are also two different phone chargers.'

'Do the cell phones work everywhere?'

'No, but the bleep does, so always carry it with you, even in the bathroom. You wouldn't want to be missing any calls now.' No pressure then, I thought.

I stuffed all of these into my pockets and swaggered out the door with a case in each hand and the maps under my arm. I had my own phone, the practice phone, a spare phone, a land line and a pager. If they wanted to get hold of me there was no escape.

I was soon miles down the road heading towards St Mary's Holm. It was a very picturesque island. The temperature of thirteen degrees centigrade was the best on record since temperatures began being recorded. The old buildings were brownstone and the more modern ones were all brown or grey pebbledash.

The directions were actually very good. The Highland Park Distillery was on the left as she had said and, sure enough, six miles down the road was St Mary's Holm. As I emptied the car of the medical equipment and my suitcase, and tried to lock the car, a man appeared from one of the chalets. He had been waiting for me and laughed as the complicated key failed several times to lock the car. He looked about sixty-five.

'Afternoon. I'm Richard.'

'Hi, I'm the doc. Looks like a Second World War Nissen hut,' I said, pointing towards an old Nissen hut in the paddock next to the chalet.

'That Nissen hut is where they made all the concrete blocks for the Barriers,' he said in what seemed like a soft Welsh accent.

'Are you from Wales?'

'Good heavens, no. Born and bred here.'

'That's odd your accent sounds just like a Welsh one.'

'Lots of people get our accent confused with the Welsh. Orkney's link was only with Scandinavia until 1468 when we became part of Scotland. So it's only recently that we've been exposed to anything Gaelic. The Pentland Firth kept us separate from Scotland until then.'

I could see the huge yard-square concrete blocks he was

talking about, lining the barrier all the way on either side of the road to the small island.

'Is that Land Holm? I asked

'Ham.'

'Sorry. What do you mean?'

'It's how you pronounce the word Holm.'

'Oh, I see. Thanks. I see it's kind of an empty island then?'

'Yes. The blocks were made just over there,' he said, pointing again to the old Nissen hut. They built the chapel as well.'

'Yes, someone mentioned it and said it's a sight to see.'

'Definitely worth spending some time in. Now let me show you around.' And with that, Chalet No 4 was unlocked. I looked out the windows … and what a view. I could see the sea, the sun setting over it with the Italian chapel to the left and a windmill in the foreground, all less than half a mile away

I took a few breaths. 'Clear air here,' I said.

'Not a bad view either,' he said. You're the only visitor now, so you've got the whole place to yourself. And you've got a double and a single room because your wife and daughter are coming to stay as well.'

'Yes, at the end of next week. Then we're up to North Ron.'

'Well, that's a bit different up there.'

'How do you mean?'

'They're hardier to stand it up there. The weather can be harsh here, but up there it's too much to bear. Where are you staying up there?'

'Oh, there's only the doctor's.'

'I was up there once, and I thought there were several places to stay.'

'Really? That's not what I heard from the doctor or the agency. I might have to re-check that.'

'You should all have a good time. We're short of doctors. No one wants to stay here for long. Don't know why. It's a great place.'

'I agree, but it's just too far for some I guess, away from friends and families.'

'It's a certain type who loves it here,' he said as he left. 'Hope you like it.'

'Many thanks.'

I began to unpack. I put all three phones on charge to make sure that they were fully charged by six o'clock. I kept an eye on my watch because I needed some food; my time on call from six in the evening was looming, and I was on call all night. First I had to get some provisions then read the eighty pages of information from the Health Authority.

At the local shop, which was the post office, garage, butcher, fishmonger, coal supplier, hardware shop and just about any kind of shop you can imagine, all in one, I bought the unhealthiest but most easy-to-cook meal I could ever imagine. A pie in a circular tin together with oven chips, which went straight into the oven. Things were going well so far; I had managed to get some food for my first meal.

The first page of my reading material was about Air Ambulance transfers. There were three categories of transfer: emergencies were transferred within three hours, very urgent within six hours and urgent within nine hours. They had to come from Aberdeen to get any casualties, which was arranged by telephoning the Air Desk at Kirkwall Airport.

The next seventy-nine pages described the size and facilities at the local hospital. It had two surgeons and two anesthetists and was run by the GPs. One anxiety provoking page described what to do in the event of one of the thirty diving injuries they have each year. The document said that there was a decompression chamber in a town called Stromness about half an hour away.

At the hospital there were all the usual facilities like a physiotherapist, X-ray and a laboratory, but I noticed that the doctors had to be good Generalists and able to work in the hospital as well as working in one of the practices. With my training in psychotherapy I began to wonder if I had perhaps picked the most challenging locum post for me. I read that there was also a cancer ward, an obstetric ward, a dietician, an occupational therapist and a pharmacy, and I felt as though they had very good facilities for most things, and I probably wouldn't be evacuating any patients to Aberdeen.

Lastly, there was the Major Incident Response Plan which I attempted to commit to memory. The definition of a major incident was, "Any incident where the location, number, severity or type of live casualties requires extraordinary resources." There was a footnote adding that this may only be three or four people from a road traffic accident. This was unusual and probably would only occur on an island where there was not enough back up. It was an excellent plan as far as any I had ever seen, and I was quite pleased because I was in the fifth category of person to be called in, just before the on-call porter and engineer.

Before my first shift began in Orkney, I decided to check with the Health Board about the accommodation in North Ronaldsay, as I seemed to have been misinformed. I got through to the head of personnel. 'I'm the locum going up to North Ronaldsay soon. Can you tell me if there is any self-catering accommodation in North Ronaldsay?'

'The only accommodation we know about there is at

the doctor's house.'

'Are you sure? One of the GPs I've just spoken about the work there said there were self-catering places, and to ask you.'

'I've never been, but you could check with the doctor up there.'

'OK, thanks anyway.' I decided to give him another call over the next few days.

Just before six o'clock, I had read all of the pages and checked the medical bags so I was familiar with their contents. I walked outside to look at the sky and see what the view was like. I had such a strange feeling. It was at first eerie, as if I wasn't alone, but I looked around and there was no one. I listened and looked around again, and in the gathering darkness I could see the Nissen hut, the sea and the sky, but what was most prominent in my senses was an awareness of something behind the sound of the wind which was interspersed with silence. It was like something calling from somewhere else, like the ancient purpose of this place, whatever that had been. I ignored it, but I had distinctly heard it.

I sat down to eat my pie and chips, and with the first mouthful of food still on my fork the electrics all went dead. At five past six I remembered what Richard had mentioned about the meter, and I fumbled in my pocket for a pound coin and remembered the last time I had done this in the '70s, in a flat in Notting Hill Gate. It used to be a shilling, but now it was twenty shillings.

The difference is that here you put the money in the meter, and when you are due to leave they empty the meter and give the money back to you. It's merely there to allow the owner of the chalet to monitor how much electricity the locum used in order to reclaim it back from the Health Authority.

'Nothing too weird so far,' I thought to myself, but I couldn't remember in the dark where the meter was. I thought it was in the main room, but I couldn't feel anything high up on the walls. I tried the hall and found the meter just behind the front door. It took me a while to find the slot for the one-pound coin and, when I did, I left six more coins on top of the meter and swore to remind myself to get more in the morning.

Chapter 2.

Mainland Orkney, South Ronaldsay and Burray
Island. Day 2

I was up at four thirty in the morning and wanted to see the sun rise. It rose at seven, slowly and beautifully, bursting into the room. There was one call at five past seven in the morning. It was an obese woman with recurrent abdominal pain, and I said she needed to be seen at the surgery, as this did not warrant a home visit at that time of the morning. It seemed like it was just a weight problem, as she weighed more than 120 kilograms. She seemed happy with my advice, and that was it for the first night. I boiled an egg, peeled an orange and drank some coffee.

During and after breakfast the sound of the wind on the windows made me keep getting up and wandering around the room to look at the different magnificent views from each of the windows, which all overlooked the sea.

The sense of solitude expanded, almost as if it filled not just the whole room but also the nooks and crannies of the rocks and seaweed I could see in front of me across the road. I couldn't help enjoying feeling calm in this stress free environment as opposed to working in a suburban town like Gillingham, where I had done the last locum.

I was happy to have chosen not to earn more money and have more security in a long term job as a doctor with all sorts of organizational, administrative, staff, financial and political problems, but to be a locum instead. I was acutely aware that this job was transient, but I saw everything as transient in life. I had more faith in fate being in control than believing in a pension being around when I needed it, so I had not bought into that system. I didn't like the thought of worrying about it for thirty years and then maybe being let down by two things: first, I might die before I got it and, second, it might be worth nothing whilst I was alive to claim it. It was a gamble which involved a lot of thinking which I couldn't be bothered with. I was always acutely aware that I could be wrong and live to regret being old and poor, but, at the same time, I always satisfied myself with the counter-balance of this being better than rich and dead. This choice was beginning to become clearer the older I got, because the result was getting nearer.

At 8.30 pm, at the end of my first Orcadian shift, I left the chalet to see the practice office manager back in Kirkwall to hand over the meagre information about the single call I had received. She was just as friendly as the afternoon before, and she told me to enjoy the day, as it was going to be sunny and warm, which I took to be unusual.

Whilst I was talking to her she introduced me to a very pleasant Australian GP called Peter, who was covering the emergencies during the day at the practice and at the hospital. This was his fifth year coming here for five weeks at a time. He said he tried working on the mainland, but it was not as interesting as the islands. He made a few suggestions for trips for me to do on empty days. He suggested going up to the north-west of the island. He said there were some old houses, a causeway and a tomb, which were all worth looking at. He circled them on a map and said to have a good time and make the most of this unusual weather and enjoy it.

Five minutes later I was on my way. I didn't have to be back until six in the evening, and so I had nine hours to explore the three things he had suggested.

I had an Ordnance Survey map of all of Orkney, but I'd left all my other maps and unread tourist guide in the chalet, and I couldn't be bothered to do a twelve-mile round trip to collect them. So I was going blind with only a basic map and the information he gave me. This seemed more fun than looking things up in a guide book.

My first target for the day was a place circled on the map called Skara Brae. It seemed to be about ten minutes north of Stromness on the west coast of the Mainland Orkney, or West Mainland as it is known. I thought I would stop there and have a snack breakfast. However, on the way I noticed a sign saying "Stone Circles", but I thought I would stick to my plan of circling the island clockwise starting with the west.

It seemed like this beautiful island was deserted of any traffic as I traveled west towards Stromness. I could see the lochs and the sea almost all of the time on the easy drive. I passed a tractor and saw a man in a car coming the other way. I was a little hungry as I drove into Stromness, and I began to look out for a café. Stromness is tucked away like a self-contained Cornish fishing village. Straight away I came across a café which sold homemade pies. A cheese and mushroom pie and a bottle of water seemed like a good snack. I stood there on the jetty, eating my pie and looking at a ferry loading up. Next to me was a fifty-plus year old man in an old oilskin, also eating a pie.

'Can't understand everyone saying the weather would be so bad up here,' I said.

'It's good now, and we have some very mild winters because of the Gulf Stream, but those days might be numbered by global warming. It can get very rough here. What are you doing up here this time of year?'

'Just standing in for a medic for a few weeks. I can't believe this place is so warm. And yourself?'

'I fish. Can be pretty bad. It's been known for a long time as a haven for ships seeking shelter from Atlantic storms.

The old well's been very good to the island.'

'How do you mean?'

'We're best known for two things, being a safe haven from storms for all kinds of ships and commercial boats, from pirates to the enemy in war time; and, of course, for our water from Login's Well. Captain Cook's Discovery was supplied here with water from the well.'

'I had no idea that he came here.'

'Well, technically he didn't come here himself, because he was dead at the time. It was on the return journey that the Discovery stopped here.'

'Still, didn't know it was an important watering hole,' I said.

'The Hudson Bay Company's ships used it from 1670 until 1891 on their way up to Arctic Canada.'

'Then, of course, there was the famous navigator from the Hudson Bay Company, Dr. John Rae, who mapped out a lot of the Arctic. He watered his boats here in 1845. He discovered the North-west Passage between the Atlantic and the Pacific, and also found the frozen remains of another explorer's forty sailors who had committed cannibalism. They were on an expedition with Sir John Franklin who had disappeared. When he got back to England the establishment, including Charles Dickens, didn't believe his story of the expedition ending in cannibalism, and he was sidelined and worked as a doctor in London. He's buried in the cathedral here.'

'Yes, I'm hoping to see that tomorrow.'

'Like Dr. Rae, many of us have worked for the company in the past as labourers and ten of us have even worked as Governors of the company. I worked up there for a bit, but I missed the family. Problem is we neglected the land.'

'Is there much to see here?' I asked.

'There's only Login's Well on the Main Street and the quoys.'

'What are the quoys?'

'They're the strange houses with private piers, which wind along the shoreline. Most of them were built during the Napoleonic time when British commercial ships used this route to get to Northern Europe because the Channel was too dangerous. There was a garrison here during that time. Hope you enjoy seeing it.'

I wandered off for a brisk walk to the end of the very windy Main Street. It was not without hazard, because there were frequent cars on the narrow street which didn't have a pavement. The quoys are very charming old houses with narrow alleyways going down their sides to their private piers, and the back of the houses have clear sea views of islands.

Stromness had a good number of gift shops and some which were relatively expensive. I assumed this was for the benefit of passengers from the frequent cruise liners and the daily ferries from the mainland and other islands.

I turned right up Khyber Pass, which is a road leading to the upper part of the town. Soon I was back where I started and in the car driving north to Skara Brae.

Just before the turning a farmer beckoned me. 'Do you mind reversing to let these cattle in? Then it's best if you carry on past here and use the next entrance as the cattle are a bit jumpy today.' He had one hand in the pocket of what looked like a sailing jacket and the other on a stick which he waved in the air to direct the cattle. He was in his early fifties and his mature beard had a three-inch growth. For the first time I thought a beard was a useful, warm thing to have, which cost nothing and saved having to shave.

'No trouble at all. What exactly is Skara Brae?' I asked.

'It's the only bloody village in Orkney without a pub. We could do with one here,' he grumbled.

'How far is it?'

'Do you see that bay about half a mile away?

'Yes.'

'Well, that's it.'

'Thanks.' I said and backed fifty yards down the road, whilst he moved the cattle across the road into a large paddock, which was part of a large hotel.

At the reception I asked the young woman, a friendly brunette from London in her midforties, about Skara Brae.

'Where are you from?' she asked.

'We live near Lymington.'

'My dad used to work in Portsmouth and then we moved to Kent for a while.'

'Did you like it?'

'No. Thought Kent was the worst place we'd lived. This place is so special. How long are you up here for?'

'Four to five weeks.'

'Sounds like you're working then, as no one comes up here for that long. What you doing?'

'Just covering for a GP.'

'Where?'

'Here for a couple of weeks and then North Ronaldsay.'

'I used to be in the NHS.'

'Oh, what did you do?'

'I was a supplies manager. Gave it up and I've been here eighteen years. It's great living here. So you're up to stay with the doctor on North Ron?'

'Yes, I think he's going away. Have you been up there?'

'Only once to North Ron for a day. The NHS here works out he can only spend five percent of his time in medicine because of the tiny number of people up there. He earns a fortune compared with the crofters on North Ron. He sometimes is the coast guard, sometimes he ties up the boats when they come in. I think it's his wife who is an ornithologist, but I'm not sure. Maybe both of them are. Can't see why else they would stay up there.'

'I'll remember that. Thanks. So can you tell me something about this place?'

'Well, it's a remarkable place.' She looked up to the sky as if to give thanks to the heavens. 'I love what I do here; and the Italian Chapel and here are my favorite places in all of Orkney.'

'I'm staying next to the chapel, but I haven't been down that way yet. I only got here yesterday, so I might go later today or sometime this week.'

'You are really lucky to be living there. I'll tell you about this place. Basically this place is one of Britain's oldest known farming villages and has stood intact for five thousand years.'

'How come it's not been destroyed by the weather or by people re-using the materials it's built from?'

'It was hidden for over four thousand years until 1850, when a wild storm stripped the grass from a high dune known as Scara Brae, which overlooks the Bay of Skaill. Everyone thought it was just a sand dune, but it wasn't. What the storm revealed was an immense refuse heap of all sorts of materials from ancient times, known as a midden. In amongst the midden they could see these dwellings. It is the best preserved Neolithic village in Northern Europe.'

'Just how old is Neolithic?'

'The village was here before the Egyptian pyramids, before Stonehenge, before the Great Wall of China. The main thing is not so much its age but the extraordinary degree to which it was preserved.'

'It must be in very good condition?'

'You'll be very surprised, especially with the furniture which has never been moved. The stages in human development are described by archeologists by the type of materials used for tool production.'

'I can't remember any of this stuff since I was at school.'

'Don't worry, it'll all come back. You start with the Stone Age, then comes the Bronze Age and finally the Iron Age.'

'I'm with you so far.'

'The oldest is the Stone Age, and it's divided into three periods. The Old Stone Age, or Paleolithic, is the earliest period, when stone implements were used, and it stretches back two and a half million years. The Middle Stone Age, or Mesolithic, dates from just after the ice melted at the end of the Ice Age, from about 10,000 BC to 4,000 BC, when people lived by hunting, fishing and gathering. The New Stone Age, or Neolithic, dates from about 4,000 BC to 2,500 BC, and is when most people farmed and when polished stone tools and pottery were used. The Bronze Age is from about 3,000 BC, which was overtaken by the Iron Age in about 800 BC.'

'That's probably enough for my head right now, but I'll be back with my wife and daughter next week to have another look around. Which way do I go to look at the village?'

'Have a look next door at the four-minute film first, and then just go through that door. The tour guide is there mooching around the village somewhere. You won't miss her, there's only you and her here today. It's going to get more windy this morning.' I exchanged a friendly handshake and moved into the room next door to watch the film.

The film gave a good synopsis of the area and indicated that nearly the whole site was open with the exception of only one room, which you could look into through its glass roof. This glass roof was to preserve it. However, there was an exact replica of this room which I was free to walk through.

I wandered down about three hundred yards to the edge of the cliff, and there, right beside the beach, was the village. I noticed how the wind had picked up a strength I was familiar with. It didn't come and go in waves. It was another force just there constantly. I had exactly the same sense of eeriness I had experienced the night before, standing outside my accommodation listening to the wind and looking at the sky and sea. The view here was sea and sky which I had experienced in many times but here it was different because it brought the same strange feeling of something important about the place which was at once ancient and in the present. I wondered if the whole area was in some way regarded as special, mystical.

In many ways the historical importance of these houses make it like one of the wonders of the world. Perhaps the only thing I had ever seen that made me feel deeply privileged to witness was when I was standing under an overhanging cliff face in a gorge in Australia, which had preserved an art gallery of colored paintings below. These had been done by men and women thirty thousand to sixty thousand years ago.

I was now looking down on a whole village right in front of me. Each of the eight houses was linked to the other houses and to the outside by stone passages. The almost perfect degree of preservation made it seem as if there must be someone still living in the houses. But really you know that this is all that they left. There are no other traces of them. There are no names, clothes, coffins or even bones, as they are gone. It is so long ago that everything has been consumed by the sea, the wind, the rain and the sun. It made me feel as though the people who lived here left nothing but these buildings, but of course this is entirely untrue. The barley that still grows in the field next to the houses was originally planted by them.

You almost wonder when they're going to come back and surprise you, but then you see that we are really them, come back to visit where we were long ago, at a staging post in our journey to civilization. I could see as I walked in the house that straight ahead there was still a hearth in the centre of the large room. Beyond this and facing you as you come in is a large stone dresser, perhaps five feet high and six or seven feet across. It was made of large flag stones which divided it into four large sections. It was easy to imagine these compartments filled with all sort of objects, such as hunting trophies, food or clothes. On either side of this were beds made of flagstones for the front, rear and sides. They are only slightly out of alignment and no doubt could still be used.

As I stood there in silence, trying to take in the sight of this unique village, I wondered what it was like then. What was the climate like? What did they eat? They must have lived off the sea. What did they wear? I noticed a figure in a large, green-hooded blue coat slowly wander around the tops of the houses and over towards me. It was almost like seeing a ghost. She walked around the grassy tops of the walls of each house of this almost subterranean village. Could she be one of the people who used to live there? Was the strong wind playing tricks with my eyes? And then she spoke.

'Welcome to the Egypt of the North,' she said in a broad local accent which I was finding difficult to get used to. It just wasn't a common accent at all. It is not the kind of accent you can describe or imitate.

'Hi there. That's one way of looking at it. This place is almost unbelievable,' I said, brought back to earth by her greeting. Here was another dark haired woman with dark blue eyes, and wrapped up well in a very thick woolen sweater.

'There's not a trace of metal here, but there are hundreds of artifacts.'

'How long did they live here?'

'The people lived here for over six centuries, using tools made from only bone and flint. We know they used horse to hunt red deer and wild boar, and they herded sheep and cattle. We also know they ate a lot of shellfish and grew an old fashioned, very yellow type of barley called bere, which still grows here.

'And was all of this furniture here?'

'Certainly was and never been moved. Most of the furniture is made from flagstones. You may have noticed lots of the houses in Orkney still have flagstone roofs. You really have to admit that the furniture in front of you looks very much like modern day furniture, especially the cupboards and the fish- tank.'

'What fish-tank?' I couldn't see what she meant.

'They found them in the floor. They were cemented

with clay to make them watertight. The fish tanks were almost certainly used to keep shell fish alive and perhaps bait alive and fresh for fishing.

'I understand now.'

'The furniture is all stone, because, like now, few trees grew on Orkney because of the wind and the salt content of the air. So they used stone.'

'The school teacher in North Ron said to bring up trees for seeds. Now I see why.'

'There'll be no trees up there, that's for certain. The island is so open it's almost always windy.'

'What was the roof made of?'

'If you go back to the replica house, which is identical in every way to the glass covered house, you'll see that the roof was made of slanting wooden poles or whale bones which sloped up to a central point through which smoke from the fire could escape. This may have been covered in skins of animals draped over the whole roof or by turf which was tied down. Grass may have grown over it, like over the house today, and further disguised it.'

'How big are the houses?'

'Each house is about thirty-five square yards, which is just over half of the average two-bed roomed semi, which is about sixty square yards.'

'The man at the desk said it survived because it was surrounded by something called a midden, which I've never heard of before.'

'It survived for three reasons. First, you must remember that there are over a thousand Neolithic sights in the Orkney Islands, more than anywhere else in Europe, and that's only because the people here at that time were forced to build their houses in stone and not wood, for there weren't many trees in Orkney and still aren't. Because they were made of stone, they survived, whilst in Europe all the wooden ones have long gone.

Third, the second reason why this village has survived is because it was deliberately cocooned by a midden, which is a pile of debris from the people living here. A midden is just a waste pit, like a compost pit, containing ash, bones, shells and all other organic matter. It insulated the houses from the weather and hid the people and their village from their enemies.

Third, the village also probably had a quick burial by advancing sand-dunes, which preserved it for over forty centuries. The sand probably acted like sandbags do, protecting it from the explosive blasts from the sea.'

'Why did the people actually not dig out the sand?'

'It may have been a quick burial and that was it ... just gone for forty centuries. But also at that time people were moving away from community-living in villages and living more as individual families on single farmsteads, and it's more likely that desertion and eventual abandonment took place over a longer period of time. Then, maybe, it was buried quickly by the sand and forgotten. '

'When did people last live here?'

'For around six hundred years from about 3,200 BC, and there may have been a break, because there are two villages, one built on top of the other. It's difficult to say why because of the sea.'

'Has the sea moved then?'

'A great deal. It's been advancing inland for thousands of years. When people lived here there was a freshwater loch where the bay is, and that would have been their source of fresh water. You can see the remaining crescent shaped parts of the loch on either side of the bay. The front of the loch would have been cliffs which were next to the sea. The cliffs were eventually eroded and the loch joined the sea. The eroded cliffs would have formed into sand dunes which engulfed the village.'

'Is that still happening? I mean will this be engulfed by the sea at some stage.

'No, because now there's a manmade protective sea wall. The sea would have been a lot further out when they lived here, but now the wall has stopped it coming any closer.'

'Did the village extend out further then?'

'This may just be the remains of a much larger settlement, but we just don't know. People may have not known what it was, as interest in archeology is only recent.'

'I think it's about to rain. So, thanks. I'm going to make a run for it.' There was a very noticeable drop in air pressure, the kind which heralds very heavy rainfall.

'I think you're right, and I've got to get my washing in. See ya,' and she was on her heels, turning to wave.

I waved and ran to the replica house. Inside I was surprised that I could not hear a sound of the very heavy downpour. It was an excellent shelter, and the silence made me think again of just how isolated it must have been thousands of years ago, knowing nothing about the rest of the world. When the rain stopped I decided I would call it a day and return to the chalet for some lunch and a rest before the night shift.

There were no calls in the evening, and I spent the time looking at the stars through a pair of binoculars. Patrick Moore always said they were better than a telescope for routine use, and he designed a special harness which rests over the back of your neck and around your shoulders. This enables a pair of binoculars to rest in the harness whilst you simply turn around to view the sky, without having to use your arms. It always struck me though: what do you do with your arms? There were a few clouds about and there was a medium breeze, so I was in and out of the chalet for a couple of hours. By nine o'clock I took full advantage of having no patients to see, and I was asleep.

Chapter 3.

Mainland Orkney, South Ronaldsay and Burray Island. Day 3

The phone woke me. 'Is that the doctor?'

'Yep.' I looked at my watch. Twenty to three in the morning.

'NHS in Aberdeen here. We've got a patient aged sixty who came out of hospital yesterday with kidney stones, and his neighbor says he just passed out.'

'What's his address?' I asked, as I found the light switch.

'Balfour, Shapinsay,' she replied.

'Any other details of medication or any other problems?'

'No. Let me give you his phone number.'

'OK, leave it with me. I'll call you back when it's sorted.' I thought this was routine until I looked on the map and found that his address was on a remote north-east island called Shapinsay. Was this a test? I couldn't see a causeway or one of the barriers which accessed some of the surrounding islands, and I had no access to a plane unless he was really ill, in which case I could call the air ambulance. There was no information about or a strip to land an aircraft there. But thinking this far ahead seemed like a bit of a drama at this stage. I didn't know enough and I needed more information. I rapidly decided the best thing was to talk to his friend and try and establish the gravity of the situation. But when I dialed the number, there was no reply. I hung up and tried again, but still there was no answer.

I rang back Eileen at the switchboard in Aberdeen. 'There's no answer on the phone. Can you double check the number is right?'

'Nae trouble at all,' she said in her broad Scottish accent.

'Also, I can't see how I can get across a mile or so of cold sea to Balfour, and no one has mentioned me covering an island which I've got no access to.'

'Apparently there are three doctors on that island. I've got the number of the surgery which is probably the doctor's home. Do you want the doctor's number?'

'I'll take it, but it sounds if you should be talking to the doctor on the island, because I'm miles away.'

I called the doctor anyway. The phone was answered after two rings with a 'Hello'.

'Who's that?' I asked

'Dr. McGill.'

'I'm a locum on Mainland Orkney, and I just got a call which I think was meant for you. It's a sixty year old with kidney stones, who was discharged from the hospital yesterday.'

'It was me who admitted him last week.'

'I couldn't raise him on the phone.'

'That's because he doesn't have one. It was probably a neighbor who called about him.'

'Can I leave it with you?'

'Yes.'

'Sorry to wake you so early.'

I called the NHS switchboard in Aberdeen to tell them it was put to bed.

'Sorry doc. It was our error as we should have called the doctor on Shapinsay, not you. Like you, we're just taking over handling the calls for Out of Hours, and we're having teething problems.' I changed out of my clothes and dozed off again in the chalet.

Half an hour later, at about ten past four, the local hospital switchboard rang my phone. 'Hi there, doctor. We've got a call out for you.'

'Ok, just finding the light. Got it. Just getting a pen and paper. Fire away.'

'It's a young lassie with kidney pains she's had before, off and on two days ago. She's been sick half an hour ago and has got a lot of back pain in her kidneys.'

'Anything else?'

'No. Let me give you her details.'

'Thanks.' I dressed as I wrote down the details. Then I called the number. 'Hello. I've got the details of your wife, and I just need to know where you are, as I can't see the address on the map. Which road are you on?'

'We're in Torness in a council estate near the shop.'

I squinted, looking all over the map of Kirkwall. 'Whereabouts is that in Kirkwall?' I asked.

'How do you mean?'

'I'm a stranger here and don't know the area. What's the nearest road?'

'I don't know the nearest road. We're opposite the school.'

'Is that near the waterfront, or …'

I was interrupted. 'It's near the school and a playground, and there's a shop nearby.'

'Ok The biggest thing that I can see on the map of Kirkwall in front of me is the boating pond. Where are you in relation to the boating pond?'

'I've never been there; have you Sue?' but no answer came from Sue, just a groan down the phone.

'Where are in relation to the very centre of town?' I asked.

'We are not a million miles from the cathedral,' which was right in the centre of town.

'Which way would I get to you if I came out of the

cathedral doors?' I asked in quiet desperation, trying to work out at four thirty in the morning if someone was making a hoax call. Then I considered that he might be genuinely so distressed that his higher brain functions were not accessible. In extreme stress the blood supply shuts down to the upper brain so that more blood is pumped to the more vital lower brain areas to do with reflexes and instincts.

'You could go left or right, but right could be quicker.'

I nearly burst out with laughter but mercifully managed to say calmly, 'Ok … then where?'

We're off the only one-way street off the Main Street from the middle of town.'

'What's the name of the one-way street?' I asked.

'Sue, what's the name of that one-way street?' Again there was just a groan.

'Do you know the names of any streets near you at all?' I asked, not believing I was really having this conversation.

'Thomas Street is near us.' I looked and looked but couldn't see it anywhere near the centre of town or around the cathedral.

'Are you sure it's Thomas Street?'

'Yes, it is.'

I looked again. 'Are you sure?' Then I saw a small road called Thoms Street, but it was spelt without an A. 'I've found it.' I said. 'Where are you in relation to Thoms Street?'

'We're not quite opposite the school.'

'There's no school on my map. What road is the school on?'

'It's next to the playground.'

'My map's a black and white photocopy and doesn't show green areas like playgrounds or schools. Let me shout some names of streets where I think you might be living. How about a big road called The Meadows?'

'That's not far away.'

'Where are you in relation to it?'

'We're off the road that leads to the council estate.'

'Do you have any idea what the name sounds like?'

There was a pause. 'No'

'Is it Linket? Lothier? Mooney Drive? Marwick Drive?'

'The shop's near Marwick Drive.'

'Is it on Marwick Drive or off it?'

'It's just off it.'

'I'm leaving to get there now. I'll phone you when I get to the shop. Can you come down and meet me at the shop?' I realised I could have made things a lot easier for us both if I had said this in the first place. But I hadn't because it was the middle of the night, and I wasn't thinking as fast as usual either.

'Yes. I'm only a minute away.'

'I'll be about fifteen minutes.' I managed to put the phone down without any comments about him not knowing the name of the road he lived on.

Then, as I drove into Kirkwall I started laughing. I had been about twenty minutes on the phone, trying to find out from him where he lived. In some way this man sounded intelligent, but he didn't seem to have any bearings about where he lived. Of course, I have dealt with distressed people who are confused but not to the extent where they can't actually remember the name of the road they live on. I amused myself by laughing all the way to the visit.

The visit took half an hour, as I had to wait until the anti-sickness medication started working before I could give her some antibiotics and pain killers for her kidney stones and possible kidney infection. She was happy when I told her to see her usual doctor later on that morning for urine and blood tests, and an X-Ray.

I didn't mention the husband's memory problem, as he was not old enough to have any form of dementia or even be pre-senile, and I assumed it was due to his distress.

'I'm ever so sorry, Doctor. I just couldn't remember the names of any road around here. So sorry,' he said in his soft Orcadian accent which I still felt they had stolen from the Welsh.

'No trouble. I understand,' I said. Here was a man who was so genuinely upset that his wife might be on her last legs that he really couldn't use his thinking function to guide me to him. I thought I should at least explain to him why he had acted out of character, if only to make him feel less guilty.

'I feel so bad about keeping you on the phone for ages.'

'Shall I explain this lapse of memory to you?' I said.

'Sure, go right ahead.'

'In stressful times, when we are worried about someone, or upset, it's difficult to access ordinary parts of our brain. We tend to get stuck in the emotional part rather than the intellectual part.'

'How do you mean?'

'Well, usually, ninety percent of the time we use the intellectual part of our brain, just thinking, but when we are in any crisis we flip over and spend ninety percent of the time using the more emotional part of our brain reacting to things with feelings.'

'I think I see what you mean.'

'Let me give you an example.'

'OK, then'

'If you work as a bank cashier and a bank robber comes up to you, points a gun at you and demands you tell him the combination number for the bank's safe, your reaction is usually terror, because you are focused on the gun, and no matter how hard you try, the number, which you know like your date of birth, just won't come into your head; and you end up with your hands shaking and your fingers fumbling with the dial to the safe when you know that usually you know the code really well.

'Why's that then?'

'You just can't access these intellectual memory parts of your brain under real threat.'

'How come they don't all get shot then?'

'They have special training?'

'How does that help?'

'For example, in training you would ask the cashier, what's a tune or a poem they sing or hum to themselves when they are happy.'

'I understand.'

'You then get them to learn to say the first verse of the poem or song, or even a hymn, and insert the numbers somewhere. If the code to the safe was 1413118. You might suggest singing the song "Ten Green Bottles sitting on the wall" losing first one bottle then two then three bottles and say to yourself it's as easy as 1,2 3.'

'I understand that.'

'Let me show you. First you say to yourself, "It's as easy as 1, 2, 3." Then you sing over and over again: "Fourteen green bottles hangin' on the wall. If one green bottle should accidentally fall, there'd be thirteen green bottles hangin' on the wall. Thirteen green bottles hangin' on the wall. If two green bottles should accidentally fall, there'd be eleven green bottles hangin' on the wall. Eleven green bottles hangin' on the wall. If three green bottles should accidentally fall, there'd be eight green bottles hangin' on the wall." And bingo, you've got the code 14, 13, 11, and 8 even with a gun pointing at your head.'

'I see,' he said. But I noticed he was looking at me strangely. I wasn't sure if he was perplexed by the explanation I was giving him or if he was more perplexed by my demonstration of it.

It was at this moment that I suddenly realised I had been singing "Ten Green Bottles" at four thirty in the morning in a strange city to someone I didn't know, who had called me out to see his sick wife, and who didn't know where he lived and probably didn't understand a word I was saying.

'I know exactly what you're saying. I mean, now I'm more relaxed, I can remember all the street names now.'

'Well, have a quiet night.' And off I went, back off to St Mary's Holm six miles away, where I tried to sleep for an hour. I gave up and had a boiled egg, an orange and two cups of coffee, gazing out through the windows waiting for the sun to rise.

I dropped the patient's duplicate note sheets into the practice and bumped into the Australian doctor again.

'How's it going?' I asked.

'Mate, it's been a busy old day yesterday, and today's even busier with a flu clinic and a ward round I've got to run.'

'Well, I'm off to refill the drugs bag which is lacking a few things that they really need.'

'Did you have a quiet night, mate?'

'It was OK, except I spent nearly half an hour on the phone trying to get a patient's address. Couldn't remember any of the street names of where he lived, not even the one he lived on.'

'Mate, here they wouldn't know if their bottoms were on fire.' And that made me laugh.

'We should hook up while we're here,' I said.

'Yeah, sure thing. How about supper Friday?'

'Suits me, although I'm on call.'

'I'll do a pasta with no alcohol.'

'Where do you live, and what time?'

'The nurses home at seven?'

'Excellent. See you then, and thanks for the circles on the map yesterday.'

'No dramas, mate. See you then.' And we both went our separate ways.

I dropped the drug request form at the chemist, then went on to the tourist office and then to the cathedral to book a guided tour for the next morning. I decided to spend the day carrying on yesterday's journey around the west and north of the island.

I drove up past Skara Brae up the west coast. I could see distant islands but didn't know their names. I stood looking at them and once again I had the strange, eerie sense I'd had twice before. This time it was not in any way uncomfortable. It was a calming sense of everything being still and as it had always been. It was as if the past was in the present, and our artificial way of defining time by dividing it up had gone. I stood and bathed in this sense of isolation, of being alone, of being still. Of just being.

I came to a sign which indicated a monument dedicated to the spot on the coast opposite where Lord Kitchener's ship had gone down with himself and many of the crew. The monument was a long walk up a steep slope. The plaque at the bottom of the slope was very informative, and, as the wind was severe, I decided to give the walk a miss.

I wasn't due to be on call until six in the evening, but at half past four the phone rang, which was a little ominous as only the switchboards in Aberdeen and Kirkwall had the number.

'We can't find Dr. McFee and there's a home visit.'

'OK, give me the details.'

'It's a thirty-three year old woman who was given some tablets for her stomach problem today and now is not well. She's dizzy, got neck ache, and pins and needles in her face and arm.'

'Fine. Where does she live?'

'Ouch, it's right in the centre of town.'

'Thanks. I'll call you back with the outcome.' And with this I phoned the number and got the patient's friend. It was the same thing. Just like the man earlier in the morning, she was unable to give me the street name. I went through twenty names in the centre of town before she recognized one near her. I began to realize that because there is so little stress normally, people here probably never have to think about street names.

'What's your name?'

'I'm Egg,' said the seven year old boy who answered the door. 'Are you a doctor?' he asked.

'Sometimes I am.' And I started climbing the stone steps up to the first floor flat of a very old house. The thirty-three year old single mother of four young children told me her story, and I listened with her friend and said nothing until she had finished.

'Have you heard of over-breathing or hyperventilating?'

'I think I have,' she said.

'I know what you mean,' said her friend. 'I've had it.'

'I want to show you how, when you want to relax, you take a very slow breath. First put your feet up on the sofa and lie back. Now put one hand flat on your tummy and the other flat on your chest bone and take a slow deep breath.'

'OK, then.' She took a big breath and the hand on the abdomen didn't move.

'Which hand moved?'

'This one,' she said, pointing to the hand on her abdomen.

'Incorrect answer,' I said jokingly like a quiz master. Only the one on your chest moved. Try it again?' And again only the hand on her chest moved. It was like asking someone to blink naturally, so I distracted her from being too conscious of her breathing, but I still wanted to show her and let her know what using her diaphragm was like.'

'Do you remember when you were a kid and you'd stand up and one of your mates would say to the rest of you, 'Who's got the biggest tummy?' And you'd all stick out your tummies?'

'Yes.'

'Can I see you do it now then?' Out came her tummy, and only the hand on her abdomen moved. 'Success!' I said. 'Well done. Let's do this for the next five minutes while I ask you a couple of questions.' I realized that she was probably just anxious about this morning's consultation, otherwise she admitted to being a pretty chilled out single mother of four children, living in a far more serene spot that her native Manchester.

After that it was another very quiet evening at the chalet overlooking the Italian chapel, and I was sound asleep, even earlier than on the previous day, by eight o'clock.

Chapter 4.

Mainland Orkney, South Ronaldsay and Burray
Island. Day 4

Thankfully, it was a silent night with no calls or home visits to be made. Orcadians are hardy and don't call you out unless they are seriously in trouble. It would be unheard of to call you out for a cough or a cold ... unlike some individuals. A tall doctor friend of mine who is six foot five did a house call at ten o'clock one evening to a house in North London. He was taken into the front room by the patient, and he asked the woman what the problem was. She asked him if he could tighten the screw holding the curtain rail to the wall, as it had become loose and was in danger of coming away from the wall. She had called him out because she'd heard there was a tall locum doctor at the surgery, and she'd thought he would probably be able to reach it.

I was having a relaxing time as a locum GP and also taking full advantage of my spare time being a tourist. After dropping the previous day's notes at the practice, I booked myself in to have a tour of the cathedral at eleven the next morning.

It was only nine thirty in the morning, and I had the whole day ahead of me with nothing to do. So I set off in the car on for a leisurely exploratory drive of what is known as Scapa Flow. It was a long drive around this harbor, and it took me to some deserted coves and an interesting graveyard. The graveyard had half the remains of a round church where some Vikings had settled and become Christians.

I had heard that Scapa Flow was a place of historic importance, but I couldn't see why. I had no tourist guide book, and I was visiting various places without any information, which I found frustrating. I promised myself that I would try and change this.

At exactly eight in the evening I had just finished reading the two local newspapers The Orcadian and Orkney Today. They both read well and carried an article about the Out of Hours (OOH) GP service, which was the job I was doing, being dropped by local GPs and taken over by the Health Authority. It was odd to find an article about a job which you were doing, which published the emergency phone number to contact me. Just as I was contemplating this, I heard the bizarre ring tone of Orkney Health Service mobile phone in the kitchen.

'Hi there, it's Jackie here. I've got a call out for you.'

'Fine. Where from?'

'South Ronaldsay, down near the bottom.'

'I'm just getting my map. What's the problem?'

'His wife says he's shaking all over.'

'How old is he?'

'It was a bad line and I couldn't tell if it was forty-six, fifty-six or sixty-six.'

'Any history of bladder or kidney stone problems?'

'No.'

'Any other information?'

'No that's it. I'll give the phone number so you can speak to his wife.'

'It sounds like he's got a kidney infection and will need a visit. I'll just ring and tell them I'll be there soon.'

I left the house at ten past eight and set off south to cross the four Churchill Barriers. I drove reasonably fast over the four barriers, very aware of the sea on either side. After the barriers the roads seemed more difficult to negotiate. They seemed narrower, and it was more difficult to feel relaxed whilst driving on them. It was misty and curiously slippery, and I thought that maybe this car was not very stable and was the wrong one for these roads. It was never my favorite make of car, but now it was leaving me feeling like a bad driver, which never makes a man feel good. The easiest way to seriously dent a man's ego is to say he has no sense of humor or he can't drive, or worse still, both.

The house was very isolated and down a very long, rough, muddy track.

'Thirteen minutes. I'm impressed,' said his wife. 'That's quick, getting here from St Mary's Holm.'

'Bit of a slippery road this time of night,' I added.

'Always is,' she said as I followed her through the porch, through three more rooms, twisting around corners until we came to a bedroom where the patient was lying with only his eyes peeping out from under the duvet. As he lowered the duvet I could see his teeth were chattering and he was shaking.

'Are you eating and drinking, peeing and pooing OK?'

'Peeing too frequently and a bit uncomfortable.'

'Any pain anywhere?'

'No, but I feel like I'm going to throw up.'

'Any problems in the past?'

'Had this twice before and had to go into hospital.'

'Anything else in the past?'

'No. I'm fit, healthy and well. Don't smoke. Hardly drink. Work hard.'

'I'm just going to take the duvet off. As I did his entire body began to shake, almost as if he was having an epileptic fit. This was a rigor due to a big rise in his body temperature; he was very hot to the touch.

'He's probably got a kidney infection and needs some antibiotics. I could give him some here, and he might well be perfectly OK in a couple of hours; but if he can't take them, then he'll need to be admitted to hospital and have an intravenous drip set up to given him the antibiotics. I can admit him, or treat him here providing he can keep the tablets down.'

'I'm not sure he will,' said his wife. She looked anxious; he was not well and they were isolated, and I didn't fancy another visit during the middle of the night to admit him, if he couldn't keep the medicine down. He now started to look better as the rigor stopped.

'If you were in London, a hospital probably wouldn't accept you as an admission. They would insist that your GP treated you at home and you be reviewed sometime in the future by a specialist. The difference is that, if things go wrong in London, you can be in an ambulance in fifteen minutes. Here it can be a lot longer, and you are in a very isolated situation. I think you would be better in hospital just for tonight.' They agreed with each other that he should go in.

'Does he need to go by ambulance?' his wife asked.

'I don't fancy being thrown about in an ambulance like last time.' He'd perked up a little more.

'No, it's not a lights-and-bells job. A car will do if they've got one,' I reassured him.

I spoke to the hospital doctor - the friendly Australian - who agreed that he needed admitting. When he put me through to the ambulance service I was told they would be a couple of hours and to try and use other transport, if it was available.

Whilst I was phoning the hospital and writing a letter to the admitting doctor, he changed and together they packed a suitcase. As I sat in an armchair writing the letter, his wife came up to me and asked, 'Is he going to be alright?'

'He's going to be alright.'

'Is he going to hospital?'

'Yes, only for tonight. Should be home tomorrow for

the weekend. One thing, the ambulance said they would be at least two hours, so they have asked for alternative transport. It's up to you. As I'm going back that way, I think the best thing is to give him a lift myself.'

'I could take him, but I'd have to drive all the way back in this weather.'

'I suppose you might as well come with me then,' I said to the patient, picking up his case. I'm driving back towards the hospital, and it will save your wife having to drive you in and drive all the way back.'

'Are you sure?'

'I'm probably not insured, but hey, it's the best thing to do. Are you alright with that?'

'No bother.' I knew they had already hoped that I would make the offer and save her the anxiety of a long car ride with a sick person and leaving her daughter behind. 'I'm absolutely sure I'm not insured, but what the heck, this is an island. Let's get him to hospital. It's the quickest way. An ambulance might be longer than a couple of hours.'

I met them both in the porch, and I noticed that they were dressed for the weather in what looked like sailing jackets.

In a minute we were driving carefully along the slippery roads. Apologetically I said, 'Sorry I seem to be driving fairly fast. These roads make you feel you are going much faster, for some reason. There are no warning signs of bends and, I don't know why, the bends are really difficult.'

'They're just as bad when they're dry, because they were built by Italian prisoners of war.'

'How does that make them so strange to drive around?'

'The camber's the wrong way round.'

'Right. Now I think about it, that's why I've been going so slowly into the corners. I've felt as if I've been driving too fast, so I've been driving around them much more slowly than usual, as if I'm about to crash.' I felt a sense of relief.

'I don't know if you know it, but just here is where the German U-boat Commander slipped into the sound and torpedoed the Royal Oak.' He had perked up and was happy to tell me about the history.

'No, I didn't know this is where he slipped in.'

'He left the same way without being seen. Over eight hundred people died on that boat. Many of the relatives come back. Even the German submarine Commander came back. There is a buoy over the wreck which is covered with a net now. It's starting to leak oil, which you can see from the air. The Navy is really not sure what they are going to do about it, and they are not saying how much oil is down there. It's also a war grave, which complicates things. It may be a potential time bomb for our wildlife, but it hasn't stopped the dolphins.'

'What dolphins?' I asked.

'When they built the Churchill Barriers, the Barriers blocked channels which dolphins had used to cross from the North Sea to the Atlantic each year. Regular as clockwork they turn up once a year to migrate.'

'After all these years! What happens to them?'

'They hang around, swimming in the area, for two or three weeks, then they swim back away. It's as if they expect their usual route to open up again, but of course it's completely sealed by the Barriers.

Minutes later we arrived at the hospital; I handed him over to the friendly Australian doctor, and then I set off back home.

Chapter 5.

Mainland Orkney, South Ronaldsay and Burray
Island. Day 5

There were a few essentials I needed to buy, and I
decided I would spend the day catching up with myself and
just looking around Kirkwall. I discovered an old barbecue
in the laundry room at the chalets, and I thought it would be
exciting to do a barbecue outside for Chrisie's birthday when
she came up next week. I decided to have some fireworks, as
we had been apart and couldn't celebrate Guy Fawkes Night. I
thought the Australian doctor might like to come along, partly
out of friendship to say thanks for dinner and partly because
fireworks are illegal in Australia. He might be good company.

I had an eleven o'clock appointment for a guided tour
around the cathedral, which I was looking forward to, and
I also felt like exploring the shops in Kirkwall town. I had a
rough idea of what I needed. I decided to eat lower down the
food chain to burn off some excess fat, and thought I would
try living off a simple diet. Breakfast: Two boiled eggs with
as many apples and oranges as I wanted. Lunch: Rocket and
green salad. Supper: Diet packet soup.

My shopping list: a warmer hat, a real coffee percolator
- I was getting fed up with instant coffee. The water was too
chlorinated to make good tea, and as tea is a more subtle drink
and more sensitive to ruin by impurities than coffee, coffee was
the next best bet.

First, I stopped in at the practice to drop off my night's
notes. Whilst I was writing a note in the back office to the
practice manager, saying just which drugs I had used from the
drugs bag, another doctor came in and used the phone briefly.
I introduced myself and we got talking.

'So how long are you up here for?'

'Nearly five weeks,' he said

'And you?'

'Oh just two weeks doing the night shift.

'Then where?'

'Four days with my family, then we go to North Ronaldsay

'Where?'

'North Ronaldsay.'

'Oh you mean North Ron. Wow! You'll need some reading material up there, or you'll have to like walking.'

'Yes, I'm looking forward to that. Not a lot to do and no responsibility; and my wife and four year old are coming up for the duration there.'

'Well, you're right. You should all enjoy it. It's the smallest general practice in the UK.'

'I know, and it sounds interesting.'

'It is a bit weird. I spent a couple of weeks up there a few years ago. The doctor usually does a surgery for under an hour a day, but, usually, no one turns up. I saw three patients in two weeks.'

'You mean I could try and break a record by seeing no patients in two weeks?'

'Wouldn't be hard up there. You should like it. Make sure you check the expiry dates in the pharmacy in North Ron, because most of them are way out of date. Where are you staying?'

'You're the second person to ask me that. At the doctor's house.'

'You know you can actually stay at the surgery.'

'No, I didn't know. The GP up there said there is no self-catering accommodation, and the only place to stay was at his house.'

'No, you can stay in the surgery. There is a flat above it which, OK, is a bit run down. But it's free. Is he charging you for your wife' stay?'

'Yes, he is.'

'Basically, he's getting paid very well by the Health Board for putting you up, and he'll then charge you London rates for your wife's stay, and lunch and supper.'

'I'm beginning to see what you are saying. Sounds like a bit of clip joint to me. Maybe I'll give him a call and ask him one more time. Thanks for the tip. What are you doing up here?'

'I've been a locum here for ten years, and I've just joined as a salaried doctor.'

'Who are the permanent partners?'

'There aren't any. They are all salaried at about half the salary of the rest of the UK doctors. Well, you know it's not busy. How are you finding it?'

'Straightforward, one to two calls a night, but the patients are well educated and know when they are ill. They listen very well and are keen to help themselves. They're not wingers or negative about life in any way. They make you feel quite positive about the job, as opposed to people with a little knowledge who want to engage you in an intellectual conversation but really only want a bun fight. They argue with you a lot down south.'

'Could never live down south myself,' he said.

'No?' I asked.

'No, couldn't be bothered. Here, my spare hours aren't spent in traffic or worrying about this or that. I can go for walks, reflect on what's happening to my family, fish, and stop for a chat with people.'

'It is an entirely sensible way to live.'

'Apart from the weather.'

'Yes. How bad does it actually get?'

'Well, if there's no heat in the summer, and no sunny days, it can be a bit grim; and in the winter you can get winds of over 100 miles an hour, which means you can't walk, especially if it rains at the same time. You're pretty much locked up. But that's a huge part of the fun of being up here. I love it.'

'I'd find that so invigorating. I used to work in a freezer at minus sixty, and I thought it was the most invigorating job I'd ever had,' I said, chuckling.

'It can get down to minus thirty and worse with the wind chill factor, when the temperature in Surrey is two or three degrees below on a frosty morning. You know we are very short of doctors here. Would you think of staying on?'

'You know, I'm just enjoying it here, but I don't want to think about it really. It's just exciting and a friendly place to be in now. Who knows?'

'I was at school with the one of the medical directors.'

'So, it wouldn't be difficult to get a job here.'

'Not at all. They would grab you. Have a think about it. And off he went with a smile.' I was walking towards the tricky front door with the button under a shelf when someone called to me.

'Are you the doc?' said one of the nurses.

'Yes, what is it?'

'I think you were supposed to see Marie Ann from Occupational Health to check your health status before you started working.'

'I forgot. Thanks for reminding me. You don't have her number do you?'

'I'll find it for you. Everyone who comes up here forgets about occupational health, 'she said, looking through her mobile phone directory. She was about thirty-five, cheerful, and had an almost permanent smile. She was Scottish with an easily recognizable Glaswegian accent.

'Thanks. You are all very helpful up here.'

'Why would we not be?'

'It's just not what I'm used to.'

'Have a good stay, and maybe think about coming up to work for us full time.' She disappeared around into the nurse's room and left me to phone Occupational Health.

'It's the forgetful doc here. I'm sorry I forgot to see you on Tuesday.'

'Can you come over now?'

'Where are you?'

'Three minutes' walk from the Health Centre.'

'I'll be there in three.' I drove and was there in two minutes. When I opened the door, a guide dog came up to me and gave me his toy.

'Is he yours?' I said to the receptionist.

'Yes, he's four now.'

'He's so very friendly.'

'Yes, he is. His name's Paddy. He sounds as if he likes you. I can hear his tail wagging.' And with that Marie Ann appeared.

'Glad you could make it.'

'I'm really sorry. There was just too much going on Monday to remember. Up at four, taxi, three planes, had to find the car, then find the way around here, find where I was living, then had to read nearly ninety pages of technical bumph, and be on call all night from six.'

'Never mind. Come in and let's have a look at you.' I followed her into her office, which was very well equipped compared with the surgery in Gillingham. 'Just got to ask you a few questions, just about your past back operations.'

'You're not from here,' I said, recognising her English accent.

'I was brought up in England.'

'Oh? Where?' I asked.

'Banbury, in Oxford.'

'I used to live in a small village about fifteen miles away - Middle Barton.'

'I've got some friends there.'

'Have they been there long?' I asked.

'Yes, they're native now. They should remember you.'

'Don't think they'll remember me from twenty odd years ago. I bought Cherry Tree Cottage, cut down the cherry tree in the front garden because of the dreadful light, and hung very large papier mâché heads in the windows, which some psychiatric patients had made. They were very colorful.'

'I'm sure they'd remember you. I'll let them know on my Christmas card. You've had quite a life before you came here, haven't you?'

'How do you mean?'

'Well, you've done other jobs - bouncer, freezer man and lots apart from this.'

'How do you know all that?'

'It's on your CV.' I had no idea that health professionals in occupational health had access to my CV, but then, I thought, so what; it's a small place and maybe it's their form of cross checking and using all the intelligence they've got; and I wasn't concerned because I had nothing to hide on my CV.

'Well, the other work supported me through college.'

'That's always a good thing.'

'Yes, makes you value it more.'

'Now, have you got your laboratory results for your

Hepatitis B immunization status with you, and your rubella status?'

'Er … no, it's on my CV. No one's actually asked me for the lab results before. I had Rubella as a child.'

'Well, I'll just have to take some blood off you now, to check them both.' And I could see the blood taking equipment. In a small white cardboard tray was a syringe with a needle already affixed. There was an empty blood bottle and a cotton wool swab waiting to get the chance to soak up my crimson blood from a leaking vein in my elbow. I am just naturally terrified of needles. I could never be a heroin addict.

'I can get the Hepatitis B laboratory report faxed over to you within a minute. The Rubella will be on my GP notes from forty years ago,' I said.

'Can you get the laboratory results?'

'Yes. I'll just phone my wife.'

I rang Chrisie, and she said, 'I'm in the shower. I'll call you back later,' and hung up. And a small shudder of panic passed through me as I realized that I might actually end up getting a needle in my arm any second. I didn't have the upper hand here, and she was free to do what she wanted. Any negative reaction on my part could be in her report.

'Um … she's in the shower … a bit of a late riser.'

'I would be too, and get up at half ten in the morning, if I wasn't here. Don't worry, I'll wait.' A wave of relief passed right through me at the thought of not having to have a needle stuck in me. I didn't mention my anxiety, but I knew she'd seen it all before and must have sensed it.

Within a couple of minutes my phone rang, and I spoke to Chrisie. The fax came down the line within seconds. Now, there's someone who understands my fear of needles, I thought. I had developed a fear of needles only a couple of years before.

I was waiting to have some back surgery, lying in an NHS hospital in Southampton, and having intravenous antibiotics through a drip in my arm for three weeks. I was having this because the back surgery I'd had a couple of months before had gone wrong, and I'd got an infection in one of my discs, called discitis.

Every two to three days the drip would need relocating to another vein in one of my arms, because the vein naturally collapses after this time. At the end of three weeks I had already had ten long-term needles inserted into my arms, and most of my veins had been used up and could not be used again for some time. In these circumstances what you really need is someone like an anaesthetist, who inserts needles into very small veins all day, into those as small as on a mouse's limb. So far I had been lucky, because all of the doctors had managed to find a vein and insert a needle without any failures.

I had been lying in an orthopedic ward when a new, very young, rookie doctor went up to a twenty year old chippie called Marco, who was opposite me. Marco was an earthy young man recovering after his broken leg which had been repaired two days ago. We'd had a few chats through the night, and he was a good guy with a well-rounded sense of humor. His wife was eighteen, and they had one daughter.

'Sir, you will need this drip replacing now, sir,' said the young doctor.

'Go right ahead,' said Marco. And with this, the tourniquet was tightened around his left upper arm.

'Won't take a minute, sir, I promise sir. I promise.' I could see he had missed entering a vein as he reached for a cotton wool ball and fumbled to tape it onto the puncture, which was bleeding. 'Sir, please hold this, sir. Put some pressure on it.' Then he tried nearer Marco's hand.

'Ouch!' said Marco, and I knew this must have hurt because most chippies are used to a bit of pain from the odd miss of a hammer and other accidents.

'Sir, just keep still, Sir, please.'

'It's not me, mate,' said Marco.

Every time the doctor tried to puncture the skin to find a vein and failed, Marco moaned and groaned in pain. Each time, I could see the doctor patching the bleeding spot with a cotton wool ball, taping it with a strip of plaster and asking Marco to hold it. He did this five times to Marco's left arm, and I could see that Marco didn't have enough fingers on his right hand with which to hold any more cotton wool balls in place.

It was painful to watch the doctor thinking, but if you've put a lot of drips in people's arms, like I had years before, it's not hard to anticipate his thoughts. Eventually, he worked out that Marco couldn't put pressure on any cotton wool balls, because Marco had no more fingers with which to do so. I thought he had finished and about to clear up and go when he started trying to take blood out of Marco's right arm whilst Marco was still using the fingers of his right hand to stop the five puncture points on his left arm from bleeding. This rookie doctor had guts.

I don't know how Marco had coped, but he was brave. However, after the doctor had tried four times to get blood out of his right arm, I started to wave to Marco and mimed, 'No, No, don't let him. No, No, No,' whilst shaking my head and waving my arms like I was trying to wave down an airplane. He saw me, and he nodded. And that finished it.

'No. Stop. No more. Just leave me. I'm not going to die if this doesn't happen. I've had a broken leg and that didn't' kill me. Nine times is enough.' The doctor made no objection, and raised his hands as he collected his tray and backed off.

The problem was he turned around and walked over to me, and said. 'Sir, I just have to replace your drip, sir. Thank you very much sir.'

'No, not today. All my veins are completely closed up, and I'll need to speak to the surgeon to see if I can have my intravenous drugs substituted with tablets by mouth. My veins are caput, closed, blocked, not working.

'Sir, it will be very fine. I just find a vein and it will be over.'

'Listen, I'm sorry mate, but my veins don't work. My veins, they're collapsed, so I need to have tablets by mouth.'

'Fine, sir. I tell boss, sir.' Mercifully he had completely understood me, and he left us. I then did something extremely cheeky. I phoned the hospital switchboard and asked them to page the on-call anesthetist. When she answered the call I apologized and explained that I was a doctor, an in-patient on the orthopedic ward with a blocked drip and a needle phobia. She came up and replaced the drip, and I was fine except for one lingering problem. I had developed a late onset needle phobia.

'And I hear your wife and daughter are coming up?' Marie Ann said now.

'Yes, for a couple of weeks. India is four and will go to North Ronaldsay Primary School whilst she is here.'

'If you want India to meet Paddy, it's no problem.'

'I might do that.' And a few moments later, with utter relief about not having my veins tampered with, I found myself around the corner on Main Street relaxing into the early morning bustle of Kirkwall.

Kirkwall's bustle was not really a bustle at all. It was quiet, and I noticed that the people were much friendlier than in the south coast in the New Forest. I found a sign pointing up an alleyway just beside the cathedral, which read, "Fresh coffee, toasted sandwiches", and I found myself walking in and sitting down, and ordering a filter coffee and a toasted cheese-ham-and-onion sandwich in this cozy little corner of Kirkwall. My diet could start later in the day. I reached into my pocket and grabbed the list of things I needed to do, but I realised that I had picked up the wrong piece of paper. It was a list of places I wanted to see in the islands. I was annoyed with myself, and resolved once again – this was not an infrequent occurrence – to try to improve. But it never works, and I laughed at my frustration with myself.

Surprisingly, there are a lot of small grocery shops in the city, and one feature is that they all seem to have a different niche market. One specializes in frozen food, but is still a general store. There are two delicatessens which are also general stores. There's one which is also the biggest bookshop, but is still a general store selling everything from butter to tinned food. There are only two supermarkets, but they are not on the main street. They are a few hundred yards away near garage workshops and a few warehouses, where there are large car parks. The high street can't really be modified for big shops and for big parking, so it has been preserved. Everyone has to go to these supermarkets at least once a week, but the dozen or so small shops remain personal with personal greetings from the people who work there. It may seem like only a small thing, but it makes you feel at home.

It was nearly half past ten when I came across the fishing shop. I went in to see if I could do some fishing in the area.

'Is there any fishing here this time of year?' I asked.

'Well, there's sea fishing, but the weather's no good out there usually this time of year. It's alright just now, but we don't know how long for. It could change today.'

'I meant just a rod or line in the water here.'

'It's good at the first or second Barrier. Get some big fish there.'

'I've left all my gear down south. Could you sort me out with something cheap and cheerful?'

'We've run out of telescopic rods.'

'What about a hand held line?'

'There's this one over here. It's OK … will do the job.' He handed me a heavyweight version of a landline.

'I'll take it.'

'You might like some flies on it if you want to catch some cod.'

'Cod?'

'Oh aye, you'll get them at the first and second Barrier before low tide.'

'I'll take some then, please.'

'And you might like a heavier lead weight.'

'I'll have that too then, please.' I'd never argue with local specialists with years of knowledge of fish, sea and weather. In fact, I listen very hard to every word they say and every intonation, because they may sound like they are joking but they are not.

'Shall I untie the hooks that come with it on the line and put the flies and the new weight and flies on?'

'That would be great, thanks.' Within five minutes I had paid less than the price of local fish and chips, and I was set up to stand on the edge of one of the great barriers and fish. On the way to the cathedral I bought a brown balaclava which I thought I might need if the wind blew up on the Barriers.

I went to the Cathedral office, and there Ingrid, who was Orcadian but looked and sounded Norwegian, informed me, 'Your guide will be here in a minute.'

'Are there many on the guided tour today?'

'Just you. We only go upstairs to the top of the tower twice a week.' Just then in walked a strange looking man with a happy smile.

'Morning, Michael,' said Ingrid.

'Hello to you, and to you too,' he said, looking at both of us.

'Hello,' I said.

'Have you shown him the photos yet?'

'No. I've been looking for the keys to the money box for change.'

'I can come back later in the week for change,' I offered.

'Don't worry, we'll find some change,' said Ingrid

'Can you look at these photos and sign the indemnity agreement? Said Ingrid.

'No trouble,' I said as I skipped through the photos which seemed normal to me.

'It's to make sure you can deal with very tight spaces and heights.'

'I'm OK with those,' I said, knowing I was now conning my way onto what was obviously an infrequent tour and meant only for the very brave, which I always hoped to be one day. I just kept quiet about my fear of heights.

'Let's go then.' And off we wandered straight upstairs to the first floor balcony where a small museum was kept.

From there Michael asked, 'How much do you know about the cathedral?'

'I know it was built in 1137 in a Romanesque style from two types of sandstone, red and white.'

'More or less right. It's regarded as the best building made of different types of stone in Britain. The name Kirkwall comes from Kirkjuvagar which means "Church Bay". It took over three hundred years to build because of all sorts of problems, like being abandoned due to lack of funds. Do you know the story of St Magus from the Orkneyinga Saga and the building of the cathedral?'

'Yes, I read about it, so you don't need to go through all that. I just really want to see the highlights of the cathedral.'

'Well, down there in that pillar in the chapel are the bones of Saint Magus. The skull has what looked like axe wounds to it. Did you know that the cathedral is owned by the people and not by the Church of Scotland?'

'No. That's a bit odd. How come?'

'It was given as dowry to King James III by the king of Denmark, but it didn't bring him any income, and, as it was expensive to maintain, he transferred it to the Magistrates Council and Community of Kirkwall to look after. It's a parish church and has had no bishops since 1688.'

'What's that?' I asked, looking at a long wooden structure on the floor.

'It's a ladder.'

'Really? Funny looking ladder. Why's it so wide?'

'It is a double ladder with 3 thirty-foot long rung holders with a set of rungs on either side. Have a look at it. Inspect it and tell me what you think.'

'Well. It's simply a double ladder, as you say, and about thirty feet long, made of wood and that's it.

'Tell me about the rungs.'

'Well they are a bit worn on one side.'

'You've got it. One set of rungs for the hangman and one for his victim, or client as they would call them today. It's seventeenth century, and if you look closely you will see one side is worn more than the other all the way along.'

'How come?'

'Well the hangman and his victim both went up the steps but only the hangman came down the steps, so his side is more worn.'

'They must have hanged a lot of people to wear a ladder down that much. Where did the hangings take place here?'

'Up on the hill behind here. But no as many as in London. I used to live near the old Tyburn gallows in London. They used to hang twenty-five people at once, every few minutes. They had crowds, eight times a year, in excess of any spectators at football match today. They used to get the victims drunk on ale on the Edgware Road so they would be sedated by the time they got on the gallows.'

'I know exactly where you mean.'

'If you look down there you'll see a triangular board rather like a board outside a pub with the name of the pub on it. Only this is a Mort Board and was hung outside a person's house to announce they were dead. It had their name on one side and a verse or two about them on the other side. It's seventeenth century and was used locally.'

We went up another story of very small steps which were perhaps only four inches in depth and I had to go up more or less on tiptoes. We both held onto the ropes on either side for what seemed like a very long way. I looked out of a window, then up another storey of even narrower stairs. My shoulders touched the wall on both sides, and I had to walk sideways, such was the narrowness of the ancient stone stairwell. I looked through a small set of double doors, and Michael shone a light in there.

'That floor is the stonework above the chapel which supports the ceiling. The stone slabs are vertical and are self-supporting like an arch. Above this unusual floor is the roof which has huge wooden buttresses. The whole ceiling was made from oak timber from wrecked ships.' We came down and looked around the area. 'This is the old clock, and this is the new one which is essentially just a large version of the old one.'

'What's in the big cabinet?'

'This is what makes it tick.' And as he opened a cabinet as big as a large wardrobe I could see an enormous swinging pendulum, perhaps one-foot wide and two feet long, of solid lead and brass. It swung about two metres across. The clock works on weights which are up there in the tower.'

I walked across the wooden floor to look up, and the floor on I was standing began to move a little. I looked down, and to my horror I could see I was standing on a five-by five-foot trapdoor, and my heart nearly leapt out of my mouth. All I wanted to do was jump, but instead, just in case the doors opened, I carefully raised my arms as if I was walking on a tight rope and walked off the trapdoors. I looked back at it and could see that I had not been looking.

'The trapdoors are used to bring things up here for the bells, the clock or for cleaning. It's a hundred-foot drop,' he said, almost casually. I felt a bit dizzy, but I recovered. We went even higher, but this time up a small, wooden spiral staircase which would usually have been made of wrought iron. This took us into the belfry. I took some photos, and then it was an even higher climb up to the top of the tower, where Michael opened a door.

'Do you like the view?' There was a very low wall; the kind you feel compelled to walk over even though there was a 150-foot drop.

'Yes, but I'm not sure how far I can go out there.' I leant out with my camera in one hand and one hand on the doorknob. I took two photos of the harbour and the town, and felt I had done my tourist deed for the day. In terms of my vertigo and fear of heights, I knew Chrisie would be impressed with the height from which these photos were taken.

'What's the time?'

'Nearly eleven o'clock.

'We'd better get out of here quick.'

'What's the rush?'

'The bells.'

'What about them?'

'They're about to sound. Quick, follow me.' A minute later I closed the wooden door behind me and a second later there was a devastating din as the bells chimed.

'Glad we weren't in there,' he said. I've been caught once before. Couldn't hear for a couple of days. Worse than after a gig.'

'Thanks for that. You were right. That is seriously loud,' I said as I listened to the noon chimes.

'So where are you from?' I asked.

'London, originally.'

'How long have you been up here?'

'I've slowly worked my way up north over eighteen years.'

'What's your day time job?'

'I teach adults part time.'

'And what else?' I asked, because he was very bright.

'I'm doing a PhD on human ecology … part-time, nearly finished. And where are you from?

'Ipswich.' I never like admitting this because Ipswich is such a tired old town.

'My mum was from Ipswich.' I could see he was very vigilant now. 'Where did you live there?'

'On Constable Road.'

He stopped and his jaw dropped. 'My mum was born on Constable Road.'

'I lived there for fifteen years. This seems like a bit of Jungian synchronicity. What was your mum's name?

'Alderton.'

'Well, that's an old Ipswich name. I know an Alderton, but he didn't come from Ipswich, his grandfather did. Where was your dad from?'

'The west of Ireland.'

'So was my mum; which part was your dad from?'

'Mayo.'

'My mum was from Sligo, just next door.' We wandered down to the ground floor.

'This is the pillar that contains the bones of St Magus who was murdered with one blow of an axe to the top of his head. And in that pillar over there are the bones of the founder of the cathedral. The tour over, we went back in the office and I was given the change that Ingrid had found. It was an odd feeling, as though I had been back in the twelfth century and going outside was like re-entering into the future. It was a powerful experience which I often have in old temples. I'm sure it's just psychological and you just put yourself in a certain mood and state of mind on entering these vast buildings raised to the skies.

That feeling was still with me when at ten to seven in the evening the phone rang. 'Is that you mate?'

'Yes, what's up?'

'Hey, mate, Peter here. Just helping the young medical officer. Supper will be half an hour late. Is that OK?'

'No worries. Give me a shout when you're done.'

The phone rang and twenty minutes later and I drove down to Peter's flat in the nursing home. There was another

English doctor – Richard – there who was an anaesthetist, who seemed engrossed in preparing a massive salad of tuna, boiled eggs, beetroot and lettuce. We all swapped stories.

'I was in the Falklands for three trips and had my own practice in NZ for ten years. I had to retrain as an anesthetist when I was forty-six.'

'Doesn't make feel so bad,' I said.

'No? Why?'

'I had to retrain as a GP last year, because I'd been out of the NHS system for more than ten years.'

'Bummer, isn't it?'

'Yes, but it's not so bad when it's all over. It's simple food,' said Peter, putting some cheese biscuits and some salmon roll mops on the table followed by a bowl of salad and a plate of macaroni.

'I think it's great. I'm trying to live a bit further down the food chain right now, to be more simple. Let's hope none of us gets called out.' And before I could complete the word 'out' my phone was ringing.

'Switch here. Got a call out for you.'

'What's the details?'

'An eighty-eight year old male. Give the rest to you later. Urgent; putting you through to his daughter.'

'Me dad saw the GP today with shingles and a bladder infection. He gave him antibiotics and something for the shingles. We just found him in the garden. Don't know how long he's been there.' I could almost smell the fear in the daughter's voice.

'Give me five minutes to get there. I'm just around the corner. If he gets worse, call an ambulance.'

'I'll put the rest of the pasta in the oven. Call me if you need me, otherwise I'll see you later for dessert.'

As I drove to the house, I took details on the phone from switchboard. When I passed the hospital I saw an ambulance with flashing blue lights take a turn behind me. When I pulled up outside the house, the son was waiting there for me. As I grabbed my bag from the boot of the Vauxhall Vector I could see the ambulance coming down the hill.

'He collapsed two minutes ago.'

'OK, let me have a look at him. You sort out the ambulance men and let them in.' He looked bad. Unconscious. 'OK you guys take over. He'll need to go in now. He's breathing, got a weak pulse and unconscious. Could be a stroke, septicemia or the medication he's on.'

I phoned switchboard at the hospital, but there was no reply to the on-call doctor or his bleep. After two minutes, I asked Switch to call Peter to ask him to come in urgently. I met him at the hospital doors and talked about his condition while he sorted him out. There were so many reasons why he could have collapsed, but it was his problem now, not mine, and so at ten I had to excuse myself and try and get some rest.

At eleven I was put through to a police officer.

'Hello there. Are you the doc?'

'That's me?'

'I just took a call from a Dutchman who, I think, is known as Jim, who was looking for the Community Psychiatric Nurse. She's away at the moment on the mainland, and so I asked him if he was Jim. He went silent and hung up.'

'What do you know about him?'

'He's a known depressive with suicidal tendencies. Once he drove to some cliffs which are a well know suicide spot. He had his wheels actually on the edge of the cliff. The wind itself could have blown his car over. He was telling me that he was going to jump. We had to get the police helicopter in from the Shetlands. By the time it got here, it needed refuelling, so they had to re-open the airport just for that. We had to get in police negotiators to talk him out of it. When we thought we were doing a good job, he would reverse six inches to a foot, and when he got angry he would go back onto the edge with his wheels.'

'So, how can I help now?'

'I want to try and ring him at home and see if he needs to talk to someone. Can I ring you back if he wants to talk?'

'No trouble at all. Be glad to help.'

Half an hour later I was woken again. 'What did he say?'

'Said he didn't need help and the police were harassing him again.'

'Sounds like he's got a few problems.'

'Certainly has, and I don't think that's the end of it tonight.'

'Ah well, what can you do. Call me later if you need me.' I bade him a good night and after that it was another quiet shift.

Chapter 6.

Mainland Orkney, South Ronaldsay and Burray Island. Day 6

It was Saturday, and I was going to be on call until 9.00 am on Monday, a sixty-hour shift, which is probably against all EEC regulations. On Saturday I had a look and a feel of the hand-held square fishing line, and, as it was a warm sunny day, I thought I should use the good weather to stand outside and fish from one of the four Barriers.

First, I thought, I should check with the GP on North Ronaldsay about the accommodation. 'Hi, it's me again, the locum coming up in a while. I'm just ringing to check to see if we can stay in the surgery. I was speaking to a doctor who did your locum a while ago, and he said he stayed in the flat about the surgery.'

'No, it's really not suitable. It's not modernized at all. In fact it is really not livable in at all.'

'Are you sure, because he said it was OK?'

'Believe me, it is not suitable for you.'

'We are not particularly fussy about it being modernized, as long as it has the basic amenities.'

'It really won't suit you.'

'Well, if you say so.'

'I've booked you in to our family room with a bed on the floor for your four year old.' He had convinced me. The last thing I wanted was my wife and daughter turning up to live in a completely run down house.

'And we can't self-cater there?' I said, checking it out one final time.

'No, we have everything you need.' I cynically thought we might end up paying for this dearly, but it seemed that I really had no choice. I still had some reservations, because two people said to double check the accommodation and that the Health Board were just trusting him. I thought a good plan would be to take a certain amount of food up with us, just in case we found somewhere which was self-catering. I planned to do a good shop at the local supermarket in Kirkwall before Chrisie and India came up.

I started the car and just started moving down the driveway towards Barrier No 1 when I heard my phone ringing.

'NHS hub from the Aberdeen Royal Infirmary. Is that the doc?'

'Yes, how can I help you?' This might be a home visit.

'It's a woman in Kirkwall who wants some telephone advice about back pain.'

'OK. Give me the number and I'll call her.'

'What's the trouble?' I asked the woman when she answered my call.

`I think I've got a kidney infection again.' I began to think that most of the call outs I had so far had been kidney stones or kidney infections. Maybe there was a reason for this is. They are pretty horrible, painful things which most people can't actually cope with without very strong prescribed medication.

'How long have you had it.?'

'I've had back ache for two days, and I've been peeing frequently for four, and it hurts when I pee.'

'I'm going to need to see you to have a look at you, but I'll be half an hour.' And off I set, but I only got to the end of the drive when the phone went again.

'I've got another one for you. It's a home visit. She can't get out of bed and is short of breath.'

'OK. I'll be half an hour. Can you text the details to me,

and I'll call you back with the outcomes.'

'No trouble.' I was less than halfway into Kirkwall when the phone went again.

'I'm really sorry, but it's me again with another call.'

'Don't worry; it's my job.'

'Well, we've had more calls today than we usually get in a week.'

'What's this one?'

'It's a sixty year old man who had a flu jab four days ago and now's got a swollen, painful, throbbing arm.'

'OK. Text me again and I'll see him last.' And on I drove to Kirkwall. The urinary tract infection got Paracetamol and Penicillin. The woman who was short of breath had emphysema and a chest infection, and, because she lived alone and couldn't get water for herself or get to the toilet, I had to admit her. The infected flu jab started a course of penicillin.

Within two and a half hours of setting out, I was standing on the pier beside Churchill Barrier No 2 and casting my hand line into the natural harbor called Scapa Flow. It was warm, but I kept my coat on just in case there was change in the weather, but it stayed fine.

The fisherman who rigged my fishing line said that Barrier No 2 would be the best place to fish. He was right in many ways, as it gave me a little shelter. Using the hand line was a simple procedure, unwinding about thirty feet of line and casting the heavy lead weight, with the coloured flies attached, off into the water and pulling it back in again. As soon as you do something like this, your mind has an entirely different set of things to focus on: temperature, wind, noise, the state of your back, time passing, thirst, hunger; and then you let go and you relax into the moment, and none of those things bother you.

After half an hour, I noticed a figure in the distance walking towards me across Churchill Barrier No 1. Fifteen minutes later he was walking along the pier, and he looked vaguely familiar.

'How are you?' It was Richard, the man who let me into the chalet on my arrival.

'I'm good, thanks. And yourself?'

'Loving the weather.'

'Just trying to catch a fish.'

'This is a great spot. I've caught a few cod here.'

'The fisherman who sells rods in town said that it was very good for cod.'

'Are you sure you'd be able to hold one with that kid's rod?'

'Well, yes, I suppose it is a kid's rod come to think of it. But I'll give it a go.'

'They can be four feet long and fifteen to twenty kilos.'

'Ouch! That is too big for me. It's just being here really. If I actually ever managed to catch a fish, I'd probably just have to cut the line anyway.'

'Oh, I didn't mean it like that. It's just that they can give you a very big fight.'

'That's exactly what I meant. I don't think I'd want to get into a fight with anything, standing on this pier. There are no sides to the pier or anything to hold on to and the fish would probably pull me in,' I said, laughing.

'Partly true, but it's more the wind you need to be careful of on this pier, because with a jacket like that it would take you up off the ground just like a kite.' My jacket was long and wide at the bottom, and I could imagine how it could fill with wind. 'We sometimes get sudden gusts which are unbelievably strong; they can actually lift you up. It's usually from November onwards, so be careful of them.'

'Thanks for the warning. I'll pay attention to the wind.' I noticed that the wind did seem to come in gusts every ten or twenty seconds but it was never a constant wind.

'Pretty nice view as well. You can see all around you here. Do you know the story of the Barriers?'

'No. The manager at the practice said I was staying next to one called Churchill Barrier No 1 and that they were built by Italian prisoners of war. What more is there to know about them?'

'Not very much, but they were involved in important historical events during World War II.'

'Like what exactly?'

'The area more or less encircled by the Islands is known as Scapa Flow. It's surrounded by Mainland Orkney to the north and west, and by Hoy to the south. It's enclosed on the east from the top downwards by the four islands of Lamb Holm, Glimps Holm, Burray and South Ronaldsay. It's a great natural anchorage and was used during World War II. It is really an inland sea of about eighty square miles.'

'I drove up the east side, but I had no idea it was so big. I don't understand the point about the barriers.'

'This huge natural anchorage had one drawback: there were several entrances between the islands through which enemy vessels could enter and leave. In World War I twenty-one Blockships were sunk at these entrance points and were still there at the beginning of World War II when a further twenty-two were added, but there were arguments and haggling over the costs of sinking more Blockships. Then an incident happened at high tide on October 14, 1939.'

'I'm interested now,' I said. I had no idea this was used as a base during World War II.

'Gunter Prien, a German U boat commander, managed to carefully manoeuvre his U47 submarine to the surface through Kirk Sound and into Scapa Flow. He torpedoed and sank the battleship HMS Royal Oak which was anchored under the cliffs at Gaitnip, and 833 people lost their lives. He escaped by the same route and wasn't even seen. It was a very severe blow to the British and so very early on in the war. So, do you see why they were built?'

'Yes, I understand now. I've passed them all a few times. It looks like they are tarmac roads on top of piles of metre-square blocks.'

'No, they are more complex than that, and there was more than one reason why they were built. Following this incident sixty thousand men and women of the Army, Air Force and Navy were garrisoned here. Breaching the entrances to the sounds was one of the biggest threats to face the Navy.'

'Is that why there are so many Nissen huts still here, being used by farmers?'

'Yes, there are hundreds all over the islands. The work started early in 1940 and stopped in October 1941 in order to build camps for Italian POWs who were going to help build the Barriers. At first the Italians went on strike because it was work to do with the war, which was against the Geneva Convention, but they eventually restarted when they were told that the Barriers would be of service to the local communities after the war.'

'How long did they stay here?'

'Nearly three years in all. They came in January 1942, after being defeated in the Western Desert, and were in Camp 60 until they left in September 1944. They were the same Italians who built the Italian Chapel.'

'I haven't managed to get to the chapel yet. What are

these barriers made of?'

'At first they tipped hundreds of tons of rocks into the channel, which the Cockneys used to describe as madness, because, as they said, we were having a go at, "Fillin in the sea." But this didn't work, as the rocks were carried away by the strong currents.'

'So they were right.'

'Yes. So, we had to think again. There were lines of broken rocks, or bolsters, which were huge, five-ton steel wire bags of rock put into place by the cableways at each barrier. These broken rocks were then filled in with infill or rubble.

On top of this were laid two very neat parallel lines of even clothing of ten-ton concrete blocks on either side of the potential road. And these and the rest of the side are covered with five-ton blocks dropped from the cableway. The ten-ton blocks are hidden. Although the five-ton blocks you can see look as if they were just dropped randomly, this is not the case, because they were not so much dropped but laid at exact angles to break up the force of severe waves before they could reach the ten-ton blocks underneath. If you look in harsh weather you'll easily see it'

'They must have used a lot of blocks for the four barriers.'

'One of the sounds was 1,400 feet across and the other three are 2,000 feet long and at places 50 feet deep. 580,000 tons of loose rock and 333,000 tons of concrete were used. They used to make a hundred blocks a day here.'

'And what about the Italians?'

'There were six hundred in the first batch to arrive. But there were also British and Irish workers, who were later needed elsewhere down south. Of the hundreds that worked on the barriers, I know that at least five people were killed and two people lost arms.' I noticed it was getting chilly, and I asked Richard if he wanted a lift back to the chalets.

'Good idea. Would you like a coffee to warm you up?'

'Yes, might as well,' I said.

'Let me just tell you about this wee place where you're staying. If you'd been here in World War II, you'd have probably not only seen Gunter Prien fifty yards from here, maneuvering his U47 submarine on the surface through Kirk Sound into Scapa Flow and sink the Royal, but you may have heard him give the orders in German: "Fire torpedo one... fire torpedo two." Even today hundreds of relatives of the dead come and visit the sea grave every year.'

'I had no idea they still did.'

'Yes. Relatives come from as far away as South Africa. But just as important is what happened in this very place in World War 1. From your room here, you can see Scapa Flow.

In July 1917 the British battleship HMS Vanguard was at anchor off Flotta. Some unstable cordite blew up in one of her magazines, and the Vanguard blew up and immediately sank killing over eight hundred men. In October 1918 UB116 tried to slip into the Flow but was detected and blown up in the controlled minefield. None of her thirty-six crew survived.

It really was the Pearl Harbor of the North. In May 1916 the British Fleet sailed from Scapa to fight the Germans in the battle of Jutland, which was the last time a set-piece Nelson style battle was fought. Both sides thought they had won, and there was an armistice which resulted in seventy-four ships of the Kaiser Wilhelm's Germany were being ordered to surrender. They arrived in Scapa in November 1918. In June 1919 the German commanding officer read a report in a four-day-old copy of The Times, which was the only source of information they had, as their radios had been confiscated by the British. The peace terms were so staggeringly severe that he decided to scuttle the whole fleet. Fifty-two out of seventy-four ships were sunk.'

'I must have missed that at school, because I had to give up history in order to study science very early on. That would have been a sight to see.'

'Funny you should say that, because a large group of schoolboys were out as a party from Stromness to look at the ships when they were all scuttled.'

'Probably the most exciting trip they ever had,' I said.

'There are over eighty wrecks down there – forty-two Blockships, three German battleships, four cruisers and four destroyers, as well as a U boat, an escort vessel and an E boat. There are also nine Royal Navy wrecks which include two battleships. There are at least fourteen other sea vessels. It's one of the best diving sites in the UK, but every summer a boat goes down to bring up live pictures.'

'Sounds a lot easier than diving.'

After Richard left, I reflected on the day and remembered that I had the usual fisherman's luck of catching no fish, yet I was feeling invigorated; and I looked out across at Barrier No 1 and Barrier No 2 with a different eye.

My late afternoon nap was interrupted by a seventy-five year old man whose plaster of Paris arm plaster was causing him pain. I suggested pain killers until the morning, when I would go and see him if he was no better. I settled in for a quiet night behind a pamphlet Richard lent me about the Barriers.

Chapter 7.

Mainland Orkney, South Ronaldsay and Burray Island. Day 7

At sixteen, I stopped going to Christian churches on Sundays, but now I was going to make an exception. As a young man, all attempts to encourage me to be a Christian had totally failed, and since then I've spent much more time in temples of the other religions than anyone else I know, trying to sense and remain constantly in touch with the common denominator of spirituality, that part of the Venn Diagram where they all overlap in the area of reality about God.

I felt happy about going over to the chapel, but I had one small task to put to bed before I felt the day was clear, and that was the man with the painful plaster of Paris on his arm from the night before. I phoned him to see if he was feeling better. He wasn't, and he had only gone to bed at six in the morning. So I said I would visit.

He lived in a big, empty house which was big enough for a family of ten, but there was hardly any furniture, and I would guess it was last swept or cleaned in any way probably several years ago. It smelt, and there were various types of alcohol all over the place. There were whisky bottles, cans of beer and bottles of wine in all sorts of strange places, but mainly they littered the floor. He had a dirty, unkempt beard, and his face was dark and grubby with dirt. From experience of other patients, I knew that one broken arm in plaster is not an excuse to not wash your face. Sadly, I think the drink had taken hold of him. I had been warned that Orkney had a terrible death rate from alcohol use, and here was a clear example.

He was friendly but, clearly, also a true eccentric who paid no attention to the outside world. His fingers were pink and he could move them all, so I reassured him that the plaster was not too tight, and then like a good boy off I went to church.

I had lived beside this Nissen hut for a week and had not ventured in, because there were other important and interesting things I felt I wanted to see and do first. But now, as I walked over to it from Barrier No 1 I felt excited.

It had more frontage than Harrods; it was meant to. The front presents as a typical whitewashed Christian church with a steeple and bell over the whitewashed portals. But when you look around the back it was still a Nissen hut. The front is only about a foot thick, and behind it are two classic Nissen huts joined end to end, which have been partly disguised by a covering of gravelly bitumen-covered sheets. If the front of the church is a little cheeky, then the inside is the most outlandish piece of interior decorating I've come across. It worked perfectly well and is a wonder to see. Almost every aspect of the floor, walls and ceiling were done in the tromp l'oeil, and it had clearly been done by an expert in this field. The floor is just concrete, but, very cleverly, the first part of the church's floor was marked with indentations, whilst the concrete was still wet, to look mimic slabs of stone.

The lower walls were stone pillars executed brilliantly in tromp l'oeil. The rest of the walls were brick, again done in tromp l'oeil, and the ceilings were Italianate and the most effective part of the whole illusion. The whole ceiling was in tromp l'oeil.

The chapel was unfurnished, apart from a simple bench down each side, although I spotted, through one of the two stained glass windows behind the altar, a few piles of chairs in the sacristy. There were two lanterns hanging from the ceiling over the passage leading up to the sanctuary. There should have been three, but the one from the front door was missing.

I was told by the guide at Skara Brae that these lamps were made from six-pound corned beef tins. The sanctuary itself was separated by a delicate wrought iron screen. The altar was made of concrete and above it was a painting of the Madonna and Child surrounded by six cherubs. It is titled Queen of Peace.

There were two windows to each Nissen hut, and these were in typical Nissen hut style, the windows projecting boldly out of the curved hut's side. The glass strengthened with wire squares was the only hint that this was a World War II building. The chapel was adorned with fourteen Stations of the Cross and a rather special Madonna; an image which all Italians hold close to their hearts. Although it had restoration work done in 1960, it was now in need of more work and preservation. It almost needed to be secured in another outer structure to protect it from the elements and to seal it in time for the future. One whole panel was damp and flapping about, and a large area of wall was very damp. It was only a matter of time before the thick inner lining, bearing the wonderful tromp l'oeil, began to peel off like damp wallpaper.

The Italians probably decided to build a chapel from a Nissen hut for two reasons. The first and most important reason was very likely simple boredom. The second was probably to have something tangible and visible to remind them of their Catholic homeland in the barren landscape of Lamb Holm.

The chapel was the only remaining part of the Camp 60. Just across the barbed wire fence was the concrete plinth of the rest of the camp buildings which were dismantled the day the Italians left. When they were living there they built paths and grew flowers to make the place more homely.

They only used redundant materials from obsolete military equipment, because the British wouldn't let them have anything else. The British probably had a great deal of interest and fun in seeing just what these Italians were doing with bits of junked military vehicles and corned beef cans. The most important Italian involved in the whole project was Domenico Chiocchetti from Moena. He was the interior painter of the striking tromp l'oeil art work used throughout the chapel. He re-visited after the war and touched up his work in 1960. The last visit by any of the original prisoners was in 1992.

Early that evening I got a call from the Police Surgeon, who was none other than a GP wearing a different hat and sounding a bit different too, a bit like a police man.

'Got a bipolar woman who's going to the GP-secure-cell bed on Nissen ward.'

'What's her name?' I asked.

'No need to know that.'

'OK, no dramas.'

'No, there aren't any dramas.' He kind of missed my humor.

'I meant no worries.'

'There aren't any.' Boy, was he serious.

'Good, then I suppose I'll be seeing her later?'

'No, only if there's a problem.' This person really was a little too serious.

'I hope you don't mind me asking, but if she's in the police secure-cell and I'm the GP who's responsible for her, what's the management plan.

'She'll be going off to the Aberdeen Psychiatric Unit on the first available plane seat with the Community Psychiatric Nurse.

'Do you want me to see her?'

'No … not unless there are any issues.'

'OK, she's got no issues at the moment then?'

'No. She's in the secure-cell bed.' But as far as I could see this woman clearly did have some issues. However, this wasn't my patch or my brief, and I was going to try to be a good boy in Orkney. I was not going to wave the flag every time human rights might be an issue. I was not going to challenge the police. I was going to write clearly. I was going to keep my mouth shut. I was going to behave and be non-confrontational.

Chapter 8.

Mainland Orkney, South Ronaldsay and Burray Island. Day 8

There wasn't a single call all night and, as usual, in the morning I made my way into the surgery to hand over the notes on my eight weekend visits and two other calls. I got cornered by a GP who seemed a bit distressed.

'Are you the person I spoke to over the weekend?' I asked as he came up to me.

'Yes. Have you got your locum agent's phone number?'

'Sure. All the contact details are on a time sheet. Here, you can have this spare one.' And I handed him a time sheet from my agency.

'Thanks.'

'Aren't you one of the three salaried GPs here?' I asked.

'Yes.'

'How long have you been here?'

'Two years, but I've had enough. I'm not sure if you're aware, but one of the doctors is practicing under supervision.'

'No, I wasn't aware of that. But doctors frequently do, especially if they are retraining.'

Alarm bells started going off in my head, similar to those in Gillingham. In Gillingham I was told nothing about the GP for whom I was standing in. Many of his patients told me he was always falling asleep, and I assumed he must have had Narcolepsy. During an evening with the rest of the Gillingham GPs I found out that, as well as working full time as a single handed GP, he was also working twelve-hour night shifts, four nights a week.

But what made me immediately resign from the post was what I heard about his practice manager. Unbeknown to me, the practice manager was a former GP who had been struck off as a doctor by the General Medical Council, for fraudulently claiming a home visit fee for a visit he hadn't done. He was only found out because the patient died and hadn't been seen by doctor. When this came to light, it also brought up a string of quite outrageous sex offenses against female patients. He had asked one patient if he could kiss her whilst he was performing an intimate examination. And this was the least serious of his offenses.

This time I was going to keep my job. Principles cost you money, and at this time I needed the work. My focus now returned to the flustered Orkney GP in front of me.

' … and he's sleeping with one of the directors of Orkney Health Board. And what's worse, her deputy is sleeping with one of the GPs at the other practice.'

'These girls sure have an interesting way of managing the GPs,' I said with a smile. 'I'm just trying to have a peaceful time here. I guess it takes all sorts.'

'Well, the Health Board here is hounding me because I've mentioned this. They are trying to get me to work under supervision because I wrote the wrong condition down for when I was off sick, and they're now saying I lied.'

'Did you?' I asked, even thought it was none of my business.

'I was depressed and took six weeks off, and said it was stress.'

'It doesn't sound too bad. I wouldn't worry about it. They can't jump on you for that.'

'You don't know what they're like.'

'I probably won't find out. I'm just passing through,' I said, and off he went to do his morning surgery. I did wonder if he was being targeted because maybe he misread a pass from one of the directors of the health board. Maybe his ego was bruised, because he was not in bed with one of these two women. Who knows and who cares I thought. They were not my problems and thank goodness I was not a GP in Orkney, otherwise it could be a bit murky.

'Morning,' said the Office Manager in a bright voice.

'Good morning. Did you have a good weekend? You seem chirpy.'

'Oh yes. I went walking. And yourself?'

'Fairly quiet, but interesting stuff. No middle-of-the-night calls. These are the notes on a couple of people who'll be coming in today to see their own GP. I've written some urgent notes, as a couple of these people have not had any blood tests done when they really should have been done a long time ago. Some people just don't like needles. It just needs pointing out to the GPs. I had to remind the patients that they needed blood tests. And here's my time sheet for the last week.'

'Thanks. I'll send it off today.'

'How long have you been using locums here?' I asked.

'Since the last partner left nearly two years ago.'

'It must be difficult, having no one sailing the ship in terms of leadership. I know Orkney Health Authority is managing the place, but that's not exactly hands-on clinical management of the practice and community. It's distant management by politicians, which, in relation to care of patients, is rudderless.'

'That's absolutely true, and there's no sign of it getting any better, except that one GP is possibly opening his own practice here next year. But he's going to be managed by Orkney Health Authority for the first year. The politics are very messy up here among the practices, the Primary Care Trust and Orkney Medical Authority.'

'Presumably none of the GPs in Kirkwall are trying to earn quality points?'

'No, that's right. They aren't bothering because they're only salaried doctors. Only partners get any of the extra money the practice earns, but there aren't any left here now; they're all salaried here. They are partners on the Isles though.'

'Quite a mess isn't it?'

'We hope it'll improve one day again.'

'I hope so. It's a beautiful spot with very good patients. It's a shame the doctors are in this position. I too hope it gets better. I'll be in again in the morning.'

At two in the afternoon, I realized I hadn't heard from Chrisie since she had picked India up from school, so I called her on my mobile, but there was no signal. The two practice mobiles were also not working, and I couldn't get an outside line on the landline in my chalet. The only solution was to go into Kirkwall to get a better signal. When I got there, I spoke to Chrisie for ten seconds before the signal went completely on both my mobiles. The only thing I could do was to go and see the Office Manager at the practice.

'I've got no mobile phone signal here.'

'Nor have we. We've got three different mobile phone services and none work.'

'Can you give the hub and switch at the hospital my land line number?'

'OK, and oh, there's just one more thing.'

'What's that?'

'The wind is going to be strong tonight.

'How strong?'

'Rumours are that it'll be more than a hundred miles per hour. If you're a sailor, you may have experienced that at sea and you'll know how severe that is. So be careful about making a choice to visit. Don't risk your own life. I hope for your sake it's quiet.'

'Thanks.' And off she went, smiling her very kind, warm smile.

There was a knock on the door, then another knock. 'Is your mobile phone working?' It was Richards's wife Louise, who owned the Chalets.

'No, none of them are, and I can't get this landline to answer.'

'That's because it's switched off.' She turned the phone upside down, and there was a button, and beside it a sign saying ON/OFF.

'Thanks.'

'You know the calls to that phone come through to me, as I'm the switchboard for taking bookings, so I'll have to re-route them to you. We are out tonight, and I can't do that, so shall I transfer the main number over to you?'

'Yes. That sounds sensible.'

'If there's an enquiry, just take the number and I'll call them back in the morning.'

'No problem at all.'

'I'll re-route the calls in the morning.'

'That will help, as the mobiles probably won't be working until then.'

After she left, I stepped outside. There was a wind, but it was the type I had got used to here over the last few days - maybe forty to fifty miles per hour. I went inside and double-checked I had everything ready for a home visit. It seemed to me that, if she was right about the weather, this could be a challenging night. Because Britain is an island, the weather can be very difficult for forecasters to get right. I was on one of its smaller offshore islands where accurate weather forecasts are unusual. Nevertheless, I made sure everything was where it should be for a quick getaway to a home visit. On the sofa were the maps in a carrier bag, car and house keys, three phones and my bleep.

I dropped my level in the food chain down one more notch and for the fifth time I was having tomatoes on rye crisp bread. At seven o'clock, just when I was biting into the last of the crisp breads laden with tomato, salt and pepper, I heard the sweet sound of music from my phone.

'Switchboard here.'

'Hi there, how's it going?'

'We're in for a real humdinger tonight.'

'Do you mean the wind?'

'It's not just wind, its weather. I wouldn't go out after about nine on any visits tonight, and if anyone who calls you is very sick, you may be better asking the police to drive you.'

'It's not going to be that bad, is it?'

'Afraid so. My family are fishermen, and they won't even go to the pub tonight. This one's a thirteen year old girl. No details, so I'll put you through to her father.'

'Thanks for the advice. I will heed it; I'm no martyr.'

'Is that the doc?' I heard a voice say when I called.

'Yep, what's up?'

'Rochine's seen the doctor today, but she's still in pain.'

'What did she see the doctor about?'

'Well, he reckons she's all bunged up and gave her some medicine.'

'Lactulose?'

'That's it.'

'And what's wrong right now?'

'The pain is still there.'

'How long's she had the pain?'

'Three days.'

'Is she eating and drinking and peeing OK.'

'Yes. I just wouldn't want to call you out later if she gets any worse because you may not be able to get here.'

'I'll be there in about twenty minutes.' These people were serious about what they called 'weather', and I wasn't going to mess with it either. Usually, I would have said that if there was any change I would see her, but I knew that if I said this, there would be a change and I would end up having to visit her later. But if I visited now, I could probably relax about it during the night and I would sleep better. So would she and her family.

When I arrived on the scene mum and daughter were there.

'Are your periods regular?'

'Yes, I've got one now.'

'A normal one?'

'Yes.'

'Where's the pain?'

'Here.'

'What's it like?'

'There all the time.'

'I just want to feel your tummy on the outside to make sure there's nothing urgent going on that needs sorting out at the hospital tonight.' After a look at her tummy I said, 'You're one of these people who should always carry a little bottle of water around with you to keep your fluid intake up because, if you don't drink enough, you can get constipated more often.'

'Can I have the flavoured drinks?'

'No, they're full of chemicals. Just drink water. And make sure you have at least two pieces of fruit a day.'

'I don't think we'll be calling you later, doc. That's what

we wanted to hear.' With that I was gone.

Waiting outside my chalet was Richard, who looked serious.

'Just to warn you about going over the Barriers.' His accent still sounded totally Welsh.

'Sure. What's the trouble?'

'If it's urgent you may have to go on your own, but you might want to think about asking the police to give you a lift over. It's Barrier No 2 you have to worry about, just when you pass the pier where we were fishing. Just past there the wind accelerates, and the sea can take you off the barrier. Be very careful if you have to go there. It is a really threatening place in the weather that's coming tonight. In the Western Isles in January this year the water was rising; and one family thought it was becoming unsafe, and so they decided to drive across the causeway. They were washed away by a wave and were all drowned.

'That's serious stuff,' I said.

'Probably best not to open any windows. Earlier this year the back window blew off the next chalet. Lost some ridge tiles too. See that one up there? Found it the next morning buried in four inches of earth. Flying objects are a real problem here. Best not to be out if you can help it.'

'Thank you Richard. I'll head your thoughtful words.'

'I hope you don't get called out.'

'I'm beginning to hope that too. Thanks.'

The wind hadn't changed, nor had the status of my phones. All three mobiles had no signal, but there was a message on the landline to call Switch at the hospital. I called.

'Someone just wants some telephone advice.'

'OK. Can you put me through?'

'Hello, I'm sorry to disturb you, but I just need some

advice.'

'Fire away.'

'Well, my husband went to the doc's today, and the doc gave him some things to put ... er ...'

'Suppositories?'

'Yes. Well, he put one in and he had to go to the toilet like straight away, and do you know ...' her words tailed off.

'And you want to know if he should take another one?' I said, trying to save her any embarrassment.

'That's right.'

'Give him another one. But coat the suppository in something like liquid soap, or any kind of lubricant. Sometimes, the chemicals in these pain killers cause an instant reflex to have your bowels open. You can sometimes delay this by covering the suppository with something else. Other than that, good luck.'

'You're a real pal, doc. Thanks, and have a quiet night.' As soon as I had gone to bed the phone rang.

'The Commodore,' I said, joking.

'Is that the Commodore Motel?'

'Sure is. How can I help?'

'I'd like to make a booking for two nights - the 8th and 9th of December for two of us in one of the large apartments with a view of the islands.'

'No trouble at all. Can I take a name?'

'Mrs Sterling.'

'Thank you for staying with us Mrs Sterling. How would you like to pay?

'Oh, cash please.'

'No trouble at all. Can I take a contact phone number, and Louise will call you back in the morning to confirm the booking.'

No sooner had I just relaxed, listening to the fierce wind, when the phone rang. I was not looking forward to venturing outside. I was a bit more serious.

'Good morning. Congratulations you've won first prize,' said the voice at the other end of the line.

This had to be some sales person from Bangalore selling insurance services of some kind, but I listened to what they had to say.

'What have I won?'

'You've won first prize in the Grand Christmas draw you entered at the weekend. You bought the winning ticket in the town hall extravaganza for all the local charities.'

'Oh, it wasn't me.'

'Who are you then?'

'I'm just the on-call doctor in South Ronaldsay. I'm answering the phone at the Commodore Apartments. Well, I'm using the phone because the mobile's not working due to the weather. I'm having to use the landline, but I have to take the calls for the Motel. I'll pass the message on to Louise.'

'We're only open three times a week.'

'When?'

'Tuesdays, Thursdays and Fridays, from 2.00 to 4.00 pm. My name is Belinda.'

'Thanks Belinda, I'll get Louise to call you tomorrow.'

I tucked myself up in bed, and by nine I could hear the weather outside. I was very happy to be indoors.

However, in the morning it was different. I wanted to go out and experience what it was like to stand and walk in a one-hundred-mile-per-hour wind. After all, I thought, when would I get the chance to experience this again? Probably tonight, said another part of me.

The wind was unusual. There was a loud noise of wind,

but there were no gusts at all. It was just continuous with no breaks. I put my tight wooly hat on, did my coat up, and walked out and stood on the inside of the porch. I wasn't yet actually in the wind, but I could see how strong it was. The dear old Vauxhall Vectra was bouncing two to three inches up and down and rolling from side to side, just as if there was a couple inside, enthusiastically following the advice of a fertility expert.

I stepped out of the porch on to the front lawn, and in less than a nanosecond, my hat was blown off. Then, suddenly, I couldn't see, because my hat had been holding down my glasses on my head and they were now flying through the air. Holy Hell! Forget the hat, I thought, as I could only just see my one pair of specs cartwheeling along on the lawn towards the road. I ran and, like a cricketer trying to stop a four reaching the boundary, I dived behind them and mercifully stopped them becoming part of Churchill Barrier No 1.

This was fun. I put my glasses back on, held them on with a finger on my nose, and spotted my wooly hat waving on a barbed wire fence. I walked over to the fence, picked my hat off the barbed wire and went back inside. I left my hat and glasses on the chair in the hall and went outside to dance with the weather. Well as near as I dared.

I found that I could actually walk in the wind and actually see what I was doing. It was as if I had just got the ball in a rugby match. My head was tucked in and I went at it with my strongest shoulder first. Yes, I did walk but with at least five times as much effort. I could sense that this would be exhausting for more than five minutes. I turned around, and it was the opposite. Having a hundered-mile-per-hour wind behind you is like walking in a gravity-free zone. You feel only a quarter of your weight, and you just bounce lightly along. As

I bounced along the long front lawn, propelled by the wind, I laughed; this job had let me get in touch with the child in me, who is so easily forgotten. It was a little reminder to have a bit more dialogue with this child, and a bit more fun.

Before I went into the surgery I could see the waves breaking at Barrier No 1 and the spray rising thirty feet over the roadway. I had to drive though this and see what it was like having the sea come over the car. But first I had to remove all of the white caked salt from the car windows. Higher up the property, I found a power hose behind a small pond and managed to get all the salt off the windows. I didn't clean the rest of the car because it would have looked too new, and I liked it looking a bit muddy like I was a local and not so much like a tourist. Driving through the thirty-foot spray was fun, and I must have gone backwards and forwards ten times, experiencing the spray hit the windscreen and the rest of the car with a crash. This was fun. If it was a solid wave, it would have only had to be two feet high to shift me off the barrier. The power I felt from the spray was enough to frighten me about the lethal enormity of the force of the waves, that Richard had mentioned.

In the afternoon the wind completely died down, and I went for a leisurely drive across Barrier No 1. I decided to find out how to get to the windsock which I had spotted on the top of the small island of Lamb Holm. I turned sharp left just before reaching Barrier No 2, and then sharp left again, and once again. I was going up a rough track to the top. On top was what looked like a well-trimmed grass strip, and there was someone coming out of what I could now see was a barn. The barn turned out to be an aircraft hangar owned by a retired farmer and fishery farmer. He had two airplanes.

'This one's a hand built English plane, and that one a

state-of-the-art fiberglass Australian four-seater,' he explained, showing me his planes.

'Did you build them?'

'Yep, both from kits. Both do about 120 miles per hour and use roughly 25 litres of fuel an hour. I've got relatives in Inverness and Aberdeen, and these are much quicker and cheaper than car, to get there.'

'And that plane over there, the amphibian?'

'That's one of two surviving Kingfishers in the UK. The person who owned it's not interested in it anymore, so I'm taking it on as a project.'

'They always appeal to me the most, because you've got more flexibility and, potentially, more fun.'

'You have to have a boating ticket as well as a pilot's ticket.'

'It makes sense. How long do you think it will take you?'

'Well, its good fun, and I would say about two years.'

'And how big is the strip?'

'Come, I'll show you.' There was a very large area of grass cut very short.

'Healthy looking grass. Looks more like a golf green,' I said.

'I keep it short and the rain does the rest. The ground is very fertile here. They're both twenty yards wide. The biggest one is 640 yards long, and the shorter one is 340 yards long.' He pulled a map of the island out and the strip virtually was the whole island of Lamb Holm. 'I call it the doughnut because of its shape.'

'What's that down there?' I asked.

'That's the old quarry, which is a hatchery now for crabs and lobsters. They send the crabs to Spain, and last year they hatched sixty-five thousand lobsters.'

It looked like a large shed, but on close inspection there were several structures containing water which, I could see, was being pumped from the sea alongside the pier where I had been fishing with Richard.

'I'd take you up, but I've got to get back to see the grandson arriving. Good luck now.'

I drove back past the Italian Chapel, over Barrier No 1 and crept into bed for an afternoon siesta. But it turned out to be a bit more than that.

It was exactly ten past six. How had I slept so long? Anyway it was the phone that woke me. I was probably more tired than I realized, or maybe it was the sea air.

'Switch here. It's the outpatient staff nurse.'

'Yes, what does she want?'

'Don't know.'

'Is it a problem?'

'Don't know, but I'll put you through.'

'Hi here. How can I help?'

'Got a suicidal person here.'

'How suicidal?'

'Well, seriously; she'll jump if I let her out of my sight.'

'That bad?'

'And I mean really seriously.'

'Any history?'

'No.'

'Can you tell me anything else?'

'Says she's got a drink problem, but she's sober now and has come here herself and brought her partner along for support.'

'I'll be about ten minutes. OK?'

'It's Room 3 in Out Patients.'

I knocked on the door of Room 3 and entered. 'Hi. I'm the doc.' There was the staff nurse who was on her way out and two individuals looking very droopy. 'Anything else you want to tell me?'

'No, she's just really suicidal.'

I walked in and introduced myself, 'I'm the doc,' and dumped my bag and coat on the floor, then sat down with my pad of paper. 'So what's up right now?'

'I don't want to be here. I want to go to Norway tonight.'

'Why Norway?'

'I can get some skis and find a good cliff, and that'll be it.'

'That's a painful way to do it.'

'My daughter jumped off the cliffs here. I've got three other kids.'

'Tell me about your daughter.'

'I had an argument with her just before she killed herself.'

'How long ago?'

'Two years ago.'

'Right now, how do you feel you've dealt with her death, as far as it is possible to deal with it?'

'Alcohol.'

'That is one way, and it is your choice, but maybe it doesn't give you the happiest outcome.'

'I know, but I've had enough of that too, and that's why I want this over.'

'So, why are you here?'

'Dave said I had to be certified sane, then he'll take me to the airport, if I really wanted to go.'

'Have you left a note?'

'I've written it in my head. I just need to put it to paper

tonight.'

'Suicide is a long term solution to a short term challenge.'

'I know, and I apologize, now but I have to do it.'

'Do you know how the rest of your children and your partner will feel after you've left them in a pile of crap for the rest of their lives?

'Yes. I don't think my daughter would have done it if she knew how we would all feel for a very long time, but she's in hell now.'

'How do you know that?'

'If you decide to take your own life, that's it, you go to hell.'

'But what if as she was flying through the air off that cliff and she changed her mind, and decided she was wrong and wanted to live, but it was too late? That would mean that her last intention was to live.'

'I think she might well have thought that.'

And there was a long silence, which we all needed. I thought. She thought.

'Let me just try and show you how you might be able to see this from another angle.'

'OK. I'll try '

'In Chinese the word crisis is represented by two symbols. One is the symbol of destruction, of annihilation. The other symbol stands for opportunity. Crisis can be either of two things. I wonder if what you are really facing is the big challenge of taking an opportunity to look at things and deal with them so that you can move on. I don't mean moving on from the memory of your daughter, but maybe you can see it in a way that enables you to honour her memory so that you can carry on with the rest of your life, instead of destroying yourself like you feel like doing tonight.'

The Community Psychiatric Nurse arrived and introduced herself.

'I'm Shirley.'

'I'm the doc. Let me leave you to it, and I'll be back in a minute. I'm just going to get a drink. Would anyone like a cup of tea?'

'You'd be hard pressed to find tea for all us lot around here,' said the CPN in a distinct Yorkshire accent.

'I know. But it's a good idea,' which enabled me to let the CPN have her time with this woman. 'Are you from Wakefield?' I asked as she had such a similar accent to a person I knew from there.

'Yes, but no-one's guessed it that close before.'

'It's quite a distinct accent in some ways, but subtle.

'Who wants tea?'

'Two sugars for both of us,' said the couple.

'Yes, but none for me,' said the CPN

In the nurses kitchen one of the nurses helped me make some tea. 'Can I help myself to biscuits? We've got a bit of a problem here that's going to take a few hours to set right.'

'Help yourself.'

'Thanks.' And I piled up a small plate with all the chocolate biscuits that I could get on it, thinking that they might make everyone smile and be a little happier in this grim situation.

'You're not kidding; you've got a problem. I know, I remember her daughter's suicide was in the papers. I feel so sad for her. She used to be a legal secretary, but now she's a cleaner at the school. I think she does other jobs … you know … to pay for the drink.'

'She's slipped down the social scale then?'

'Don't know if I could cope with my daughter killing

herself. Don't think I'd ever be myself again.'

'I brought the tea in, and after I had handed everyone a cup I said, 'Can we be totally transparent here?' I handed around the biscuits.

'Yes. I think she'll need to stay in the safe room tonight and go to the Royal Cornhill Hospital in Aberdeen tomorrow,' said the CPN.

'That's exactly what I think,' I said, backing her up.

'No. I want to go now. I need to leave.'

'You are free to want to go, but I can't let you leave and go and just kill yourself without offering you an alternative for tonight. The last thing I want you to do as an adult is choose to be locked up, because that would be just ridiculous. You're in enough pain already, and you know better than that. I would prefer if you chose to stay here so you're safe here for tonight, and tomorrow we can get you to a supportive environment first thing in the morning, where you can get the care and attention you need.'

She nodded and grunted, 'Humph.'

'Have a think about it whilst I try and get a bed for you here tonight, and for the morning. If you want, I can give you tablets to make you feel calmer, but you don't have to take them.'

I rang Ninian Ward with the safe bed and then spoke to the duty doctor in Kirkwall to let him know there was going to be an extra patient in the hospital, whom I had to look after. I then called the duty consultant psychiatrist in Aberdeen.

'Hello, I'm the locum GP in Kirkwall tonight. I've got a fifty-three year old female, very high risk, suicidally depressed patient who needs a bed tomorrow as an urgent admission.'

'I can't give away a bed for tomorrow. You'll have to phone back and speak to the duty Consultant tomorrow,' she said.

'Is that usual?'

'You seem worried about this woman.' This was not the answer anyone would expect when all you want is a target everyone can aim for the next day. It seemed to me that this female psychiatrist was unable to understand the nature of one of the most basic psychological emergencies and help in a practical way. I didn't have to time to engage with this

'I'm going, bye.' And went back to the patient, her partner and the CPN, and just lied. 'They've confirmed a bed for you, and we'll get you to Aberdeen first thing in the morning. We'll work times out when I come back at half seven.' And she nodded.

'Are you alright for the night here for the duration?' I said to the CPN.

'Yes. I've got no cover, so I'll have to stay the night. I've got your number.'

'Any other questions?'

'How about some tablets?

'I've written you up on the ward for 5 mg valium whenever you need it tonight, but here's 10 mg for right now.'

'What's that?'

'Do you remember a Stones song from the '60s - Mothers Little Helper?'

'Yes.'

'Well, that's them. They'll make her feel sleepy and relaxed, so you should have a very quiet night. I'll be back at half seven.'

Chapter 9.

Mainland Orkney, South Ronaldsay and Burray
Island. Day 9

I thought I was going home to bed for a good night's
sleep, but I got called at 5.00 am to see a seventy year old man's
knee. He didn't want to call me out in the middle of the night,
not until I had some sleep. This was not the first time I had
come across a really considerate patient on the islands. We had
a warm encounter, talking about the fifties and sixties dancing
and music whilst I just wrote a letter to his GP. I went from
there across all four Barriers, past my chalet and straight to the
hospital.

I realized that the only person who had had any sleep
and was fit enough to take her on the plane to Aberdeen was
me.

'You'll need a pressurized aircraft, because she could
easily jump from the helicopter or the light plane they usually
use, which only flies at a couple of thousand feet. Ask for a
King Air,' said the CPN.

'OK. Thanks for that.'

'Can I get a King Air?' I asked the Air Ambulance desk
at Kirkwall Airport.

'We've got one arriving in the Shetlands at ten, picking
up and leaving at about ten thirty. It could drop down to
Kirkwall and be with you at about eleven. It's a King Air Beech
Super 200, with enough room for two stretcher cases and six
passengers. We'll arrange the ambulance at both ends - for ten
forty-five to pick you up in Kirkwall, and to meet the aircraft
in Aberdeen.'

'That sounds fine. I'll wait for the pickup. We are on
Ninian Ward.'

My passenger seemed much calmer after her partner had spoken with her and explained the non-negotiable situation.

I sat and reflected with the CPN and had a mini debriefing where we both expresses our feelings and reviewed what we had done, what had gone well and what had gone badly. It seemed that life for this woman was a choiceless path, and, whatever she decided, she had really brought herself to get help in Aberdeen. We were relieved that we hadn't had to exercise forceful use of a psychiatric detention order, because it is never the outcome you really want. It's on someone's records forever and works against them, preventing them from being fairly and meaningfully employed.

The ambulance was precisely on time, and we had fifteen minutes to get on the plane, so I called the Air desk and asked if the plane was on time. I was told it was on its way and would arrive on time.

Five minutes later, we were through the security gate, and the ambulance pulled up right behind the wing of the plane. I just had time to say hello to the paramedic who was with a sick man on a stretcher. No words were spoken; no safety drill was given about seat belts and life jackets, just the captain turning around once to make sure we were sitting down. Even as I was fastening my belt, we were already on the runway. And within two minutes, with a perfect view through the pilot's windows, I could see all of the oil rig helicopters below, looking like ants. On the short flight, not a word was said between the six men on board, communication was by hand signals between the pilot and co-pilot.

There was no ambulance at Aberdeen, and the fuel tanker could not refuel the plane on its way to Farnham until we had left the aircraft. There was nowhere for us to sit and wait for the ambulance, so the tanker took off to refuel a helicopter. The pilot of the air ambulance was disappointed; he had been running ahead of his schedule, but now he was probably going to be delayed. What was worse, if the tanker crossed the runway to refuel choppers on the other side, where it was very busy, his plane could be waiting hours for the tanker to get clearance to re-cross the runway to refuel him.

Eventually, the ambulance arrived exactly on time; apparently we were very early, and within ten minutes I had dropped my patient off at the psychiatric ward and was in a taxi to have a very brief look at Aberdeen. Neither the charge nurse nor the taxi driver could think of anything that was worth looking at apart from the granite building.

'Second biggest granite building in the world,' said the taxi driver who was taking me into town.

'Where's the biggest?'

'Don't know, probably Russia. They've got big buildings there.'

I relaxed and enjoyed the much colder air in Aberdeen. My phone rang once.

'Hi. It's Clare here from the agency. Would you like to do two more weeks just before Christmas?'

'It would suit me perfectly. I'll come back to you in a while.' I felt very pleased to be offered more time in these islands, and I phoned Chrisie to see what she thought.

'It'll be like an extended holiday,' I said, and we agreed it looked like a good place to be for a short while longer. 'But probably a short while only,' she said, and she was right. I was probably indulging in being a big fish in a small pond, but at the same time I was consciously beginning to wish I was anonymous again.

I was in two minds about Orkney now. I was in no way

trying to sell the place to Chrisie and, instead, wanted to try and perceive the place as accurately as possible to see if maybe it might be a place to come for some small breaks and rent a cottage in the wilderness away from tourists. It didn't seem to me that the weather kept the tourists away, as it had been pretty fine for most of the time there, so far.

Chapter 10.

Mainland Orkney, South Ronaldsay and Burray Island. Day 10

I was called at half past two in the morning to certify a man dead, and the carer said she was going to ring the undertaker. Although it was mandatory to call me before calling the next of kin, I would have expected the undertakers to be left in bed until about seven or eight in the morning. But I was told that they removed the body pretty much straight away.

I went into the surgery where I did my usual handing over. There hadn't been any dramas, and I only had one night to go. I was going to prepare three relaxing days for Chrisie and India, and I spent the day planning on buying things.

I dropped in to the butcher's to order some bacon and Cumberland chipolatas, and asked him if it was too late to change the order I had requested the day before for the three T-bone steaks which would be arriving on Friday morning. I had realized that the barbecue I had found was small, and, moreover, the weather forecast was terrible – eighty-mile-per-hour winds. Although I was determined to have a barbie on Saturday night I was aware that I might only be able to put the meat on it for a minute or two as is might be too dangerous, so I thought I would ask him for thinner steaks.

'They arrived this morning, but I had to send them back,' he said.

'Why?'

'They were so thick you would never cook them. They were this thick they were,' and he indicated three inches with his thumb and forefinger.

'I see,' I said.

'I sent them back, and they're going to cut them in half and send them back here for the morning.'

'Can you tell me where I can buy fish? I know it's a bit cheeky asking a butcher this, but I haven't seen a fish shop in town. Can you help?'

Davidson from Burray is supposed to fill that counter up with fish for this weekend. He works from home, and you can give him a ring and order what you like. He'll deliver it to your home.'

'Is it fresh fish?'

'Oh yes. Gets it every single day from the fisherman who comes over from Westray.'

'Thanks for that.' My next stop was for provisions for North Ronaldsay. The doctor who had worked there joked that he often used to miss the shop, because it's only open for an hour a day, and the hour it opens varies with the days of the week. I thought they might not have much fresh fruit, so I bought some pineapples, melons and bananas, and some chestnuts. I bought some extra chestnuts as I figured that as they had probably had few trees, these might be unusual and interesting for the school children.

My phone rang again later that afternoon. 'I'm the fisherman from the Pear Hotel. I'll drop some fish off for you tomorrow if you like.'

'Thanks. What have you got?'

'Haddock, cod, bream, skate, mullet and squid.'

'Can I take a kilo of the haddock and a kilo of the cod?'

'The only thing is I'm not sure about getting there tomorrow. I'm going to take the ferry, if it's running. We've got some bad weather coming in. The best thing is to meet on the quay between ten and ten fifteen if the ferry is in. If not I'll be there Saturday, and you can call me.'

After this serious concern about the next day's weather I decided to ring the airport to ask about flying conditions. 'I'm just enquiring about the weather because my wife and daughter are coming in on a flight tomorrow at seven fifteen in the evening, and I know bad winds are predicted.'

'Yes. I'll put you through to the control tower.'

'Hello. Yes, my wife's coming in on flight tomorrow at seven fifteen. I'm just a bit worried, you know. I want to know if the planes are likely to be able to land.'

'As long as there are no crosswinds it should be OK. The strong winds should be later tomorrow night and the next morning. So your wife should be OK.'

There were no calls from patients, and so I took the opportunity of trying to catch up on sleep and not be tired when Chrisie and India arrived. When I woke it was nine in the morning, and my work was over. I was very upbeat; I was going to see Chrisie and India later on in the evening. I spent the whole day clearing up the chalet and getting things just right, especially for India who was missing me. I bought them both presents which I wrapped in pink, and left a small bag of chocolate buttons under India's pillow. I hung up three "Welcome Home" signs, and I turned the light down to low and the heating up, so that it would be warm and cozy when they arrived.

When I went to the surgery I met the Australian, who was going for a very long walk on Hoy, and I said if I didn't have to meet the fisherman I would have liked to have gone with him. And this was a preparation day to make sure Chrisie and India's landing on the island was smooth and comfortable.

First, I stocked up on provisions for our trip to North Ronaldsay, just in case we found some self-catering accommodation. I concentrated on pasta, jars of pesto, lots of dried foods and fruit, and some chocolate and sweets for India.

The fish looked excellent, but I decided not to cook chips; instead I went to the local fish shop and bought fresh hot chips for four people an hour before they were due to land. I put these in the oven and then drove to the airport to meet them. I was not anxious about their landing, as I had rung the control tower the day before and again that afternoon. I was going to drop into the airport to ask if they were going to be able to land.

Before I left for the airport I switched on the weather and could see that the Orkney were in the eye of what they were describing as hurricane conditions. On the way to the airport the car was blown four feet across the road, three times, and I wondered what these treacherous conditions on the road were like in the air. What I was experiencing was really bad news.

The airport announced that flight would be five minutes early, and I noticed that the airport fire engine drove close to the runway and sat there with its lights flashing in what I could only see as anticipation of bad tidings. This was even more bad news.

Ten minutes after it was due the plane's lights became visible. It was a very well controlled approach, but at about two hundred feet I saw what was like a second away from a disaster as the nose and tail went up and down almost independently, whilst the wings seemed level. It was about to go out of control when there was a sudden acceleration, and the landing was aborted. The fire engine took off leisurely back to its garage, and I knew they would be flying back to mainland Scotland.

My worried state was totally relieved when Chrisie phoned and said that India was very upset, but only because she wasn't going to see me that night. Mercifully, she had slept through it all. Chrisie described the flight like it was a disaster movie; the aircraft was going all over the place, almost upside down. Three tough Orkney men had chucked up into their chunder bags. The pilot had said that there was a twenty-minute window, and I could only conclude that he had just missed it. The good thing was he had the grace not to try and land a second time. People from Orkney, who took the flight every day for years, said they had never experienced anything like this. The pilot said that he was unable to attempt the landing because of an instrument failure. I'm sure he was right, and I would have said the same thing, but how do you say I can't land this plane right now in these conditions except by blaming the plane.

All hopes of Chrisie and India taking any kind of liking to this place, even in terms of an occasional holiday cottage, vanished. In the furthest corner of my mind a little thought bubble appeared, warning me to be careful of what I say about flying: 'Don't forget you're the one who is scared of flying sometimes.' But another part of me accepted this as just part of what was going to happen to me, and I wasn't going to back down off being here because of the weather, or its effects on flying. I had four weeks to go now, two in North Ronaldsay and two back on the mainland Island, and I wasn't inclined to not live up to my commitments as a result of being beaten by this weather.

I felt miserable as my frustration subsided, and I switched on the news to blur my feelings into oblivion. Within fifteen minutes sleep took over, and I moved from the armchair to bed.

Mainland Orkney, South Ronaldsay and Burray
Island. Day 12

In the morning the arrival lounge was full of the same
people from the night before. We all chatted as the flight was
delayed, and delayed again. The pilots were now concerned
about the safety of the aircraft because of the extreme winds
from the night before. No one could remember when an aircraft
had failed to land at Kirkwall Airport. There were memories of
planes not taking off, but an aborted landing was most unusual.
It finally landed.

The day was spent recovering from the journey, and it
was only the next morning that we were able to go exploring to
the Tomb of the Eagles. It was a perfect place to show Chrisie
and India on the way into Kirkwall city.

The woman who showed us around would have talked
all day if we'd let her, and within five minutes we both gave
each other the signal - a question mark and a cut throat - which
meant if either of us asked any questions to prolong this then
that person would have to suffer the consequences.

She was a very good tour guide, relating history
through the artifacts which we were able to handle. We handled
a male and a female skull which were both over five thousand
years old. I had never experienced this before. The skulls were
over two hundred generations, or two hundred times my
grandmother. Another way of looking at it was that this skull
had been buried for fifty centuries. All the while India was
quiet and not involved, as she was told to play with some toys.
But she would have preferred to have been more part of the
tour. However, her excitement was yet to come.

When we went outside in the hurricane, Ronald Simison,

the man who had discovered the Tomb of the Eagles, showed us around. He was brief and gave us basic information, but his humour showed through. He had originally been looking for new fencing posts on the beach and was looking at the rocks off the cliffs, which were all slanting the same way, except three which were horizontal. This is when he started to dig. The authorities told him he couldn't dig, but he managed to find a loophole in the law, which said that after he had written to them they had three months to respond, after which time the responsibility of the land reverted to him, which it did.

Ronald Simison uncovered the Bronze Age site and the Tomb of the Eagles over a twenty year period. Most of the Tomb of the Eagles is still buried under fifty centuries of earth, because he has not been given permission to dig any further. He was very frustrated by this, but his daughter was of the mind that this was a good thing, and she said that maybe it should be explored and dug in a hundred years because only then it would be likely that they would have new technology to explore further. She said that all the most modern technology had already been used, and if there was a further dig now, it would add nothing to the knowledge of the site. Her father knew that she was right.

The tomb had to be entered by lying on a trolley on four wheels, which was like a large modified skate board. In turn, we each lay on our backs, and, one by one, we pulled the trolley along by the rope which was attached to the ceiling of the very thick stone tunnel. Pulling yourself on a trolley by a rope makes you realize that the only reason you can't just climb through is because the walls are several metres thick in these ancient places. Suddenly we found ourselves in a tomb over five thousand years old with several skulls in one of the recesses. We took a few photographs and just stood there in total awe of the age of the place and the giant stones which lined the walls and floor.

As I stood in the tomb, there was a powerful sense of almost knowing these ancient people. Perhaps our guide had given us too much detail and it had just stimulated my mind. But then I had the same sense here as I had on other occasions when I sensed the ancient purpose of these islands. I felt detached, still and calm. This place had a strong attraction for me. I was aware it had been a very important place and still was. I savored this feeling for as long as I could, until I was called by Chrisie and India to look at something.

The history of the Tomb of the Eagles, or Isbister Tomb, was quite amazing. In it they had found twenty-six kilograms of pottery, thousands of fish bones, barley and wheat, masses of disarticulated human bones and the bones of the white-tailed sea-eagle. It was estimated that it had taken 12,500 man hours to build. The tomb of Maes Howe, which we had not yet seen, had taken 38,000 man hours to build. In the Tomb of the Eagles they found the remains of 342 people. It is believed that the bodies were left on slabs of stone at the entrance to the tomb, and when they had been picked bare they were then interred further inside the tomb. It is thought that this allowed grieving time. Essentially, a body was put out of sight when the person was no longer in living memory. The white-tailed sea-eagles are believed to be the sacred totem of the people who lived there over five thousand years ago.

At other sites in Orkney the people had different totems, such as dogs, songbirds and the still very plentiful cormorants. White-tailed sea-eagles, which have wing spans in excess of two meters, have just been re-introduced to Scotland, and there is a theory that they may come back to breed in their old hunting ground. The ancient tribal people almost certainly took their name from the eagles and would have probably been known as the Eagle Tribe. Romantic though this may seem, there were downsides to having been born then. Analysis of the bones showed that life expectancy was less than twenty years.

It was impossible to introduce Chrisie and India to this island in any way that was in my control. This island introduces itself by its weather. It is the hallmark of the place, with no compromises. Take, for example, my attempt to show them one of the most impressive stone circles in the world, Brodgar.

This Ring of Brodgar is between a freshwater and a saltwater loch and is remarkable in size. There are twenty-seven of the original sixty stones left, and some are twenty-five feet tall, but it's an incredibly slippery and boggy walk, certainly in the winter months. The horizontal wind can upset your balance as soon as you lift one foot off the ground, and so each step requires total concentration. This kind of intense physical concentration switches your thinking mind into neutral and enables you to be free from thoughts for a short while. We didn't get past the entrance, but it was still a sight to behold.

Part of me which I don't like listening to was sending me some kind of uncomfortable message. I didn't know what, but something along the lines of 'you've been here before,' or 'There is more to this than you can see,' as if I had some strange connection with the place. It was the same as the feeling at Scara Brae. The difference was that this was more intense, like a louder drum beat. I looked at it and chose to acknowledge, but ignore, it.

On Chrisie's birthday I let off rockets, none of which went straight. The wind in the garden came from everywhere, and so each rocket went, well, anywhere. It was almost impossible to find a still place to light a match. Rather horrendously, I had to light the rocket inside, take it outside and place it in its take off place holder for lift off, and I only just made it every time. One rocket got stuck and exploded on the lawn in front of everyone, which made me think twice about ever having fireworks again.

Peter turned out to be a very pleasant, upper middle class Australian doctor. He very seriously wore a dear stalker hat and matching coat. When India was in the bathroom having her bath, he asked Chrisie where the toilet was, which was in the bathroom. I said for him to just go and have a pee outside, because, after all, there was nobody for miles; but he declined. This was not good news for an Aussie, but it made me smile, and I put him into an it-takes-all-types category. We managed to entertain him, however, with our humor and rather unusual food. I served him a starter which he was almost certainly not going to eat.

'This looks like you've got the menu the wrong way round mate.'

'What do you mean?'

'Well there's something under the cream and there's a raspberry on top.'

'Yes, it's a tromp l'oeil starter.' He slowly explored it, discovering that it was crème fraise and that under it was an upside down avocado hiding its stuffing of caviar.

'I see.' He didn't like the idea of this, but he still finished it out of his unbelievable politeness. He sounded like the Australian PM Johnny Howard and looked like him too. He had a wealthy uncle who lived next to Madonna and Noel Gallagher in Marylebone, and he knew London very well.

Chapter 12.

Mainland Orkney, South Ronaldsay and Burray Island. Day 13

On my last day in Mainland Orkney I received a call from the agency, asking me if I wouldn't mind covering an island called Rousay instead of Mainland Orkney for the two weeks before Christmas. This suited me. I hadn't been there; and there were only two hundred people, so it would be a leisurely job, albeit twenty-four hours a day. I wondered if it was the second smallest practice in Britain.

On a tour around the Highland Park distillery, the guide perked up when we said we were going to North Ron. 'Oh the doctor there keeps a good collection of single malts.'

'Really, I thought he was on call twenty-four hours a day.'

'He keeps over sixty single malts.'

'That sounds strange. What are the people like?'

'Very interesting and very sociable. You'll see.' This made me happy. I was having an interesting time, and it looked like it was going to improve. Almost everyone I met suggested I move my family up to Orkney. Although the work was straightforward and there are lots of great things about the place, I couldn't but help feel several entirely different reality buzzers going off in my head when I started thinking about us all moving up here.

The weather was unusual; the people were easygoing, friendly and not stressed out in any way. It was an interesting place, and we could have a very peaceful life up here. The few people there lived a long time and were hearty and hardy. I had not come across much in the way of aggression and crime was very low, because it's an island and there aren't many ways off it where you wouldn't be spotted. There were no speed cameras and the medical services were well funded. There were lots of properties for sale at almost giveaway prices.

Because the Orkneys are even further north than the Highlands and Northern Scotland, there are some extremely short days. OK, there are the days in June when the sun never sets as well. There is some extraordinary weather with 100-mile-per-hour winds. It's also isolated because of the time it takes to travel there, and even though the flying time with connections is less than two hours, in reality the traveling time for any kind of door to door trip to London is probably five hours. If you have children here, the chances of them eventually leaving and you not being near them are high? I can't say work opportunities were worse, and some of the doctors were excellent.

It's easy to imagine being in Orkney for a period of withdrawal from the world. After all that's what I'd done so far. For the first week I'd probably spent less than one hour a day with people, and, despite talking to family on the phone, it was still a long way from them. However, it was a good place to lead a simple life and to just have a sense of being. But, eventually, you do begin to feel the distance. But that sense of an ache about distance is part of the nature of the ebb and flow of things that change. It's a feeling that comes and goes with places which are usually good for you. And, although you long to leave, you know that at some time you will also long to return. Places don't change, only we do, and maybe one of the reasons we go back to places is to measure how much we have changed compared with when we were last there.

Elsewhere in the world, if there is a thirty- to forty-mile-per-hour wind blowing outside, you can see with your eyes that it's severe because the trees are moving about and bushes are horizontal; but in Orkney there are neither of these because there really are so few trees or bushes to see moving about. Because of very good double glazing you are easily lulled by the absence of the sound of the wind into a semi-sedated state of false security ... that is, until you open the door and find you need all your strength to close it.

The light is unusual because it is so far north. It is as far north as St Petersburg, Hudson Bay or the southern tip of Denmark. In the winter it doesn't get light until nine in the morning, and it is dark by three in the afternoon. In the summer, I was told that you can read a paper all night outside. I was here for November and December.

There seemed to be only two types of building used for dwellings, the old ones made of stone and the modern ones that are covered in pebble-dash. Both come in shades of brown or grey. The old stone ones make you feel cozy and secure, whilst the pebble-dash ones make you want to paint them white or blue, like the houses on Greek islands, to cheer everyone up.

Pebble-dash, horrible though most Brits think it is, is used out of necessity. It is the toughest material to withstand the horizontal winds and ice storms. If it is removed, the building falls down. There is always a constant nightly whooshing of the wind and with it some salt. It is the salt that breaks down everything with the rain and wind. There is salt on every pane of glass. And the wind ... anything that is unfastened or loose is sent flying or broken. This gravity defying horizontal wind brings gravity defying horizontal rain and, of course, salt. The wind in Orkney would destroy any kind of umbrella in seconds. Perhaps this is why I never noticed anyone using one in Orkney, or even carrying one. If you were seen carrying one, you were obviously a tourist.

There appeared to be no autumn in the conventional sense, as there were no trees at all anywhere. Believe me, I looked. Orkney could easily be quite honestly renamed the Nullarbor Islands after the Nullarbor desert in Australia.

Chapter 13.

Mainland Orkney, South Ronaldsay and Burray Island. Day 14

I always try to leave a place, feeling at peace with the people I have served or have come across sometimes in the line of duty and care. I think it is important. Therefore, I tread carefully, not to leave on bad terms in any way. But for some unknown reason I had worries about this job. The double messages I was receiving about the accommodation had started it, and I hoped it would settle down.

At first it may seem that many things would take a lot longer in these remote islands of the north, like communication. You would be entirely wrong to assume this, because it could not be more the reverse in this very small oceanic island community. There is almost a natural desperation to feel part of the rest of Britain. I can only understand it, and see it, as the most expressive way for Orcadians to have a competitive spirit in modern day times, which I think is really good. Whist we were waiting for the plane to take us to North Ronaldsay I had a communication from Orkney Health Board via the locum agency who were employing me. It was Clare.

'I've received an e-mail from the Health Board, and I've sent it to you in North Ronaldsay.'

'Fine, but what does it say?'

'I'll read it out to you.'

'OK'

'"I have received a call from Orkney Health Board regarding the amount of fuel used in the hire care provided to you 1st to 12th November. The bill the Health Board has received from the hire company for fuels is £158.97. They are unhappy to pay the bill, as it is higher than the normal figure they receive. Please could you confirm/deny you used the hire care for personal use in the day time whilst not on duty? The Health Board are happy for locum doctors to use the hire cars provided in their time off, but are not happy to cover the costs of fuel used in the car for personal use. If you did use the car for personal use Orkney Health Board feel a contribution towards the fuel bill should be made.'

I laughed. It was a bit of a cheeky phone call from Orkney Health Board to my agency, but the agency were only doing their job in letting me know. I thought about it for a bit, chuckling to myself behind my black and grey beard, which had grown since leaving Gillingham. Then I told Chrisie about the e-mail, and immediately suggested I asked our four year old daughter for her guidance.

'They say I used the car for personal use. What should I tell them?'

'Daddy, you only came here because of the work, didn't you?'

'Yes. What are you saying?'

'You used the petrol for work didn't you?'

'Yes, I did, but I also had to make sure I knew where I was going, because I was going to be working at night when I couldn't see anything. So I did drive around a bit, finding out where all the houses were, and I wasn't quite sure about the boundaries of the practices I was covering.'

'Well, daddy you used their petrol then.'

'Yes, for work.'

'Can you have free petrol in your job in North Ron too?

'I'll try,' I said.

I felt absolutely reassured because kids like fun too. I very much enjoyed formulating my response to Orkney Health Board, and I based it on my sense that … well … yes, they had received a rather larger than usual bill, but the post had changed, with an extension of the patch covered. I remembered thinking that it was scary being given six maps of the different islands and not knowing a single road. This is why I drove around so much. I also thought that having a rest in a Neolithic monument was acceptable. I was not going to deny or admit anything they had any suspicions or queries about. I was merely going to give them information in a friendly reply. After all, I had other jobs to do for them, one job in North Ron, one in Rousay and the last back in South Ronaldsay, finishing on 23rd December. I sent an e-mail from the airport.

Dear Clare,

Re: Car Hire Kirkwall Out of Hours Locum November 1 - 12, 2005

Thank you for your e-mail regarding petrol expenses for the hire car for the new post of Out of Hours, covering Kirkwall, East Mainland, Burray and South Ronaldsay, which I understand is a new extended Out of Hours position for Orkney Health Board, which may of course explain the increased fuel bill of £158.87.
I was based six to seven miles out of Kirkwall at St Mary's Holm, and my use of the car, as I understood it, was different from other locum doctors who were previously based in Kirkwall and did not cover the new extended area.
I was told by the car hire firm that the Vauxhall was not a very fuel economic car. My use of the car was as follows:-

1. All home visits to and from Kirkwall, East Mainland, Burray and South Ronaldsay. On one occasion, I had to use the car as an ambulance in the early hours to give a lift to a patient from St Margaret's Holm to the hospital in Kirkwall, as the patient had acute renal pain and needed urgent admission. This was done because there was no phone signal from that area due to bad weather.

2. One return trip to the airport.

3. Twelve return trips once a day to drop off my notes to Practice Manager at the Scapa practice.

4. Three return trips to Kirkwall to the garage to find out how to fill the screen cleaner, how to work the rear wiper and how to open the petrol cap.

5. One return visit to Kirkwall to see the Occupational Health Nurse.

6. One return visit to Kirkwall to see Maggie in HR

7. One return visit to Kirkwall to replenish the emergency drug bag.

8. During the first two days of the OOH post, I did a long drive around the OOH geographical area, covering the six maps which I was given, so that I could familiarize myself with the various islands and roads in order to get to and from visits easily.

9. Because of the rather different and interesting weather conditions of winds of 80-100 mph whist I was doing the locum, and because of the absence of any street lighting or torches at night, for my own health and safety, I thought it wise to leave the car running with its headlights on whilst I was doing my visits.

I do hope this explains the increased fuel consumption of the car. I also hope that Orkney Health Board are aware that considerable monies were saved by my agreeing to stay on for an extra four days in

Orkney without pay and then go onto another locum for them instead of incurring my expenses for the two days travel and a further flight from Kirkwall to Southampton and back. If it helps Orkney Health Authority, please pass this e-mail on to them.

Kind Regards

I got an almost immediate reply.

Dear Doctor,
I have just heard back from Orkney Health Authority. Now they have read your e-mail and understand why the fuel bill was more expensive than usual, they are happy to cover the cost.

Kind Regards
Clare

Chapter 14.

Locum 2. North Ronaldsay

It was a straightforward fifteen-minute flight, with the Islander pointing clearly to the north all the way. I sat just behind the pilot, beside a musician who was spending the day at the school, teaching the children to play the fiddle. Again I saw the yellow helicopter at the airport as we were waiting for our flight, and I hoped this wasn't an ominous sign that I would be medi-evacuating someone from North Ron. It was perfect flying weather compared with the hundred-mile-per-hour winds of the last few days. It was a surprisingly quick landing. There was a drop in the engine's power, and the plane dropped down, curled over the roof of a house, gently swooped down further and stopped just before it ran out of runway on the very short strip.

To meet us were the outgoing six passengers, as well as the doctor and his wife, who each had a short wheel base Land Rover. Chrisie was escorted into hers which was red. The doctor's wife was thin and a little scraggy in her old jeans, an old orange jumper and short, curly, brown hair. She had poor eye contact, which always alerted me to depression. The eye contact she did give was dark and cold, and reminded me of a patient I once saw whom I could not really make contact with.

As the ex-health worker mentioned when I visited Skara Brae, it was now abundantly clear that being a GP was only one of many things that the doctor did. His wife told Chrisie, in the three minute drive to their house, that he was also the Chief Coastguard, the Chief Fireman, Chairman of the Community Council, as well as a crofter and the owner of a B&B. He also helped loading and unloading the ferry which docked at a pier at the bottom of his land.

My drive to the doctor's house was different from what I had expected. The GP was a bit of a shock. My first thought was that the doctor looked very unusual indeed. Then I thought, well, maybe he's just a little unconventional. The only parts of his face which were visible were his forehead, eyes and his purple-red nose. His head of hair, beard and moustache, and the rest of his facial hair were long, and if you didn't know he was the doctor, you would at first think that he was a pleasant, old fashioned vagrant, rather than a modern homeless person. I noticed immediately that he seemed angry or, at least, agitated. He looked like the kind of person you had to be careful with. His eyes had that look of hidden menace, but I dismissed the thought from my head. It was just his looks, and sometimes they meant nothing at all.

I have never seen anyone with such a head of long hair and such a long beard, apart from Rasputin. Yes. Rasputin was the only person who came to mind. The doctor had old, baggy blue jeans, dirty boots and a jumper that was baggy with large holes in it. At first he seemed straightforward enough. Perhaps he was just eccentric. I was certain of one thing. We had found ourselves in an extremely odd person's company in a very remote part of some very remote islands.

'I'm keen to hand over right now and switch off,' he said nervously, as if he was under some kind of stress, even before we had got into the Land Rover. There were signs of all not being well.

I was a bit surprised at this premature and rather sudden need to hand over, as I wasn't due to begin the locum until the following day, but I replied, 'No trouble, if you feel you need to shut down.'

'We're going to drop your bags off, and then we can visit the surgery which is just past the air strip.'

'Where's that?' I asked. It was quiet and the wind had ceased. It looked like a peaceful place which could easily turn to mayhem.

'Its three to four minutes down the road.' I was a bit surprised that he felt so stressed out in such a small, apparently peaceful community, but it was none of my business, and so I deliberately didn't ask him how long it was since he last had a break from the island. I wondered when he was actually leaving the island.

'When are you going away?'

'We're going away for a bird ringer's conference for the weekend and then on for a two week holiday, so I'll be here for two nights in case you need to know anything. You can use this Land Rover; it has an emergency kit and an emergency drug bag in it. Your wife can use the other one.'

'That all sounds good,' I said as I tried to open the passenger door. 'I can't get the door open.'

'The passenger door has only been used once and never opened again.'

'Really?' I said, thinking it just a bit strange that he had never bothered to get it fixed. I assumed that this was perhaps an eccentricity which came with running the smallest General Practice in the country. I had to climb in the back of the Land Rover with my case. There were several emergency cases. It was cramped and I tried to make some conversation during the rough, fast drive.

'The bags, are they medical?'

'That bag's got resuscitation stuff in it. That large case's for emergency drugs, and that one's got all sorts of emergency things in it like intravenous drips, various fluids, needles and syringes. We're fully equipped.'

'Seems like you've got a lot of stuff in the wagon,' I said.

'Yes, never know when you might need it.'

'Rarely, I should think,' I said.

'Seven years ago a fishermen got his foot taken off down by the jetty. Managed to patch him up and medically evac him out.'

If he was friendly, he would have said 'Yes, rarely,' but he didn't. I think he saw me as a threat. Perhaps he felt inferior for taking a job where you get almost no opportunity to practice your medical and surgical skills. I wasn't really impressed much with this tale, because if you lose your foot in a blunt injury, you probably won't bleed a great deal, and you only need some pressure on the wound until proper care is available. But another part of me thought I was being a bit mean, because, with only fifty-seven people, the chance of something happening that was going to impress me was small.

The doctor's house, which was originally a tiny, stone, crofter's cottage, seemed to have a few extensions attached to it and an out building for backpackers. It was a large complex by any standards. However, none of it seemed particularly well planned. It was very higgledy-piggledy, but had a good kitchen. There was a strange hexagonal dining room/lounge bar which had a good view of the south-west part of the island and the ocean. There were two impressive white windmills, neither of which worked. One was lying flat, as if it had been blown over in these utterly desolate surroundings. I immediately thought he must have got grants for these; they were not small wind turbines, and if you had personally invested money in them you wouldn't just leave them there to rot. Maybe I was wrong, and maybe he did do just this.

The engines of the Land Rovers were not switched off whilst we dropped our bags up in the room. I noticed the doctor's house was rather shockingly characterless, like a hostel where the owners have got just the basics with nothing personal showing. There were no pictures with any personal connection or connection to anything. It was as if there was nothing that could be stolen by people who stayed there. No B&B I've ever stayed in was like that. They are almost always just like an extension of someone's home. This was like living in a naked building where everyone was just camping but not really living. The feeling was of a cold atmosphere, rather like an army barracks. There was something unfriendly, and a little niggle began in my stomach of possible danger.

We were going to be shown the surgery next. We both came down stairs and jumped back into the vehicles again. North Ronaldsay's surgery was a house standing quite alone at the end of a precariously slippery, narrow concrete path less than sixty feet long and perhaps two feet wide. I couldn't help noticing, in the strong cross wind which suddenly began, dozens of eight-inch long and half-inch thick reinforced steel rods just sticking out of the ground on either side of the path. This was a potentially lethal walk in wet, windy weather. In the dark it would be even worse. If you fell there, it would be lethal, as you would land on at least one of them piercing your chest or abdomen. Forget health and safety. This particular scene was the most lethal man-made environment I had seen for a long time. Mentally, I swore I would take some photographs of this, because no one would believe the path to a doctor's house could be as dangerous as this. I wondered what the patients thought of it. Maybe these pieces of steel sticking out of the ground, angled perfectly at anyone who fell in the wind, were there deliberately to keep patients away. Maybe he didn't like patients.

The surgery was a former minister's house. It was spacious but wasn't kept in a good state at all, simply because it was embarrassingly … well, surprisingly, very dirty and untidy. It was otherwise a large, comfortable looking house.

The large, doctor's room had no examination couch which usually, but not always, indicates that the doctor is not keen to examine his patients. Instead, there was a couch in the small room for minor operations, but it was covered with boxes.

'These are just some out-of-date drugs we are getting rid of and re-stocking,' said his wife as they showed us around. I remembered what the GP in Kirkwall had said about them having a lot of out-of-date drugs.

'There's a cargo flight on Tuesdays and a ship that comes in on Fridays with supplies, but everything has to be unloaded at sea, as there is no proper jetty.'

'Presumably you can order anything?' I asked.

'Yes, and there's a shop which is open from four until five in the afternoons. It is conveniently situated by the runway, and the owner will order most things very quickly from the mainland, but there's a small charge for that.'

'How often do I do a surgery?'

'There are two surgeries a day on Mondays, Wednesdays and Fridays from nine thirty until ten in the morning, and in the evenings from five thirty until six o'clock. The surgery is closed on Tuesdays, Thursdays and Sundays.

'So, there's no surgery on Saturdays?'

'There's an extra-long surgery on Saturday mornings of one hour.'

This GP's weekly work came to a grand total of four hours work a week!

'You'll be lucky to see three patients a week.'

'Right. Do people just show up or phone?'

'There are no appointments as it's a walk in arrangement.

If the doctor isn't at the surgery, patients call at the house or just turn up there.'

'I think I understand,' I said.

'It's a dispensing surgery and different from most GP surgeries. We have a good stock of emergency drugs. If you want drugs they have to be ordered from the mainland pharmacy who will get them on a flight during the week. But if you want them urgently, they have to be posted to you.'

'That seems odd, that posting is quicker than a phone call?' But he didn't reply. I knew it wasn't me, and it would be blindingly obvious to anyone that here was a very strange man indeed. However, the circumstances were unusual, and I accepted this as completely normal in these abnormal circumstances. 'There but for the grace ...' I thought.

As he was showing me around the ground floor I noticed there was an old dentist chair in the filthy scullery, which he pointed out. 'We have a lot of equipment like this chair, but there hasn't been a dentist on the island for many years. The dentist used to visit once a year, but not anymore. I do what I can,' he said, as if he was reluctantly but heroically having a go at dentistry.

'Presumably it's not part of your contract?' I said.

'I haven't had a contract for nearly two years,' he said. I decided not to say what I thought: that this was a very bad sign; they probably wanted to close down the surgery on the island. My tour had convinced me that the surgery building had very little time to go. The Health Board were probably just waiting for the numbers to drop so low that they could no longer justify keeping a full-time doctor on the island.

'Fairisle hasn't even got a doctor,' said the GP, a very good guess at what I was thinking about.

'How many islands have one?' I asked.

'Eight.'

'Well, it's that a bit hypocritical because Fairisle has over sixty people and they haven't got doctor but North Ronaldsay has. Is there a reason for that?

'There's a GP in Westray, Papa Westray, Stronsay, Sanday, Eday, Rousay. Then there's Hoy and Shapinsay, and of course there's the practices on Mainland Orkney where you've already worked.'

'So there's about a couple of dozen GPs covering how many people?'

'Well, twenty-six of us for around nineteen thousand people, with eight on the remote isles. We cover twenty-four hours a day, seven days a week, but we get seventeen weeks off a year.'

'Really! That's amazing. Most GPs only get six weeks a year,' I said. 'What do you do with it?'

'I usually do my own locum at £3,000 a week, sometimes more. But you have to get off the island sometimes.'

'Why on earth don't you go away for all that time? I mean you could have all the children's holidays – three or four months – abroad every year?' He looked around as if there was someone behind him, as if to avoid answering my question. Then I realized he might have taken offence. 'I thought that was a thing of the distant past, doing your own locum?'

'No, lots of the isles doctors do it to boost their income.'

'You must earn a fortune. I mean, seventeen weeks times £3,000 is over £50,000 extra a year on top of your salary, which alone must be £100,000 to £150,000.' It seemed an outrageous expenditure.

'Well we are all stuck here 24/7. And it provides a service.'

'And the number of patients is way below the UK

average, whether it's London, or Southampton or in the middle of nowhere. Most GPs have 1,500 to 3,000 patients.'

'So you think it's really an extravagant expense?' There was a touch of annoyance in his voice which I hadn't picked up on before.

'Yes. It just seems to be an exceptional decision to have made, to have a GP for fewer than sixty people. Twenty thousand people would usually need around twelve doctors. They would just absorb the extra work and cover for each other when they were on holidays. They wouldn't use locums, as it's too expensive.'

'But you have to do the numbers, and it's no different from anywhere - London or Southampton. At the end of the day it's all the same country.' He was incorrect with his figures, but I didn't want to get into an argument. He seemed potentially volatile, and he was highly competitive. There was more than just a hint of irritation and impatience, which concerned me, and I was beginning to feel uncomfortable. He was really in an indefensible position, so I left it there. I had nothing to prove.

I was left to look around the main practice room on my own. I very much felt that this was it, the buck stopped with me, especially when he showed me the chest drain. 'What the heck am I going to do with that?' I thought. I'd never inserted one before, and in a place like this you would be in seriously deep trouble if you found yourself needing to do that. Even if you could insert one, it would be unlikely that someone would survive the wait for a plane or a chopper to evacuate them. Then he showed me some airway tubes, which I had never been able to insert very well. I felt I was either being made to feel deliberately out of my depth or this was just professional anxiety keeping me on my toes; and I decided it was the former. He was trying to wind me up and make me anxious.

However, there was one aspect which was unique, which my four year old daughter pointed out by way of a question. 'Daddy, where are the children's toys?' There was a complete absence of children's toys. She knew there were only four children on the island, but even she thought they still needed toys. This was a really serious omission for a GP who saw three patients a week and earned £1,000 per patient whilst doing his own locum. This was either lack of insight or naked meanness. I even carry child's stuff in my bag.

The practice was organized in the most unconventional way. There were fifty-seven patients on the island and each was filed not by their name or by their address, but according to their house name in two drawers of one large filing cabinet. There were thirty-four house names. These were ancient names that I had certainly never come across before, mostly Viking names. I was, however, given a beautifully drawn map of the island with all of the house names written on it in ink that had faded with age.

'Who drew this map?' asked Chrisie.

'Oh, just a local crofter,' said the doctor's wife.

'It's extremely well done. It's like it's been done by a professional artist,' said Chrisie.

'It's got art and history coming out of it everywhere,' I said. It was a really very finely executed drawing.

'The technical detail has been executed perfectly, but, apart from that, it's really a perfect drawing. Nothing could be improved. This person must be very talented. Where do they live?' said Chrisie.

'Oh, two houses down the road,' said the doctor's wife.

'Could we meet him?' asked Chrisie.

'He's often out.'

It was as if she didn't want us to meet this person, and I

found this odd but quietly chuckled to myself at the eccentricity of the smallest practice in the UK.

But there was one limitation of living on the island, as the doctor's wife pointed out, which we didn't really need to know, but which was obviously a problem for the doctor and his wife.

'There's only one downside to staying here. When the children reach twelve years, the children of the Isles, including here on North Ronaldsay, have to go to Mainland Orkney to the school.'

'That must be good for them, getting off the island, and it means more pupils and more friends,' I said positively. I looked at their faces and realized I had said completely the wrong thing. They were looking at me as if they wanted to hurt me. He seemed so put out that he couldn't speak, but his wife bravely confronted me.

'No, that is not true at all. We have to pay for them to stay in a hostel five nights a week, and for their flights, and they have to do all their own washing. All they are given is food. And this was not really what parents would really want.'

It seemed to me that they really wanted everything they could get. They were working on an island, which in the national scheme of things didn't really deserve a full-time, 24/7 doctor. They were living on an island, even being paid to do their own locum at locum rates. My guess is that they were probably being paid well for all their other official roles on the island as well. Their income would probably dwarf that of most other GPs in the UK, and that for a miniscule workload.

'One of the children is coming up to attending to the mainland secondary school next year, and we have been considering leaving the island before the summer and taking up a position possibly in Mainland Orkney.

I didn't say anything at the time but I felt this might be a tough one for him, or any potential employer, as he was nearly sixty and had only ever done this job for twenty-eight years, with less than sixty patients. If he did take a job in Mainland Orkney he would be seeing over two hundred patients a week. He would also be dealing with house calls; the administration of a practice of between seven thousand and fifteen thousand patients, as well as seeing to staff problems and severe budget restraints because or NHS Orkney's imminent financial cuts. It could be a very tough thing with which to be suddenly be faced. He would also have to reduce his holidays from seventeen weeks a year to six. This would be a very tough call, and I thought he could be in for a massive shock. I decided he was not giving me the whole truth.

In contrast, I remembered what Peter, the Australian doctor who was also doing a locum in Kirkwall, had said about independence. His daughter was spending a whole year living in the bush as part of her school education. I thought he had a healthy sense of balance, in stressing the importance of basic needs behind before an adolescent embarks on modern life.

The Australian doctor was a true doctor's doctor. He could deal with most medical emergencies at the hospital as the admitting hospital physician. His management of chronic illness was far more comprehensive than most GPs in practice in the UK, because he was used to having to cope on his own. I felt I was far less able and confident than him.

The doctor's wife then said, 'If everyone on North Ron could persuade the Health Authority to prevail on the local government to start night flights to and from North Ron, it could help the island.'

Wow! I thought. What an extraordinary sense of feeling one was owed everything. I couldn't quite remember when I had last come across this sense of entitlement. Maybe I wasn't so conditioned to get the maximum I could get out of my circumstances.

'How come?' said Chrisie.

'With night flights, the island might start to re-populate, because a number of business people from Mainland Orkney are very interested in living in North Ron.' I found this was stretching even my belief in the people I had met in Mainland Orkney just a bit too far. I couldn't see how they would want to be even more remote than they already were. But I was open to being wrong, because I was only passing through.

'If they want to live here why don't they simply commute?' asked Chrisie.

'The problem is that the last flight comes in to North Ron from Mainland Orkney at around four thirty, which is too early for businesses or schools to finish for the day. Also in order to get night flights, the pilot would have to get rated for night flying, the runway would have to be extended, and it would have to have night time runway lights, which are all difficult to justify for one child, but perhaps not for business commuters.'

I remembered what the very experienced ex-RAF pilot of the King Air medical plane who had ferried me down to Aberdeen had said: he hated flying at night. When I had naively asked him why, he had turned around to look at me eyeball to eyeball, so as to make sure that I heard him. He said, 'You can't see anything.'

I then wondered why the people of North Ron had not got together with the doctor and his wife and petitioned for this. Maybe there was some friction, or they didn't get on. Or maybe it was just an idea which the other islanders didn't agree with. Maybe there simply were not enough children at the moment to justify it. Maybe the people on Mainland Orkney knew that no one would ever want to go and live on an island like North Ron.

The daylight here was different. The sky seemed bigger and more expansive on North Ron than it had done on Mainland Orkney. It is probably because the island is so low lying. The highest point is a mere twenty meters above sea level. It was a bit like New Zealand, in that it made you realize that with this rare sense of beauty came the silence of intense isolation. This was a little slice of paradise which was a lot closer to home than New Zealand, and I was looking forward to every moment, partly because there was a lot of time to explore this very small island. There was no rush whatsoever. I was keen for the doctor and his family to leave so we could feel more at ease. I was acutely aware that I had to be careful with him.

'What's the food like at the pub?' Chrisie asked.

'A tourist once ate there and said it was off,' said the doctor. 'I wouldn't eat there. You only get pubites there. I would recommend that you don't go near the place.' It struck me that he didn't seem to have a particularly good relationship with his patients, and I began to wonder if he was actually liked. He was openly trashing their services, and I sensed he was in competition with the pub. Why else would he speak so unfavourably about their work? He had already created a potential them and us situation. I couldn't accept this, because I had not seen it for myself; it was coming from a particularly odd man in very odd circumstances in a very remote place.

'Well we would like to see the only restaurant and pub on the island at some stage,' I boldly said. 'Can't come all the way without trying it out.' He ignored me and wandered off to do some bird things on his computer in the reception area before coming back for supper.

Supper was very light, and the three of us would have gone to bed hungry if we hadn't dug into our own provisions. Essentially, the portions his wife served to all of us were child portions and not enough for an adult in this climate. Over supper the doctor explained that they ran a B&B, especially for people interested in birds, but it would be closed for the two weeks when they were away. There was only one other person staying, whom we had already bumped into. He was friendly and on benefits, and did some work for the doctor, and some birding which he was very enthusiastic about.

'The B&B will be closed when we're gone, but there are a few things you need to know, which my wife will show you before we go.'

That evening Tommy dropped in and introduced himself. One of his duties was to drive the school bus and pick up the doctor's two children and now, of course, India as well. He was a well built, warm, hearty man who wore a bright red smile.

'I'll pick India up at about nine in the morning as I drive the school bus with one of the teachers.' So far, he was the only person to actually say anything to our four year old daughter, for neither the doctor, his wife nor children had acknowledged her by interacting with her in any way. I wondered if that was a simple effect of living on an isolated island, where you have to tap into your inner resources to survive, with the result that it is too easy for everyone to become loners and see other people as intrusive or a threat.

We unpacked our things and put them all away, and put all the provisions into the kitchen. We had brought a small but good range of meals, which, it was now clear, we would need. We chatted as we went to bed about how tense the doctor and his wife had seemed over supper.

In the morning the first thing we did was ask about breakfast, but it was 'help yourself' to anything you want in the kitchen … but you had to mark it up and pay for it. So I wasn't getting bed and breakfast, even though the Health Board was paying for my B&B, and I was paying for Chrisie and India's B&B. It seemed to be more like self-catering, which I preferred. I thought that he would pick up the details of the expenses of my breakfasts and pass this on to the Health Board.

Next we had to introduce India to her school, her teachers and fellow classmates. We followed Tommy and his crew to the local school which was just a little way from the war memorial. For a school with only four children, it was huge. The youngest boy and a massive mobile trolley load of toys and other amusements sat in the large gym which was about twenty yards wide by thirty yards long. There was a pool table and more computers and staff than pupils. There was a cook, janitor, cleaner, administrator and two teachers, and a new headmistress, who was due to start in a couple of months.

India was really excited about meeting the other pupils and was looking forward to starting school, particularly because this was the first time she would use a school bus. She would be in the kindergarten in the morning and in the main school in the afternoon.

After we introduced her to the school, we tried to decide what to do for the rest of the day. There was the lighthouse to see and the sheep that ate seaweed. There was an old church, a new church and one pub. That's it.

If you are into birds, of course you would have a busy time in North Ron, as thousands of birds are ringed every year on the island. About 800 thousand birds are ringed each year in Britain by only two thousand ringers. It takes two years to train each ringer, and ringers have to renew their licenses every year. Only one in fifty of the ringed birds are ever spotted. And the birds in North Ron were all unusual. There were few of the common birds which you see in your garden in most of Britain. All classes of birds are seen whilst they rest on this tiny island on their way to and from their summer holidays in Iceland, Greenland and Scandinavia. The only impressions I think I made on the locals were about the birds we saw in Australia and New Zealand. The only bird that no one had heard of on North Ron was the More Pork bird, named as such because it's call sounds exactly like it's saying, 'More Pork, More Pork.'

My first surgery was half an hour and consisted of two patients. The doctor's wife came with me to show me how to use the computer, so neither Chrisie or I had a chance to look at the flat upstairs, which we had been dissuaded from staying in. It was not possible to get the computer to work. I wondered if this was a one off incident, but part of me sensed it was not used at all. I did wonder why she had insisted she come to the first surgery with me. No reasons were given for any fault. I was just told, 'It is not working.'

I was beginning to sense something less than honesty and not revealing the truth. There was something uncomfortable about secrets and people in a community not being open which un-nerves you. However, it was new to me, and, perhaps, that is why I felt so uneasy. I dealt with it by saying it was just me not being used to the psychology of tiny island communities. Just like any small community, there had to be smaller splinter groups within the already small community. There was bound to be between different groups in such a place as this. I kept on telling myself to get used to it and to make adjustments. Perhaps then, I thought, it might be more fun.

No one on the island seemed to have just one job. I found this very odd. If you asked someone what they do on

North Ronaldsay they would always name several jobs, which usually included crofter, fireman and coastguard. Most men had at least six jobs. Men and women seemed to also be Directors of the wool company, member of the North Ronaldsay Association and the North Ronaldsay Trust. Everyone had many roles, and they were flexible about how they spent their time. Apart from the shop, the pub and the doctor's B&B, there didn't seem to be any other ways of making a living other than by being a crofter or one of the very few local artists.

However, there is much more to North Ron than meets the eye. It is an island which not only presents a very low profile to all shipping, but cunningly conceals a huge submerged reef, known as Reefdyke, on its north-east side. The reef is as large as the island and has been the resting place of many shipwrecks and their sailors over the years. The first recorded was a Swedish East Indiaman called Svecia, which was wrecked on Reefdyke in 1740 with the loss of ninety-one lives. She was carrying cargo worth £1,500,000. Next, in 1744, came the Danish East Indiaman, the Crown Prince, which was wrecked on the other side of the top of the island, called Savie Geo. No one was lost and neither was the cargo of silver coins. I concluded that the Vikings must have lost many ships on that reef.

Then in 1822 came The Royal Oak which ran aground in dense fog in Bride's Kirk, in the south of the island, carrying dressed timber which was then used to build houses on the island. Famously, in one night in 1926 three German ships managed to avoid Reefdyke only to be wrecked on the most easterly part of the island known as Dennis Head. The last victim, in 1957, was a coasting steamer Mistley which was wrecked on the reef.

But perhaps the most amusing local shipwreck yarn,

which is also a documented historical fact, is the story of the survival of the captain of the Lena. The Lena was wrecked near Senness. Many lives were apparently lost, but the local islanders went to help any survivors. On the beach they found a semi-conscious man and took him to a nearby house where they left him under the care of a woman. They returned to the wreck and left her to resuscitate him. She placed him in the still warm bed in which she had been sleeping. Despite giving him brandy, there was no sign of him recovering, and so she decided to help him by using her own body heat. She took off her clothes and warmed him up, successfully reviving him. When he woke up he thanked her and told her that he was the captain of the wrecked ship, and promised that he would repay her once he returned to his home. On returning home he sent her a beautiful silk dress, which had to pass through the local Receiver of Wrecks, whose wife, thinking it was too good for a crofter's wife, substituted it with a cheap printed cotton dress. Her reputation for meanness seemed to have outlived her.

The sheep on North Ron are rather enigmatic because no one knows how they got there or how they came to live off seaweed. Some things were known about these sheep, but, first, let me get one thing off my chest before telling you about them. It seemed, from watching various popular chefs on television, that mutton was making a big comeback. I had never really tried it, except perhaps in Irish stew, because it's regarded as old meat, not young meat. On our first night in North Ron we had mutton stew at the restaurant in the local pub. I have never tasted anything like it in my life. It is stronger than venison, hare or even heart. It had a powerful taste which is unmistakably mutton, but it smelt of lanolin. I don't think any of the chefs knew how dreadful the meat of North Ronaldsay sheep tasted. I could not in my wildest dreams imagine how the sheep industry survived for so long. You would only serve North Ron sheep to demonstrate how disgusting it tasted or to put someone off eating mutton. The sheep were interesting and to be admired, but not for their palatability. I had never heard of the meat being served in a restaurant, and I'd never met anyone who has tasted it.

North Ron sheep are the very last of the British native sheep known as Northern Short Tails. There is only one other large colony of these sheep on a Norwegian island. No one knows if the early Vikings brought them to North Ron or took them from North Ron to Norway. They are also very odd because they are so small, and in North Ron they regarded them as lambs for a full three to four years, which is when they reach their full size, which is still small. They are less than a third the size of normal sheep. Because they are basically old mutton, they have to be cooked slowly, for a long time to tenderize the meat.

With one exception, all of the sheep lived on the beach, kept there by the dyke, parts of which date back to before 1000 BC. At lambing time the ewes are brought inside the dyke to feed on the grass for up to four months. They leave the beach only three times, and that is for dipping and shearing, which is done communally – a rare thing these days – and for slaughter. Because this breed of sheep is unique to the island and there are only a few of them, any woolen garments are probably the rarest in the world. If you wanted to make someone feel special you could buy them a North Ron sweater or scarf.

When I mentioned that there is one exception to all of the sheep, well, there is only one. And that is the single sheep who managed to escape from the beach by louping the dyke. Loup is the Orcadian term for jumping, and they refer to foreigners on the island as people who've louped the ferry. This castrated sheep had been living in a huge field for a long time, and he ate grass rather than seaweed. No one could catch him, and his coat had not been cut. It was matted, almost Rastafarian-like, and so long that it trailed behind him on the ground like a very long coat.

But that was not the only interesting thing about this particular Rastafarian looking sheep. If sheep live longer than four years, eating grass, they get Wilsons Disease, which is copper poisoning. This quickly kills them. This sheep had been eating grass for only two years, and had two years to go. Although they can live a long time, for up to twenty years, this only happens if they stop eating seaweed. If they remain eating seaweed, they die from starvation, because the sand wears their teeth down to nothing within eleven years.

I didn't know enough about these sheep, or indeed about any sheep, but I wondered what they ate if they couldn't eat grass or seaweed to survive. Although there were nearly four thousand sheep on the island there were only twenty that were geriatric; and these were kept by a couple who were retired university lecturers in Biology. Nothing about this island was quite what it seemed.

We felt partly settled in after our first day. In the evening the doctor said, 'We're all off to punding at ten tomorrow.'

'What's that?' I asked

'Punding the sheep,' said the doctor's wife.

'What's punding the sheep?' I asked.

'We've got to get them off the shore into punds, to get them on the boat,' said the doctor.

'What are punds?' I asked, still mystified.

'They're stone wall enclosures at various places on the dyke. The dyke is twelve miles long and about five feet high, but seven feet in some places. The flock of sheep is thought to be one of the very last in Europe that is still communally farmed.'

'How do you catch them?'

'With difficulty. It's always done at high tide so there is less room for them to manoeuvre. But, first, I need to take the diesel tank down to the quay. You can all come and help us pund if you like. It's a community thing. You'll be expected to be there.'

'We would be interested to come along,' I said. This sounded exciting, as I hadn't been involved in anything agricultural since I was a small child in the west of Ireland, where I spent all of my summers working on relative's farms.

In the morning we just followed the doctor and his wife. He attached a tow rope to the front of an incredibly rusty, forty year old tractor.

'What's the tow rope for?'

'Won't start, so it has to be jump started. Can you tie a clove hitch to the back of the Land Rover?'

'No trouble at all.' Chrisie jumped in the Land Rover, and I decided to walk behind the tractor trailer which held the empty thousand litre diesel tank.

'Everything is diesel on the island,' he said as he tried to bang out a drop-down bolt that held the trailer onto the elderly tractor.

'Any reason for that?'

'Because of new regulations last year, the ferry boat now can't transport petrol, so it's all diesel.' He continued banging with a large lump hammer.

'You have a go. Too tired,' he said, and I took the hammer and banged vigorously from underneath, but there was only a foot of clearance from the ground and I couldn't bang upwards quite hard enough. After a further minute I handed it back to him, but there was no difference even after him hitting it for another minute.

'If you've got a jack to jack the bolt up, the weight of the trailer would probably force the bolt out,' I suggested.

He stared at me for a fraction of a second, then he really lost it and shouted at me in a rage, 'I know what to do!'

He was clearly operating on a very short fuse, and it was like holding a lit powder keg. The problem was that my family and I were now trapped with him.

'Damn thing's rusted with salt,' he shouted.

I tried to calm him down by speaking every word in a lower volume and taking slower and slower breaths as I slowly went down on my haunches again. 'Salt pretty much attacks everything. I did some work on Grand Turk once, and everything just fell apart with the salt.' The psychological defusing technique worked very well, and he had no idea I was using it.

He then pulled out a can of de-rusting spray, but the oil from that didn't work either. 'I'll come back to this a bit later,' he said in frustration, and we all set off to pund the sheep.

The Land Rover stopped at a gate in the dyke, and the doctor got out and said, 'I'm going to run the sheep north along the beach. You drive and turn left along the track and stay in the car or in the pund, but don't get on the beach, because the sheep will get scared and will turn around and run backwards, and won't come into the pund. They're a bit sensitive or stupid, whichever way you want to see it.'

'No trouble at all,' I said as I jumped in the driver's seat and accelerated off. A couple of minutes later the sheep came running along the beach but didn't stop at the pund. They raced past us, and an elderly man who stood there shook his head. He was about six foot four and in his eighties.

'Never get them first time,' he said.

'Too clever aren't they?' I added.

'Just sheep, they won't stop.' The doctor appeared and started waving his arms and screaming at the sheep, but they simply ignored him, heading south and running past him. He jumped in his Land Rover to get to the end of the bay before they did, which was about a mile away. The beach was made of rocks about eight inches across, and for the last five metres it was covered with what looked like brown bones, but which was, in fact, a very odd type of seaweed. There were four seals looking curiously at a bunch of adult men and women chasing sheep on the beach. I was sure the seals were having a good laugh.

After the sheep were chased from the far end of the beach by a man called Jim, they passed us once again, going north. The elderly man signalled for us to help him unroll a long length of metal fencing across the beach so that when the sheep turned around again they wouldn't be able to go back again.

'Never get it right,' said the elderly man's wife. In all the years I've lived here it's always the same, up and down the flipping beach all morning. Always the same.' This made me smile. Humans are fundamentally irrational, even though they are totally convinced they are predominantly rational.

We drove to the pund on the northern part of the beach, and there were all the sheep.

'How many have you got?' I asked the elderly man.

'Probably two hundred. Give us a hand with this, can you?' He seemed to be feeling how big their bottoms were. 'Here you do it,' he said to me, 'and pull the biggest ones over there,' pointing to a small fenced enclosure within the pund.

As I felt the sheep's bottoms I began to wonder if I

could be prosecuted for this. "Doctor gets life for assaulting rare sheep in Britain's smallest general practice."

Honest M'Lord I was only feeling their bottoms to see who had the biggest one.

'Take him downstairs.'

I hoped no one was taking photographs. Curious, on the way back I asked, 'Who is the local policeman?'

'Oh, it's Tony. He's the special constable.' And I hoped I wouldn't be meeting him.

'They're strange looking sheep,' I remarked to the elderly man.

'North Ronaldsay sheep are the smallest and hardiest sheep in Britain, and they are thought to go back to Neolithic times. There's a strong belief that they were originally Siberian. They are also known for their longevity. Over hundreds of years they've not been interbred, and their short tails are a mark of being an ancient breed.' I thought they probably hadn't interbred because it would have been near impossible to get a different breed of sheep to this place. Fly them in? They could be smuggled in, I supposed.

'They look more like goats in the way that they negotiate the slippery rocks on the beach,' I said.

'They're known for being very competitive in trying to reach the most freshly exposed seaweed first. The hardiest ones will sometimes swim to get to the very best seaweed.'

'How much seaweed do they eat?' I asked.

'Seaweed has always featured highly as the main raw material which has enabled North Ronaldsay to be a self-supporting economy, but now it supports the community only as food for the sheep. In the past it was used as fuel for fires and for manure for the fields. It was also burned and the ash shipped to Newcastle or Grangemouth in cargo loads of 150 to 300 tons. Each sheep still requires five pounds of seaweed a day, which amounts to around 3,000 tons a year.'

I stood on the beach, looking at the seaweed, the sheep, the sky, the sea and the seals, and I wondered how this was any different from thousands of years ago. It had that sense of silence, making me forget where I was in time and place. It was very still, although I could hear the wind and the sea. There was the sense of inner silence. Detachment. The spirit. That is what these isles and islands were all about. They weren't merely remnants of Stone Age towns. They were a spiritual centre.

Back at the doctor's house, the doctor's wife said, 'You'll need to collect the eggs every day.'

'Where from?' I asked

'The chickens.' Numbskull!

'Chickens. I haven't seen any yet. Where are they?'

'Out the back. I'll show you.' Chickens are always out the back ... another numbskull question.

All three of us followed her towards the northern part of the property along a path which was made easier to walk on by broken roof tiles and other rubble that had been tipped along the lines of the land rover tracks.

'How many have you got?'

'Thirteen, and you'll need to feed the chickens with your leftovers.'

'What's that cat doing over there?' I asked, looking at a black cat lying in the doorway of a rundown house in front of us, who seemed not to have noticed us coming.

'Dead,' she said. 'I found it yesterday. It's one of thousands of feral cats on the island. They just die of starvation.' And clearly this dead cat was not going to be moved from the house. This house had a roof, windows and doors, which was not the rule but an exception on North Ron. It was still and silent, a deserted house from many generations back 'The old lady who lived here decided she'd had enough and moved to the rest home in Kirkwall.'

'When?' Chrisie asked.

'In the late '80s. She had no toilet and one running tap in a shed, and she lived here. Take a look inside. It's in good condition.' And we followed her in through the open front door.

'What's this?' Chrisie asked, looking at a wall with a large recess in it.

'It's a box bed.' And indeed it was a five by five foot boxed space along one wall. The doctor's wife said it was particularly difficult to examine her in this, because she was always on the far side.

'It's amazing that she lived here,' said Chrisie. The house was full rubbish, such as old mattresses, and I realized that this was another hallmark of North Ronaldsay. As there is nowhere to dispose of rubbish, no one seems to collect it, and there is a great deal of rubbish in unexpected places, but mostly in the empty houses.

I wondered if everyone just left their rubbish where it lay. There seemed to be whole century's worth of rubbish. Everywhere, there are buildings which had been deserted. At the airport the old terminal building, which is a windowless wooden hut, had been filled with rubbish, and more rubbish lay outside. Most of the rubbish was metal, as the salt had dissolved and rotted anything made of plastic or wood. It was in stark contrast to the new airport building, which was essentially one room that was used as the traffic controller's room, the waiting room, the fire officer's room, the weighing room for passengers and cargo, as well as being a shelter from the wind, rain and sun.

The chickens were around the back of the house in a new chicken shed. 'The old one's roof's fallen in, so we don't go in there.'

'Do they lay in there?'

'Yes, but that's the only place where we don't pick up the eggs. There are four areas where they lay, so you'll need to check the other three which are safe to go into,' she said as she picked up two eggs from a bucket with a false egg in it. The sheep eat the eggs if we don't get here every day, so make sure you empty them all. The roofs of the out buildings were made of flagstones about three feet wide by six feet long. They made the outhouses look like death traps, but there was one exception.

'What's this?' Chrisie asked, pointing to an oval structure which was a stone walled building of some kind with flag stones laid on top of the wall. In the middle of this oval building was half a rotting boat lying upside down.

'It's a boat building.'

'What's that?' I asked, another stupid question. The answer had to be: a building made with a boat.

'It was a building they made when a boat could no longer be sailed. They built the stone wall to the size of the boat, and then used the boat as the roof. But most of them have rotted away now, and this is probably the only one left on the island.'

My thoughts went now to physics and the law of entropy, where everything just gets worse, and I wondered how long it would take to depopulate the island; and how long it would it take for me to stop asking dumb questions.

'How long do you think people will live here?' I asked her.

'Well, the answer's in the children. Twenty-five years ago there were

seventeen children in the school. Now there are four, five with India.'

'That's pretty much a death knell then,' I said. But she didn't answer me.

When we got back to the house, the doctor's wife said. 'You'll need to feed the dog and the goldfish. And any bookings for the B&B, you can either make in the diary, or you can take a message and we'll phone them up when we get back.'

'What if someone just turns up to stay?' I asked.

'No one ever does,' she said with such finality that I didn't dare ask 'What if?'

When we dropped the doctor and his family at the airport, there was a huge feeling of relief. Not just for us, but for them, because they really seemed to need the break. Part of me heard the whole of North Ron collectively go 'Phew' in relief that they were going. The weather seemed to get calmer, and I even imagined that the sheep looked happier. It was just my imagination, of course.

The only creature that was not calm was the collie. The dog was having a major panic attack at the airport. The more I looked at her, the more I thought I could identify with her, except I didn't understand why she was so panicky. First, she wouldn't get out the car; then, even on a lead, she wouldn't go anywhere near the runway. Then it all clicked into place when the doctor got a muzzle out of his pocket and put it across her nose. She used both front paws to try and remove this mandatory aircraft device. These were the regulations; no one wanted a dog on a plane to bite the pilot or anyone else. So this lovely collie was going to have to endure a little bit of hypoxia in order to stay with its family.

I felt some sympathy for this doctor working on a very remote island with all the responsibility and pressure that it must bring, not to mention the various divisions and camps which must form on a small island. As I wallowed in my empathy and sympathy for him I was suddenly jolted by a single realization. He had chosen to come and work here for twenty-nine years, shunning all the chores and responsibilities of a normal GP. He could follow hobbies, like ornithology, nearly all day and he got seventeen weeks holiday, for which he virtually gets paid double by doing his own locum. I realized that my attitude was too soft and I needed to be tougher, and not always assume that all people were decent and principled.

We were at last on our own, even though we had to look after their chickens, dog, cat, goldfish and the phone for the B&B. It seemed like Chrisie would have to be the receptionist at the surgery, to let patients in and out, and to answer the phone.

Although it was an enormous relief to drop them at the airport and be on our own, it was also to be the beginning of a lot of surprises. Just as we were walking past the airport building, Chrisie noticed an advert in a wood-framed glass box on the side wall. It was an advert to rent a self-catering house on the island.

'I thought he was not telling us the truth all along about there being no self-catering accommodation,' I said to Chrisie. We were both shocked, and I was just a little fed up with this man who was the island's GP. I was more than fed up. I was disgusted with him, his dishonesty and naked greed.

'There are more of them,' said Tommy who had just given another passenger a lift to the airport in his car.

'Where are they? I mean this doctor said his was the only self-catering accommodation on the island.'

'Did he really say that?'

'Yes.'

'Well, well, well. That really does confirm what we thought was going on. Many of us always say there are two islands on North Ronaldsay. There's North Ronaldsay ... and there's the doctor's B&B. But we have to just let him get on with it, because he has a lot of power, especially over our health. '

I had no idea it was so bad. All the hunches I'd had when I talked to him three times before on the phone before we arrived were confirmed. He had lied to me on three occasions, and he was acting against the survival of the rest of the community in every way, but particularly financially. He was not a fair trader; he was not honest and didn't radiate trustworthiness. He had no principles. He was a liar, dishonest, greedy and cold.

'He's quite something, isn't he?' said Tommy, breaking into my thoughts.

'Someone ought to report him to the Office of Fair Trading, the Trading Standards and the Competition Commission. I bet the RSPB wouldn't be very happy about recommending people to stay here, if they knew what he was doing. I'm sure Orkney Tourist Board and the Highlands and Islands Enterprise would be interested in how he uses their resources, sneakily deceiving one and all.' I had vented my spleen about his lies, and I felt relieved; and I saw Tommy, who had listened carefully, nodding his head.

'I'll show you the old croft I rent out, if you want. It must be a shock for you coming across a doctor like this.'

'A man like this,' I said.

'Yes, we'd like that very much,' said Chrisie, who, I could tell by her look, was as fed up with the doctor and his wife as I was.

'You can follow me,' said Tommy, stepping into his

Land Rover.

'The house is called The Brig. It's only two minutes away.' We took off, going north towards the lighthouse. It was a beautiful house on one floor.

'How old is it? Asked Chrisie.

'No one really knows. We know it's over three hundred years old, but it probably goes back much further than that. We renovated the inside this year. So it's very cozy and warm. There's central heating, a modern kitchen with a microwave and a washing machine. There are two bedrooms and plenty of room to kick around in. There's an open coal fire with plenty of fuel.' He opened the door, and we could see that the house was large and had a spacious main bedroom with a spare place for extra people to sleep in.

'This is just the kind of house I had imagined we would find up here. It would have been ideal for us, but we are stuck at the doctor's B&B now. I am so disappointed with him.'

'How much is this to rent?' Chrisie asked.

'Well, it's not a very busy island, and it's only an interest of mine. We charge £28 a week, but you have to pay for the coal.'

'Is that £28 for each person?' Chrisie asked.

'Good Heavens, no. Don't be silly. It's for the whole house for as many people as want to stay in it. Six is comfortable, but we've occasionally had ten birders.'

'That's incredibly cheap. Chrisie is being charged £30 per night for Birders B&B at the doctor's house.'

'And I expect he's got you taking the calls for his B&B, and looking after his pets and his chickens, all for nothing.'

'You said it all in one. We feel as if we are victims of a con artist. Are there any other places where you can self-cater on the island?'

'Yes. There are four all together.'

'He is almost unbelievable isn't he?' I said.

'I think you are in for a shock. There's Hoybanks, Dennis Hill and the Dolls House.'

'Oh heck. I hope he isn't a psychopath,' Chrisie said.

'No, I'm sure he's just an eccentric island GP,' I said reassuringly. Now, however, much though I really wanted to believe this, I didn't. I had a very uncomfortable feeling that I might have set myself to come home one night to find him waiting in the bushes for me.

'Hoybanks is oldy worldly, warm and cosy, and its £5 a night per person. It's got 8 beds, and a lot of birders who just show up come here in the short season to live in it. Dennis Hill is very modern and a bit more expensive. Then there's Dolls House which is owned by the landlord and his wife at the pub. But you would need to eat at the pub because it is very small. All of them are really good enough for a passing king or queen.' I was even more disappointed and felt totally cheated by the GP.

'What's the food like at the pub?' Chrisie asked.

They serve good soup and their own really tasty home grown lamb, pork or beef. The puddings are pretty good too. It's really good food.'

'Is it expensive?'

'Not really. You should try it. If there's anything else you need to know, come over and see us for a coffee or tea.'

'Thanks for your information. I feel I'm getting to know the people a bit better.'

'No bother,' he said and went back towards the lighthouse.

'I suppose we might as well have a look at the flat above the surgery,' said Chrisie.

'It'll be interesting,' I replied, feeling a little more positive.

This time, without the doctor or his wife present, we had a more thorough look around. The surgery consisted of two large rooms downstairs. One was the main surgery room and one was the waiting room, which was covered in anti-smoking stickers and warnings about drinking alcohol. And there seemed to be a lot more stickers than you would usually expect to find in a GP's surgery. They were even all over both sides of the doors. Most of them were about nicotine gum and nicotine patches. This told me something about the doctor – he disliked pub culture.

He certainly didn't seem the kind of religious fundamentalist type or an evangelical smoking cessation doctor. But I was taken with his display of enthusiasm to help patients quit smoking and curb their alcohol use. I felt a sense of guilt for having generalized my opinion of him. Walking around the public areas of his surgery, I could see an abundance of evidence that he was doing everything he could to help these islanders develop and maintain healthy lifestyles. He was obviously a GP who belied immediate impressions and, deep down, really cared about the welfare of his patients. I felt really awful for pre-judging him and I was working on how to make it up by building up a positive image of him which I could give to anyone who mentioned him. I could then forgive myself my error in judgement.

The smaller minor ops room had more junk on the floor than I remembered. In the kitchen were three more boxes full of all sorts of out-of-date drugs. I now thought about what the GP in Kirkwall had said about the out-of-date drugs and wondered if the doctor or his wife had removed them from the shelves of the pharmacy for my benefit and put them here. I had no way of knowing.

The kitchen was quite good and had everything you would need. Out the back was a stone shed, probably used for hay storage at some time. The wallpaper was probably late '50s or early '60s and was brown with age. The stairs led up to three bedrooms. One had a large double bed and it was a good room which would have accommodated the three of us. One bedroom was an office. In the third bedroom there were seventeen large dustbins full of rubbish. This was not what I was expecting.

The surgery was ... well ... a bit of a mess and a depressing place, simply because it was untidy, dirty and full of junk. There were many boxes on the floor in the treatment room, as well as a couple of large free standing gas cylinders, which at a glance looked precariously balanced, especially dangerous if they were to fall on to a child. This combined with the steel stakes sticking several inches out of the ground beside the path made it a dangerous place to be. But it was better than the housing we had been given, because here we could have had privacy away from the doctor and his wife. We both felt too intimidated by the doctor to request a change, because we had to spend a day with him when he returned from his holidays. We would be able to cope for just one day.

I thought I would just run through and familiarize myself with the contents of the emergency drug bag. I opened it and found an unused syringe and a dirty needle but nothing else. My reaction was to laugh; bizarre. This was either some kind of silly joke or an extremely serious error on the doctor's part. Fortunately, thinking I might need a really serious drug bag, I had my own very small stash of emergency drugs.

For the rest of our first day on our own we gently pottered around the house and the rest of the island. I went fishing off the quay and got a bite straight away, but the fish got away.

'I wonder if they really need a doctor here,' said Chrisie.

'It would be cheaper to fly one in when someone is sick,' I said. 'I'm sure all the people know that they would get an experienced and skilled doctor visiting them, but the downside is that they would have to cope well with emergencies, which hardly ever seem to happen.'

In the afternoon we went to have a guided tour of the lighthouse given by Billy the lightkeeper.

'Well, I've been here for thirty-nine years. I was the last full time lightkeeper until 1998. There are two lighthouses, the old one and the new one. The old one still stands and was only seventy feet high and was built in 1789. That one became redundant when a new one was built on the island of Sanday in 1806. Eventually, it became obvious that North Ronaldsay still needed its own lighthouse, and the new one, which is nearly twice as high at 139 feet, is this quite beautiful building. It was built in 1854 by Robert Louis Stevenson's grandfather's family, who built nearly all of the lighthouses in Scotland and many in India and New Zealand. His trips to remote lighthouses are thought to have inspired him to write the books Treasure Island and Kidnapped.'

'It's also the tallest land-based lighthouse in Britain, and the tower is made of red brick with two massive white stripes around it, so it can clearly be seen in the day. The walls are over five feet thick and all the 176 steps inside are red. It is, however, an easy climb, but not if you had to do it once an hour to wind the mechanism up like they used to. It flashes every ten seconds and has a range of twenty-four miles. It's powered by a 400 watt bulb which is magnified many times by a massive French Fresnel lens. Fresnel is the name of the maker of crystal lenses in those days. The intensity of the light is equivalent to over half a million candles and flashes every ten seconds. There is a foghorn which blasts every sixty seconds.'

'What's the big book?' I asked, looking at an old, large book.'

'It's the original Shipwreck Recording Book, which boasts only twenty shipwrecks since the new lighthouse was built in 1854. Each report begins with a sombre sentence such as, 'I beg to inform you that at 4.00 am…' They are all terrible stories. It cost £6,181 to build then but would now cost £6.2 million. In the early days the Principal lightkeeper was only paid £45 a year. My job, along with the other two lightkeepers, was to keep the bearings oiled, the reflectors polished and the windows clean of salt. We had a large workshop, which you can see down on the ground.'

'What are all the buildings around the lighthouse?' I asked.

'The old lightkeeper's buildings are being converted to luxury holiday houses for tourists, but this is a long term project. They are going to be let by the National Trust. What a fabulous location right at the top North Ron where, on clear nights, the Northern lights are clearly visible. There are some great walks to do around the lighthouse.'

'And what's in the sacks?' I asked.

'The lighthouse also boasts a wool mill and a shop selling various woolen garments such as hats and scarves, and sheep skins. I'll walk you around the place.'

'What's this wood?' I asked.

'This is part of the cargo of the ship Svecia which was wrecked on the reef in 1740. It was redwood, known as dyewood, from the forests of Eastern India. The trees are now extinct, but before synthetic dyes appeared they were used by the locals for dying North Ronaldsay wool. Part of the cargo of wood still gets washed up on the beaches. The wreck was found in 1975, and surveyed and archaeologically excavated in 1983. Now, before you go to the old lighthouse I must tell you one last thing. Come back and look at this lighthouse and stand under it at night. I won't tell you why, but it's worth it.' I could only think of moths or birds being attracted to the light, but I was later to be proved wrong about this.

On the way to the old lighthouse we saw seals craftily hiding amongst the sheep on the beach. They really seemed like quite defenseless creatures, but as I approached one of them barked and growled at me. The old lighthouse had a large seagulls nest in the top window and, although it was possible to go inside, it would mean negotiating an enormous, two hundred year old pile of bird droppings.

There is only one large house on North Ron, called Holland House. This was owned by the Traill family, who bought the whole island in 1727. There are three cannons in the front garden, which came from the Crown Prince, which was wrecked in 1744. Eventually, they reluctantly had to sell off all of the crofts to anyone who wanted to buy them. They only come to North Ron in the summer now.

Driving is risky on North Ron, and for a whole variety of reasons. Most people have provisional licenses, and they are exempt from having to have a licensed driver with them. Unbelievably, vehicles are exempt from having MOTs, so the island is a veritable museum of ancient cars, some without doors and windows and some with just one seat. Most of the residents had never driven anywhere else, so we were very careful when we approached other vehicles. The roads are treacherously narrow, and there was no margin for error, even in the two Land Rovers we were driving. Any lapse of concentration, and you would be in a ditch. There were rabbits everywhere and lots of dead ones just lying in the fields. Had they been hit by cars?

The whole area was an open museum of Neolithic sites. For example, in the field beside the house is a Neolithic standing stone thirteen feet high and four feet wide, but what is a little strange about this one is the hole in the middle. Archeologists believe it was part of a primitive sundial.

The other unusual stones were the cooking stones. Thousands of years ago stones were heated in fire and then put into stone water containers in the ground. The hot stones would boil the water, and all manner of vegetables and meats were cooked this way. In North Ron there is a large mound of these cooking stones, which is called Sameul Stand Knowe.

On our second evening we got two calls.

'Hi there. I'm ringing to invite you to come bulbing tomorrow morning.'

'Yes. Thank you, but what is it?'

'Meet at the Community Centre in the morning after surgery, and we will all go bulbing. It's a community thing, followed by soup,' the woman said and hung up, leaving me mystified and amused. I made a note of it, and as soon as I hung the phone up, it rang again. It was the doctor's wife.

'The surgery answer machine needs a message on it. The key to our flat is on a hook in the back storeroom by a picture. There is an inch-thick manual if you can't work out how to change the message.' She hung up almost as if she was trying not to spend money on her phone.

Now I found myself slightly irritated at this. She had not said, 'Sorry, we completely forgot to put a message on the answer machine. Could you please leave one?' She didn't ask me to change it. She was assuming I would obey her orders.

This was quite funny, because it seemed she was not used to interacting with people and having the grace to listen to what they had to say.

Answer machines are not my favorite things to tinkle with, and certainly not a strange one. I suppose my irritation stemmed mostly from the fact that we were minding their house and animals for them for nothing, and yet they intended to charge Chrisie for B&B on a daily basis.

We went into the back storeroom, and, to my utter surprise, I saw dozens of cases of single malt whisky stacked nearly to the ceiling. I remembered being told about the doctor keeping a large stock of over sixty different types of malt whisky. I assumed these were bottles not crates. I had also naturally assumed that the doctor, with his anti 'pubite' attitude, kept this hoard of expensive whisky for his guests.

Chrisie found the key to the doctor's flat as directed by his wife, and I followed her in search of the answer machine. When we switched the light on, we both slipped at the same time and bumped into each other. We had slipped on whisky bottles on the floor. There were about eight or nine lying there. Some were a quarter full but most were empty and simply strewn on the floor, along with dirty clothes, empty biscuit packets wrappers, crisp packet wrappers and other rubbish. We were both in total shock. It was like the home of derelicts. It made me remember my initial sense that their children didn't look very happy at all when we met them.

That night we took the four-mile drive back to the lighthouse, to follow the lightkeeper's suggestion. We got out of the car and stood right under the lighthouse. It was a magnificent sight. High above us were sixteen beams of brilliant, white light coming from the top of the lighthouse, moving slowly and majestically in unison, lighting up vast areas of the island and the sea. It was as if we were standing under a massive umbrella, but, instead of the black dome being supported by metal spokes arising from a central hub, the spokes were made of light. This can only be experienced by standing directly under a lighthouse, which is rare, as many are offshore and you can't get this close. Also, this one is the biggest and, therefore, probably the most impressive lighthouse.

The next morning after surgery we dropped India at the school, which was also the Community Centre. And off we went to join three school teachers and the school cook and plant a hundred yards of daffodil bulbs on either side of the main road. It was a really good feeling to know that they would probably outlive us and our children. Lunch was not just soup but sausage rolls, tuna sandwiches, vegetarian sausages and vegetable soup, all freshly prepared by the cook. They were all friendly, positive people, although one or two were somewhat introverted. The cook was the most outgoing and the happiest, dancing to highland reels and jigs in the school kitchen whilst she cooked.

After being on the island for nearly a week, we decided to eat out. The only place was the local pub/restaurant. I was told that I was the first doctor to go to the pub in living memory, that is in twenty-eight years, and everyone inside was aghast when we walked into the pub. There were two taps on the bar, one for Guinness and one for bitter, but they hadn't worked for years. There was, basically, no beer. However, there was draught canned Guinness and canned beer. I just stuck with the food which was excellent. We were given a warm welcome and felt much more accepted by the locals than by the doctor and his family.

The next day we went to see one of the other houses which could be rented, which was wonderfully simple. It slept eight but could accommodate sixteen in its four bedrooms. There were beds which slid out from underneath other beds, and others that folded down from walls. There was no mains water, but fresh water from a spring was available, which was tested every year. There was a '60s bathroom, a kitchen and sitting room, and many outbuildings. It was right on the coast, protected by the five-foot high dyke wall. It was only £5 per person per night, which sounded very attractive. It was mainly used by birders during the migratory season. I was tempted but had to think about it before making a decision.

The unofficial traditional national Orcadian costume, which I first spotted in a shop on Mainland Orkney, is a very thick, padded blue boiler suit, which almost everyone wears, with no other outer protection. I thought if I was going to spend more time here, it would be wise to buy one of these, as I would probably have to carry less clothing on any return winter visit. This seemed sensible; winter was now only a few weeks away. Even the school children wore them when they played in the playgrounds. I soon learnt, when discussing these Dickies – as they are better known – that some of the locals have a 'working' padded boiler suit and a 'good' padded boiler suit. It's a bit like in the military, having number ones and number twos. I resolved to try one on when we passed through Kirkwall on our way to Rousay. I would seem like less of a visitor.

At the end of our first week, some visitors arrived on the island. The first was an American Vietnam veteran. He had lived in Orkney for fifteen years and this was his first visit to North Ron. He carried a six-pack as an emergency supply in his rucksack and was on his way to the pub to have his morning four pints. Vietnam veterans stand out in places like Alaska or Orkney, particularly if they are visitors. Alaska has more Vietnam Vets than anywhere else in the world. Many of these ex-military personnel suffer from various forms of traumatic stress from their combat time and find these lonely outposts the most welcoming for them. This is because they can be most avoidant. Of course many are heavy substance abusers, whilst others just take advantage of the general absence of people and prefer the elements, birds and animals for company. They prefer to be left alone with nature.

On the way to the pub, a Vietnam Vet had bumped into two visitors, who were two firemen who had come to repair the radio at the airport. They serviced the forty other fire stations on the other islands. They were very happy with their work, and I thought, how could one fail to be happy going around these islands all the time. I took them to see the old lighthouse which they had not seen before. There we found a seal puppy who had a large chunk of his bottom bitten out. I decided to try and find out what veterinary services they had on the island, apart from my own, and to return to see him the next day.

In the afternoon we were the guests of two retired research scientists who were the world's experts in North Ronaldsay sheep. They have some sheep called Westons, which are the smallest sheep in the world and originate from Brittany. These sheep are viscious. They attack each other worse than wild dogs, and the wife had many moderately serious injuries from them. Some of them had horns that curled around twice. The couple looked after a spare flock of North Ronaldsay sheep, just in case the ones on the beach perished in a catastrophe, such as an oil slick or a bad storm. Genetically, they would be preserved. They are fed a small amount of seaweed every day, which contains alginates that stops them absorbing copper and getting copper poisoning.

Once, whilst they were at a conference, they spotted a woman who had Wilson's disease, and they probably saved her from getting the dreadful dementia that comes with it by suggesting she try a chemical which only they, as research scientists, could procure. This is now licensed by the pharmaceutical industry to listed patients only. This couple has been consulted by vets the world over about suspected copper poisoning in various flocks of sheep and are internationally known for their extraordinary practical experience of the problem with the North Ronaldsay sheep.

They were not just fine hosts and experts on North Ronaldsay sheep but also experts on the unexcavated Viking village in their garden on the seashore. They allow the public to visit free of charge and the village is always open. They also had the only smithy with a working pair of bellows on the island.

Walking on the seashore and looking back up towards the village, we were shown the midden, or the ancient village's rubbish tip. It was about six feet high, and we were asked to keep sharp eyes out for anything the weather had very recently uncovered such as broken combs or Pictish painted stones. A wonderful cross was found there a century ago, which is now the symbol of Orkney.

Their fascinating Chow Chow dog was called Otto. Apparently Chow Chows come in white, black or red, but the white albinos die early, as they carry a fatal gene. They have purple tongues and have the strongest bites of all mammals. They look more like bears and indeed they might well be a kind of bear. Their first set of teeth has the same number as a bear's and they are built in almost the same way.

There is a price one pays for living on an island. The ups are the price of property itself. Each property is a croft, and they seem to come cheap. An eighty acre croft with a three to four bedroom house, and with barns and one or two older cottages which have not been lived in, will go for less than a tenth of the price of anywhere else in the UK. The downside is that you will usually have some prehistoric or Viking buildings which you can't excavate unless you employ an approved archeologist. There can be wonderful summer days, but there is also the wind and rain to contend with, as well as frequent droughts. But most worrying to the locals is that, if the weekly ferry doesn't come in, there are severe problems immediately.

That evening we were concerned about what to do to help the seal I had seen earlier, but we were not sure who to approach and ask. The pub came to mind, which the doctor had told us not to visit. We drove there in the early evening and sat watching Manchester United play a goalless draw against a Spanish club. Two birders who had immigrated to the island said that there was a local seal rescue number which I could call on the mainland, but that they would probably just instruct one of the islanders to find the seal and shoot it.

The next morning after surgery I decided to venture back and see if the pup was still there. He was, and he still looked too young to be in the water. If they are not old enough, their coats are not well insulated enough for them to survive the winter waters. I decided to leave him to his own devices, knowing that any interference on my part would probably result in him either going into the water too young or in him being shot.

One thing that the Orkneys still have and can boast, because they are thankfully stuck a little in the past, is NHS dentists. I met one of them, and he lived in Mainland Orkney and worked in Kirkwall. Most dentists have around 1,500 patients but here they have at least 3,000 and, as a result, they are very busy. When I told him the story of the injured seal, he strongly advised me not to tell anyone on Mainland

Orkney about the seal, because, although it is totally illegal, the fishermen, and in particular those of South Ronaldsay, still shoot seals by the dozen. He had seen three dead ones washed up that week on the beach where he lived. They had all been shot.

I also learnt from him that it was only in the late Victorian times that the islanders of North Ronaldsay had stopped using the old calendar, which is twelve days later than the newly adopted New Gregorian calendar which the rest of the world uses. Just as interesting, and as strange, was the fact that most of the islanders, excluding those who work at the airport, did not adjust their clocks for daylight saving. I wondered who else was aware of this interesting fact.

Our second week in North Ron began, and we waited for a winter storm to hit the island. Warnings were given out by all the locals, and they said that all they do is buy a few extra cans of food and drink, and sit it out. We knew that we were due some snow, which was supposed to be very unusual for North Ron. However, it was obvious from the casual encounters with islanders on the lonely road of North Ron that the exciting thing for them was looking forward to seeing what the storm would wash in on the beach. But the incoming storm took everyone by surprise when it came, simply because it was more severe than forecasted.

The storm was like hell on earth. The planes stopped, the ferry stopped, the phones stopped, and the birds were nowhere to be seen. The dentist from Kirkwall said to us as we took refuge in the pub's restaurant, 'A while ago the Health Board decided to scrap all these island doctors and just have one based on Westray, who would visit the other islands every week. But the islanders objected and Orkney Health Board just weren't assertive enough.'

'I wasn't told that,' I said.

'I'm not surprised. All information is closed here,' he replied.

'It all seems a total waste to have a doctor based here. I read the other day that they've had a doctor here since 1914 but only because the government was forced into the decision because of the death certificates.'

'I wasn't aware of that,' said the dentist.

'Apparently people were being certified as dead with cause of death unknown, as there was no doctor in attendance. It seemed like pressure from another doctor on the mainland.'

'It's all very weird up here.'

'How do you mean? I asked.

'Well, the health authority is more concerned with the jobs of health workers rather than with the care of patients.'

'I got that impression in Mainland Orkney when I was doing the Out of Hours job for a couple of weeks.'

'I nearly got myself into trouble with the health authority over the dental X Rays.'

'Really. How come?'

'I said that the fixer and other liquids should be properly disposed of instead of being thrown down the sink or toilet, but they said it was approved by Scottish Water.'

'And was it?' I asked

'No. I phoned up Scottish Water, and they were shocked. They told me that the most serious danger from the silver fixer was to the most important farming – shell fish – as they can be totally destroyed by silver.'

'And how did it all end?'

'To my horror, I discovered that the local hospital's X-Ray department was also disposing all of its silver fixer down the sink, and it runs straight out into the sea.'

'Did they stop?'

'Yes. They now use digital X-Rays.'

'Well done for saving the shellfish.'

'It nearly cost me my job in these parts.'

After breakfast the storm stopped, and we went to do a surgery; but, as usual, there were no patients. At the end of the appointed hour of eleven o'clock, we locked the surgery, leaving the light on just in case I got called out, because it was a notoriously difficult house to see. It was set back about fifty or sixty yards from the road. It could be a fatal error to forget your torch, because you needed your vision and to be very sure footed, in order to walk up the path at night with a 100-mile-per-hour wind on your side, to prevent being blown onto the reinforced steel stakes sticking out of the ground.

Now, I'm not a bird person, really. I like them and care for them and have four bird feeders in my garden, where there are only tits, woodpeckers and a few insect eating birds who need a bit of help with surviving the squirrels and cats, whom I also love, sometimes. I would always choose birds, though. I'm not an ornithologist or a 'birder'; I'm certainly not an anorak extremist like the 'twitchers', who will travel thousands of miles and spend large sums of money just for a very rare sighting of a rare bird. I can't get my head around any of that; my head is concerned with ordinary, everyday mortal things like asking myself, am I cooking breakfast or is someone else?

Before we returned home we thought we would slow the morning down by dropping into the old Kirk, which is the old church. The new one was beside the surgery and didn't look particularly interesting. It was still windy, but we knew the planes were going to take off that day and that it would be less severe.

I jumped out of the Land Rover, and Chrisie said, 'You

have a look and we'll come out after just to have a peep.'

'It's pretty windy, about sixty miles per hour, so you stay put. I'll go around and come back.' I walked around the chapel and peeped in the window, and took some photographs with my camera, pointing up, down and around where I couldn't see through the high broken window. I could, however, see the old pews, rows of them, and I could see the beautiful oak pulpit which was perfectly preserved. Suddenly, a feral cat jumped right out in front of me from the window, making me jump in fright. I thought she must be using the old Kirk as her home and had kittens in there.

There was a three foot wide, neatly mowed path around the old Kirk, and just beside the building was an area of concrete. There was evidence of dead animals and birds, and I tried to make out the difference between the bones of rabbits, cats and birds. There were no dead sheep, as there was no way in. The old Kirk and its two graveyards were fenced off. I was a bit bewildered about why there were so many dead cats, as there were four just along one side of the old Kirk. I decided that I was not competent or knowledgeable enough about the local wildlife to know what was behind the dead animals.

Because of the surprising anti-pubite advice given by the doctor and his wife we decided to go to the pub at lunch in order to book an evening meal for later that day. We wanted to see if there were any reasons why he did not like the local people who lived on the island. Although the island was medically his patch – and some GPs don't like living on their patch in cities – this doctor had chosen to live amongst his patients, and I was mystified as to why he should give out so many negative messages about them and be so anti-social.

During a quiet moment before lunch, we got back to the cottage and I sat down to record my reflections on the people of the island, just so that one day when I was long dead India might be able to tell her children what it was like to have visited this island. So, what was it like to be the GP in the smallest general practice in Britain? Well, first, it meant not just living on the patch but actually living and interacting with the people you shared a house with, people in the shop and in the restaurant, and on the windy beach, picking them up and giving them lifts back to their houses or to wherever they're going. It was quite a unique position to listen to everything they wanted to say. At times it required patience, having to fit in with their unique social ways, without being free to assert yourself and criticize in any way whatsoever their attitudes, service or living standards. I found one thing about living on the patch particularly negative, and this was you were at all times always the doctor first and foremost, and anything else afterwards. You were there as the doctor not as an islander. Your professional life took absolute precedence over your social life. This must be one of the only places left in the UK where this is the case.

My thoughts went back to the sheep on the island and what they must be like. Imagine living with a group of introverted animals who, because of their special geographical location, make excessively outrageous demands on more well-rounded folk, who know it is a mistake to live in such parts. Imagine how these inward turned sheep actually think and occupy their days. Curiously, they are probably obsessed by things they don't have because of where they live. They don't like in any way being chased by the authorities, or being clubbed together and thought of as a group. They are not just extremely eccentric; they actually seem like independent individuals. In this respect they seemed more like goats.

As I thought about this I wasn't really sure anymore if I

was thinking about the sheep or about the people of North Ron. This island was making me think in strange ways, as the sheep were only animals who gave the appearance of being unique and complicated, whilst all the time they were nothing more than simple old North Ronaldsay inhabitants. I think I was being over-influenced by the local island thinking too much. They only appeared complex because of their history; but all sheep have history. It's just that these one's rather unusual traits were not annihilated by proper breeding which dilutes such negative qualities. These North Ron sheep had escaped that. The wild sheep of these islands were probably bred out, but this little group of inbred sheep had survived.

After watching the All Blacks win the rugby game, I got a call out, not on the phone but by a man who called in on his way back from their visit to the pub. He was sober and a little bit worried about one of his friends on the island.

'She's called the pub three times. Not like her,' the brown eyed, grey bearded North Ronaldsay local said as he handed me the patient's number on a very small piece of paper. 'Got no paracetamol or anything. But I haven't seen her for a few weeks.'

'What seems to be the problem?' I asked.

'Just doesn't feel good, but that's a bit unlike her.'

'Anything specific?'

'It's not like her to call the pub unless it's something. She keeps herself to herself.'

'She probably needs a visit, so I'll go,' I said. Half an hour later I had picked up some antibiotics from the surgery, just in case she had a chest infection, and I drove to her house. It was remote, and I reckoned I could probably find it myself down several small turnings from the main road. Her house seemed like it was in the centre of the island, but actually it was isolated and on the edge of the island. She certainly lived in a remote place; there were no houses around for a long way off, for I couldn't see any lights. It was a difficult track even in a Land Rover.

I knocked on the door, and all I could hear was a groan, so I turned the door knob and walked in. It was a very busy, rustic house with all kinds of gear all over the place – guns, fishing rods, fishing nets, boots, overalls, wooly hats and several of pairs of gloves. What was immediately obvious was that it was spotlessly clean.

'Hi, I'm the doc. You alright?'

'They said you would come and visit, even though they don't know you.'

'What's the trouble?' I was listening to a very pleasantly mannered, middle aged woman who was obviously very independent. She was as perfectly kept as her busy house.

'This cough. Smoked since I was in Class 7, but I gave up before I got to forty, and I'm happy. This cough's got me, though. Feeling aches all over. I'm shivery too. Just like flu. I've coughed up a bit of blood with some green stuff, but I think it's because I've been straining so much.'

'Good job you stopped smoking, and you're probably right about the blood,' I said.

'Best thing I ever did.'

'Are you eating OK?'

'Haven't eaten for two days, but I'm drinking fluids and keeping them down.'

'It's a bit remote here,' I said looking around.

'Like it that way. No people, just the birds. They're no bother.'

'Anything else?'

'Just a bit of earache … and this green stuff I'm coughing

up. '

'How long have you been unwell?'

'About two to three days, can't quite remember. Just can't shake this off.'

'Do you live on your own here?'

'Yes.'

'How old are you?'

'Fifty-nine.'

'Is your diet good?'

'It's excellent, but I could lose one stone.'

'You look pretty fit to me.'

'I stock up the freezer every two months with fresh food from the mainland, and I've got a good routine of eating nuts, honey and a little dairy, but mainly fish.'

'Any family?'

'No, just me. Oh, and a brother who still lives down south; but I haven't seen him for years.'

'You on any medication?'

'No.'

'Apart from coughs and colds have you had any other illnesses or other problems?'

'No. I've been lucky and also looked after myself.

'Do you mind if I have a look at you?' She did have a funny cough, and when I examined her she didn't look too well either. But that wasn't unusual with flu. Her chest sounded like she had a chest infection on both sides. The ear she was complaining of was normal.

'I want you to try and blow into this meter which measures the peak flow rate of air from your lungs. Put your lips around the cardboard tube and blow as hard and as fast as you can just for a second. You can have three goes, and I'll take the best of three.' She took the peak flow meter and blew. The first one was 120 litres per min, the second was 110 l/min and the last was 110 l/min.

'What's it supposed to read, doc?'

'For someone your age and size probably about 550 l/min. 120 is bad.'

'What do you think, doc?'

'I'm not sure. Can I just ask you a few more questions?'

'Fire away.'

'When did you last see anyone or touch your post or anything from anyone?'

'What are you getting at?'

'Well you seem to have flu, so you must have seen someone over the last few days or the last week.'

'No, I haven't'

'Are you sure?'

'Absolutely sure. Know exactly when I last got my mail and got my supplies off the ship.' This was a little bit worrying, as I had assumed this was flu.

But then I had to ask her directly 'They tell me you're not a birder but you do help them out. When did you last handle a bird?' I hoped she was going not jump at the obvious.

'Well now, let me see,' she said, stroking her hair. 'When did I last touch a bird? I would say I don't know really,' she coughed and spluttered.

'Roughly?'

'Well, it was some time ago now.' She coughed and spluttered again, and I could see there was blood in the tissue as she pulled it away from her mouth.

'How long?'

'Oh, not that long ago.'

'I understand. You think it was in the last few days, a week, a month or more?'

'Oh, I've not actually touched any bird for at least a week. You don't think it could be that bird flu? Do you Doc?'

'No. If you had bird flu, I wouldn't be standing here dressed like this. I'd have a fully protective suit on and a mask. It's probably not bird flu, but I have to ask you a few more questions before I can rule it out.'

'Thank heavens for that. I was a bit worried with all this talk down South.'

'Do you know who you got if off?'

'What?'

'This infection.'

'I can't recall anyone having a cold or flu. But I haven't seen anyone for a while. Just can't remember when.'

'Start taking these antibiotics – one, three times a day - and I'll be back in the morning. But call me if you feel worse.'

On the way back to the house a large blue tractor was coming down the lane with two huge forks attached to the front, and I had to reverse the Land Rover, as there was no passing place. It took about two minutes; I couldn't see anything, as there were no reversing lights on the Land Rover, and I ended up coming to an abrupt stop when I hit some kind of immovable object. I couldn't see any damage in the dark, because the lights, which I knew were not working, would have been obliterated anyway by the massive impact of hitting the concrete wall of the jetty.

I didn't bother to get out and look, because I had too many things on my mind to deal with, one being getting annoyed at the doctor for giving me a car to use without any reversing lights. I thought that, if I got out, I would only feel anger at him or maybe some guilt for bending his Land Rover in two. Considering the driving regulations in North Ron I wasn't sure how the world of insurance worked up there; if, indeed, it did work or apply to outsiders as well as locals. As far as I was concerned, anything I hit at night in his car whilst on duty was his responsibility, as he had no lights on his car.

At one in the morning I woke up soaking in a sweat, worrying if I had some kind of bird flu. I started to think about the dead rabbit and the dead birds around the old Kirk, which was less than half a mile from the patient's house. I reflected many times on my decision to conclude she had flu and not bird flu. If she had bird flu, it would be catastrophic for the island. It was just a niggling doubt which came into my mind to make me re-check I was right and hadn't missed anything. This multiple checking, which can keep you awake at night, is common in doctors and is a particularly annoying thing about medicine, because it matters a lot if you get something wrong, whereas so many other jobs seem to carry little anxiety or responsibility.

First thing in the morning I returned to the patient with flu.

'You seem a bit more chirpy?' I remarked.

'The sleep helps a lot, and I think I'm getting enough nourishment from all the juice I've been drinking.'

'Can I listen to your chest?'

'No bother,' she said. I listened, and now there was a change in the both lungs. They sounded clearer and more air was getting in. I was really hoping she was going to be better and not worse, otherwise my dream could become a nightmare. The peak flow was better, and we were both pleased.

'I'm going to leave you and see how you get on. I think you've turned a corner,' I said positively, hoping that things would continue to improve.

'Well, just when was the last big flu epidemic?' she asked me.

'In the past the Spanish Flu of 1918-1919 killed between twenty and forty million globally and twenty-five thousand in the UK, and it killed mainly healthy young adults aged between twenty and fifty years. The Asian Flu of 1957-1958 and the Hong Kong Flu of 1968-1969 each killed between one and four million globally and around thirty-three thousand each in the UK, killing the very old, the very young and those with underlying medical conditions.'

'Interesting numbers,' she said.

'I've got to go and do a surgery, but I'll be back if you're not getting better.'

That evening I received a call from a woman who worked for the ferry which operated between Kirkwall and North Ronaldsay. 'Can you come down to the ferry building to collect a delivery?'

'I'm not expecting anything,' I said.

'There's a delivery for the GP,' said the woman.

'I haven't made an order,' I said.

'It's for the GP who's here permanently.'

'Oh, OK. No trouble. I'll be down in a few minutes.' Within three minutes I drove one of the two Land Rovers onto the quay and backed it up to the ferry building.

'You the locum, then?'

'Yes.'

'You've got a delivery. Here it is.' The woman in a set of blue Dickies, who was in her midfifties handed me a box which felt quite light. 'There are two larger ones here with beer and casks of wine in, so be careful lifting them.'

'Thanks, but I should be fine. They don't look too heavy.'

'You don't have to take them,' she said. I thought that this was a peculiar thing to say, because clearly there was no choice but to take them, as they couldn't be left in the open ferry building.

'What's in this one?'

'Bacci and fags.'

'I didn't think he smoked,' I said, quietly sizing up the weight of the contents.

I noticed that she didn't answer me. 'I'll drop them at his house,' I said. And I put the four boxes on the floor in the back of the Land Rover. On the way back to the GP's house my phone went off three times, and when I arrived there were five people waiting for me trying to give me money.

'What's all this about?' I asked.

'We've just come for our stuff from the doctor.'

'What, you mean this is for you?'

'Yes. Well, what's wrong with that?'

'Everything,' I said. 'You're his patients. He's being paid to try to stop you smoking. I can't sell you this; you are my temporary patients.' A light switch went on in an upstairs room, as well as inside my head, and I remembered that there was a birder staying in the doctor's house as a guest.

'What's up?' said Chris the birder.

'Won't give us our bacci and fags,' said an elderly man.

'Is that right?' said Chris, looking straight over to me.

'Yes. I'm not selling this. I'm having nothing to do with this. This is a disgrace. No monies will change hands on my duty.'

I was in a state of utter shock at what I had just seen. I couldn't see how a doctor could ever sell tobacco and cigarettes to his own patients, and in bulk for profit, whilst at the same time wear the badge of the local medical man, accepting payment for services which included encouraging smoking cessation. He could only do this if he imagined that no one would ever notice or pay any attention to it because North Ron was so far away from the usual policing of society.

Having never heard of anything like this before, I had no clear idea what to do about it, as this seemed to be a long-standing arrangement between the doctor and his patients. I could only guess that the reason they bought their tobacco and cigarettes off him rather than from the local shop was that he probably sold it cheaper. I wondered if they had lost all respect for him as a doctor. Would they even listen to a single word he said about health, if he was willing to sell them cigarettes for profit? It took me some considerable time to regain my usual composure. I was bitterly and personally disappointed by this fellow doctor. I felt sorry for the local North Ron residents.

To make up for my disappointment and distress, was my meeting with a special man who was also a local artist, and particularly one on such an unusual island. I knew nothing about him until I met him, when all he said was that he had specialized in Sculpture in Aberdeen. I asked no probing questions, because he had his own gentle way of communicating his reality which I deeply respected. He kindly offered us his hospitality.

He was clearly an enormously talented artist. I could tell from the way Chrisie asked him things that she had a very unusual degree of respect for him. She had a first in Art from New Zealand, and I could tell that she had never expected to find a 'Master' in North Ronaldsay.

He had a quiet way of speaking without overtones of authority but, instead, as if suggesting in his wisdom, 'This is what something looks like or seems like, but this is what is behind it.' He had his own way of letting you, in your own way, experience his world. He had chosen not to desert his island and be tempted by commercialism. He would very obviously be on everyone's A list to have at various functions, but he had chosen differently from most.

He lived in a beautiful, old house which had a wonderfully unique style. There were a lot of mementos of the many people whom he had once known well but had now passed on. Spiritually and technologically he had bridged the past to the present. We had coffee and some chocolate biscuits with him and sat with him for maybe an hour, but it seemed like a whole day.

It was a cold, very windy day outside as we sat on comfortable old chairs a good distance back from the range, which had one of the front doors open, exposing red hot coal, radiating hot rays onto our hands which we rubbed together. Leaning against the range were two shotguns. He had two large accordions. The red one was his, and the black electronic one belonged to an old friend who was now dead and about whom he spoke with kindness.

He played us three tunes on his huge, red accordion, which he said he could only play by ear. I seemed to remember that most of the Beatles didn't read music. He played a couple of reels and ended with a very sad tune, but they were all very moving, as he played not only by ear but from his heart. It was like being in a world I had not experienced for over thirty years, when lots of towns had folk clubs and some pubs had folk bands. He made me remember that back in the 1960s most people were expected to have learnt an instrument or to sing at school.

We talked about many different things: the population of the island, the weather, art, and his family. He also worked as a crofter and had a few cattle and sheep. He was a published writer as well as being one of Scotland's best artists. He was a gifted man in more ways than one.

He gave me a poem to read, which he had copied and

written out in beautiful calligraphy, adding that he was not a religious man but that it made a lot of sense in the world we live in. It was called 17th Century Nun's Prayer. And it went like this:

Lord, you knowest better than I know myself, that I am growing older and will some day be old.
Keep me from the fatal habit of thinking I say something on every occasion.
Release me from craving to straighten out everybody's affairs.
Make me thoughtful but not moody, helpful but not bossy.

With my vast store of wisdom it seems a pity not to use it after all, but thou knowest Lord that I want a few friends at the end.
Keep my mind free from the recital of endless details; give me wings to get to the point.

Seal my lips of my aches and pains.
They are increasing, and love of rehearsing them is becoming sweeter as the years go by.
I dare not ask for grace enough to enjoy the tales of others pains, but help me to endure them with patience.

I dare not ask for improved memory but for a growing humility and a lessening cocksureness when my memory seems to clash with the memories of others.

Teach me the glorious lesson that occasionally I may be mistaken.
Keep me reasonably sweet, I do not want to be a saint - some of them are hard to live with - but a sour old person is one of the crowning works of the devil.
Give me the ability to see good things in unexpected places and

talents in unexpected people.
And give me, O lord, the grace to tell them so.

He then showed us the island's list of the fallen in the First World War It was a piece of parchment about three feet wide and four feet long. It was done in the most beautiful calligraphy, and there were elaborate multicolored borders which were intricately done. He was very proud to have got it restored for the new church. Here was a true community man. He had elected to stay on this island, even after he had been a student in Aberdeen. He was a true son of North Ronaldsay.

Before we met him someone described him as eccentric. After I met him I realized that the person who said this, and probably we ourselves, were the eccentric ones, for he was not. He was well rounded, not odd or extreme in any way. Leaving his house and waving goodbye brought a tear to my eye. It was one of those situations where you know you will never see this person again, and I felt sad.

Chapter 15.

Locum 3. Rousay, Egilsay, Wyre and Gairsay
Islands

On the morning we were due to leave North Ron there
was an expectant feeling of great relief. We crept around,
packing our things, and placed them into one of the Land
Rovers. I had left the other Land Rover at the airport the night
before. I'm not sure why I call the shed on the grass strip the
airport.

We took the one and a half minute drive to the airport
and waited for the Islander aircraft to arrive. The three of us
were excited, because the doctor and his family would get off,
and we would get on, the plane.

Just as we were about to stop at the strip a patient
flagged me down and stopped me in her car. She wanted me
to sign a claim form for her to go by plane to Mainland Orkney
for medical treatment. I signed it through the window of the
Land Rover.

One minute after the plane was sighted it had landed
and taxied, and the door was opened. Out stepped the doctor
and his family. There were no greetings from him, his wife or
children. No hello … just a look. We welcomed them with a
'Hello' from each of us. There was still just a look. I don't think
they were pleased to be back home.

I handed over a piece of paper to the doctor, with the
short list of patients I had seen together with all of the treatments
I had prescribed. He wasn't particularly interested; and there
were no niceties, such as, 'I hope you had a nice time,' or 'thank
you' or 'how are you?'.

'What happened to the Land Rover?'

'How, you mean,' I asked. I had left it at the airport

overnight so that he and his wife could drive both his family and luggage in the two Land Rovers back to his house.

'Come and look.' He looked very tense and on edge, and I felt just a bit uncomfortable in his presence. My eagerness to get away from this man had made me forget reversing it into something the first night I saw the woman with flu. I could see the rear wing panel sticking out.

'Well, I'm glad I wasn't in it when that happened. I would probably have got a bad whiplash. Must have been something big, like a tractor, to have bent the rear chassis like that. I'm sure someone will own up to it.'

'Wow, must have taken a bang,' said Chrisie, who came over to inspect the damage, which I could now see had totally buckled the nearside rear wing which had been pushed out by the bent chassis. The chassis was so bent it was never going to be repaired in less than a week or on the mainland. And with that we were beckoned to get on the plane.

On the plane, when I relaxed, I remembered reversing the Land Rover and hearing a bang. I told her about the bump. 'Good job you didn't tell me before,' Chrisie said. 'I don't think I could have hidden it very well.'

'Nor could I,' I said, and I was at last able to smile about North Ron.

I was never so relieved to get on a plane. I sat in the back with India, Chrisie sat next to the pilot, and we were all three huffing and puffing with big sighs of relief, our body language wordlessly expressing our relief to be leaving North Ron.

When we got to the Mainland Orkney airport there was no one there to meet us. The itinerary which I had from the agency had stated, 'A representative from the car hire firm will meet you at the airport.' We waited for ten minutes, but no one came. I found another car hire firm and asked them if they knew anything about the other car hire company. 'They are all at a funeral today,' I was told.

'Right. Not much I can do about that.'

'The funeral's starting in an hour, so they'll all be getting ready now. I'll get one of the girls to come up to the airport.' They were taking this funeral as seriously as I remembered funerals having been in Tubbercurry in the west of Ireland when I was a boy. When the girl arrived with the car she was in a very sombre mood and didn't want to talk. She was not a relative but an employee. But I thought I should say something. 'I admire your respect for the dead up here. It is unusual.'

She turned and looked at me eyeball to eyeball and said in her Orcadian accent, 'Why, that's kind. Thank you.' I could see that she had clearly liked the man whose funeral it was, and she had a deep respect that was not so obvious down south. This time I got a blue Peugeot.

We decided to go to the best hotel in Mainland Orkney and have lunch before getting the ferry from Twingness across to Rousay. We bought the local weekly newspapers, the Orcadian and Orkney Today to read any local gossip, but we were a bit too tired to look at them. We took a long drive out to see Captain Cook's Well in Stromness and then headed for the ferry at Twingness. Sitting beside us, waiting to reverse on to the ferry was a breakdown vehicle which had signs indicating that it served almost every breakdown organization in the UK.

There to meet us off the 4.30 pm ferry was the doctor, and at first he looked quite calm. 'Spot the doctor,' said Chrisie, as he was dressed in the smartest conservative clothes we had seen anyone wear for weeks. He wasn't quite so outrageous at the Aussie doctor in full Sherlock Holmes gear, whom I had met a few weeks before, and I remembered how much I respected that Aussie doctor's clinical skills.

'Can I do a handover?' he asked.

'Yes, fine.'

'I just need to get my car on to the ferry.' It was his car the breakdown truck had come to fix.

'We're not in a hurry,' I said.

'I am. I've got to get off on the boat here.' He seemed panicky, almost as if there was someone after him, but I took it that he was just fussing and in a rush due to the need to get his car on the ferry.

'Look at these notes, because that's all the problems at the moment, otherwise there's nothing to worry about. I've got to go for surgery on my knee. Sport is a curse.' He handed me some notes on a single side of A4 paper, which summarized a few medical problems. There was nothing that looked particularly challenging.

'Well, hope it all goes well with your operation. Rugby was it?'

'As a matter of fact it was.'

'Who were you playing for?'

'I was a spectator.'

'Oh, one of them.'

'My team scored a try and my cruciate ligament was torn in the applause.'

'Ah, well, the surgeons in Aberdeen are pretty good. See you in a couple of weeks then. Nothing else is there?'

'No. Oh, and there's a visit.' I was a little surprised by this, as usually you would hand over a clean sheet of paper with no actual outstanding work. I just let it go by, because I assumed there wasn't much else to do.

'What is it?'

'Salmonella. I've alerted the Public Health Officer. He might be getting better. I don't know where it's coming from.'

'How many other people have had it?'

'Just one.'

'I might as well go and see him now.'

'You can't, because you've got an evening surgery in half an hour.' This was another unexpected surprise. 'I'll take you to the surgery and then to the house a couple of miles away, where you're staying. Follow my car and I'll drop you there.'

We followed him to the surgery by the sea. It was on a small promontory, next to what looked like a disused church, a disused school and a graveyard. Parked outside the surgery was an old white ambulance with a red cross on all the doors.

'Whose is the ambulance?'

'It belongs to the surgery.'

'Who is the driver?'

'You are. If there's a problem, you have to use it to take someone on the ferry across to the mainland, where another ambulance will meet you.'

'Sounds like fun. I'll have to have a practice run in it. Where is the house we are staying in?' I asked.

'Go straight back up the hill and turn left onto the main island ring road. It's about three miles along on the right.'

The ring road was a particularly steep hundred-yard drive uphill, but we found the house very easily. We were then shown around the house by the young female owner. It was a modern, minimalist, two bedroom bungalow with a Neolithic twelve foot standing stone in the driveway. We could just see the glimmer on the sea which looked about two hundred foot below us. It looked as if we were going to have a good view in the morning, which might give us a lift in our spirits, as I had to drop Chrisie and India at the airport in Kirkwall the next day, so that India could return to her own school and be in a nativity play.

I went to see the person who had had Salmonella for two days, and, although he was still unwell, he was managing to drink liquids. I then went straight to the evening surgery, and there were no patients during the hour, so I tried to get some information on the island of Rousay from the receptionist. She looked much older than thirty-five, and, as she wasn't over-friendly or forthcoming, I thought it best to avoid exchanging any information other than the essentials.

'How often do you do surgeries?'

'There's an hour on Monday morning from ten until eleven. Then Tuesday is from five until six in the evening, Wednesday is six until seven, Friday is from five until six and Saturday is ten until eleven in the morning.'

'What happens on Thursdays?' I asked, as she didn't volunteer the information.

'You usually go to the mainland to shop for the day. You just have to let one of the two nurses know.'

'Is there a phone?'

'No, you have to use your own mobile. Did he give you the bleep or handover folder?'

'No. He didn't mention either.'

'Well, you'll have to look for them.' I found her mildly amusing, as she seemed just a little uptight, a bit like her boss.

I wasn't sure where to look, and she got up and started searching through all of the open space where he might have left them both. She found them in a drawer in his desk.

'There are phone numbers and instructions for the computer,' she said.

'And I see I'm covering four islands, Rousay, Egilsay, Wyre and Gairsay. What's the population on each?'

'They are only small populations. We're a hundred and seventy. Egilsay and Wyre each have about twenty-five people.

'How many does Gairsay have?'

'I think it's just a family of three. Sue, the nurse, visits once a month unless there are other problems.'

'What about shops?'

'There's a pub, a restaurant, one shop which is good and a post office.'

'Can we eat in the restaurant tonight?'

'I think it's closed now. I don't really go out to eat, so I'm not sure.'

'And what's the pub like?'

'I don't really go out much, so I don't know.' I was cautious and took this to mean not to be recommended, or there was some reason why she didn't go to the pub.

'What time does the restaurant open?'

'It's closed for a bit.'

'When you say a bit, how long do you mean?'

'I think it may open in a few weeks.'

'Why has it closed?'

'Don't know.' She appeared to be monosyllabic, and I decided to leave it at that.

I only had enough food for two days, and we would need to eat that tonight for the three of us. Because I hadn't been told where the Salmonella came from, it wouldn't be safe to eat out. I would also need to stock up with food for a week, as it seemed like the restaurant was closed and the pub wasn't really highly recommended.

I wondered why no one told me this. The doctor could have, so could his secretary, let alone the agency who should have been told by NHS Orkney, who could also have told me. But this was not the only thing they had not told me. I began to wonder if maybe no one likes doctors in Orkney.

After supper, I picked up the local newspapers Chrisie

had bought me to read, and they carried interesting stories. The Orcadian's headlines were: "NHS Officials Hired GP Reported to the GMC." It was all about the doctor at the Scapa practice, which was one of the practices I had covered a couple of weeks back. The health board official he was allegedly having a relationship with came out publicly and supported him in the article. I wondered if that was linked to the previous article which said that the NHS Orkney had just been reported and was under a police investigation. All of this had apparently been initiated by a locum GP. I thought that the truth would eventually come out, if there was any connection between these two stories. It didn't actually involve me, and so I just cracked on and ignored it.

But this was just mild compared with the inside page. On Page 3 there was an even more worrying article titled, "Second Orkney GP under supervision". It was about the doctor whom I had just shaken hands with and whose practice I taken over for the next twelve days.

When I opened a copy of the other paper there was an article on Page 2 titled, "GPs Involved in GMC Inquiries." The first thing it mentioned was that the Rousay GP I had just shaken hands with, had taken heroin from this single-doctor practice without a prescription. The GMC launched an investigation, but the two witnesses were not prepared to cooperate. The police were now launching an inquiry of their own. I showed it to Chrisie. 'Well, I hope he comes back. He did seem in a bit of a hurry.'

'I'm sure he'll be back. Funny, the receptionist didn't mention it to me during the hour I spent with her. But she wasn't exactly the friendliest or most helpful person I've met recently. Perhaps this explains her being so monosyllabic.'

'It is very odd that no one mentioned any of this,' said

Chrisie. 'It's actually a shocking withholding of information.'

'I'll let you know the outcome, because there's bound to be some talk going around about it on the island.' I laughed to myself and wondered how a dispensing GP could be so casual and not write a prescription for the most seriously controlled drug, heroin. However, I was merely the locum. I had no power and no responsibility. It wasn't my problem, and I thought I would just get on and enjoy my short stay.

The next morning we woke to a truly spectacular view. It was rather like the best views you get in the Bay of Islands in New Zealand, and it looked almost as unpopulated. There was a view from the front of the house of Mainland Orkney, and also of Wyre to the left and beyond it Egilsay. Beyond this I could see two or three other islands to the south-east. Nearly all of the houses on Wyre were visible.

It only took half an hour to drive around the island, and we could see lots of brown and white Scottish Tourist Board signs indicating historic sites to see. There was not a single person about. However, today was not the day to see these sights. In order to get Chrisie and India to the airport with enough time for me to be back safely on the island, we needed to get the eleven o'clock ferry.

It was truly magnificent weather. The sky was blue with no clouds, the sun was warm, and there was a certain amount of heat in the air, probably from the Gulf Stream. We reversed onto the ferry with all its friendly local crew from Rousay and Wyre. The crossing was like gliding over a completely calm sea. There was no wind and no waves, and the ferry seemed silent. Stromness was a welcome place to return to for lunch, but with regret at four thirty I kissed my family goodbye for twelve days.

As I was sitting parked in a reversed position to board

the incoming ferry I got a call regarding the case of Salmonella. 'He's stopped drinking and had nae liquids since yesterday and looks even more poorly,' said his wife.

'Can you get him down to the ferry, and I'll give him a lift over in my car.'

'I ken what you're saying, but I can nae drive.'

'What about your neighbour?'

'I can ask her.'

'Get her to meet me in half an hour.'

I then phoned the on-call doctor at the hospital, who said that I was taking the very last bed at the hospital, which meant that any other admission would have to go down to Aberdeen or Inverness. That was not my problem, but I took on board what he said. I then called the ambulance who said they would meet me at the ferry.

I phoned the ferry office and tried to speak to the captain of the ferry, but there was no signal on his cell phone. When the ferry docked, the weather had completely changed to severe wind. I asked one of the crew if I could see the captain, and he pointed me to some vertical steel steps at the front of the tower. The ladder was about fifteen feet high and at the top were two chains about two feet high, which were difficult to scale over in such fierce winds. I stood there for a moment and looked at the large waves and the wind, and I managed to get over the top of the ladder and found myself in the Captain's cabin.

I shook hands and introduced myself. He was very friendly, and I could tell he was working out his route. He said that the passengers for Egilsay and Wyre would not be able to get straight to their islands first. They would have to come with me to Rousay, disembark, and wait until the ferry returned after I had dropped my patient off at Twingness. He said that a few minutes wait might make a difference and that, if it was his spouse who was ill, he completely understood where I was coming from. He was very friendly about it.

No one seemed put out, as it was only forty minutes delay. The only problem was that it was a really rough sea, as the weather had changed from bad to dreadful. As the ferry chugged on through the sea, there were frequent sixty-foot high sheets of spray from the waves. But what I had learnt at the Churchill Barriers was that as long as its spray it's OK. It's only if it's waves of water that you have to worry.

I examined the patient in his neighbor's car and then transferred him to my car, and back we went on the rough crossing. I was the only car and passenger going back to Rousay, and it was an even rougher crossing. The friendly ambulance crew was there on time to meet me.

In the morning I was woken twice by my phone, but the person didn't leave a message. I got dressed and my pager went off, and at the same time there was a knock at the door. I wondered what on earth could be going on in such a small island. I opened the door and there, being blown in by an extremely strong wind, stood a young woman dressed in a nurse's uniform.

'Got a bleeder.'

'Come in. What did you say?

'Just down the road – this man's nose has been bleeding for a while. He's also got angina.'

'I'll just get my boots on and follow your car.' Within a couple of minutes I was entering a house which had standing stones a foot away from the main wall.

'How long has it been bleeding?

'Since half seven.'

'This morning?'

'Yes.'

'That's a while. Have you had them before?'

'Since I was six.'

'Do you take any drugs?'

'Loads.'

'Where are they?'

'Over there in my suitcase.' This was a good sign. This person knew he was going to hospital and he was in control.

'Can I have a look?'

'Help yourself.' There was blood coming out of the small punctum on the inner edge of his lower eyelids, which is usually for draining the tears to the nose. There was a lot of pressure in this bleeding, which worried me.

'Can I get you to hold your nose at the top not the bottom?' I said.

'Show me how.'

'Just squeeze here.'

'Right.'

'How young are you?'

There was a laugh. 'Eighty-eight.'

'When did you last take one of these?' pointing to the pack of aspirin.

'When I woke up at five.'

'Can I have a word out the back?' I said to the nurse.

'What is it?'

'Well, the hospital in Kirkwall probably hasn't got any beds, and he'll probably have to go to Aberdeen.'

'That's seems a bit dramatic.'

'Afraid not. Attila the Hun died of nose bleed.'

'Really. I didn't know that.'

'I'll tell you about it later. I need to call Aberdeen.'

'Are you sure?'

'I love a good joke, but this is serious.'

'Hi Switch.'

'Is that you?'

'Yep, in Rousay.'

'How was North Ron?

'I'll tell you about it in two weeks, when I'm back with you doing Out of Hours. I need the on-call doctor.'

'Well I've been trying to get hold of him for an hour, and there's no reply.'

'Keep on trying, and when you get him tell him to try calling me, and give him this message. I'm sending him an eighty-eight year old patient with angina, who is on aspirin, and who's had a nose bleed from both nostrils. I've stopped the aspirin, which is probably the main culprit for the bleeding. Tell him he'll need some blood taken and a drip put in before he's sent to Aberdeen. Tell him I'll arrange an ENT bed in Aberdeen. And can you get him to call me?'

'No bother.'

I then turned to the nurse. 'It's all arranged. Is your car OK, or do you want the ambulance?'

'My car will probably be more calming.' The patient looked deathly pale, but his vital signs were pretty good.

'OK. I'll follow you and make sure you get on the ferry.'

When the gate was finally closed on the ferry, I went back to the comfortable house that I was staying in and reflected on the last day. In the last twenty-four hours, I had managed to leave North Ron alive, taken over from a doctor who had some issues with heroin, waved goodbye to my family and admitted two patients to hospital. I felt calm, because there really wasn't anything dramatic about any of it. It was just bizarre. Yes, the heroin thing was something I hadn't come across before, and I still couldn't work out how he could make an error like that. Maybe he was trying to bring attention to a problem with it, because you don't mess with that stuff on your shift.

The next day there was only an evening surgery, so I spent the day preparing myself for a pleasurable stay. I wanted to do some leisurely hand-line fishing just to spend some time by the water, and I wanted to do some walking. I spent my day just getting familiar with the house and my surroundings which were interesting. Because of the presence of such a large standing stone beside the driveway, I wondered if this house was built on a Neolithic site or a Neolithic grave. It was likely it was one of these, as no one here would attempt to move such a large stone.

The house I was staying in was about two miles west of the ferry. The main road on this round island is about three hundred feet up a steep incline, and is thirteen miles long, which makes the circular island roughly five miles across. Because it is very hilly with the highest point being 750 feet, farming is only on the edges of the island, below the road which was formed in most parts by a natural terrace. In the centre of the island is moorland. Behind the house was another hundred-foot incline, which was very steep and only just possible to climb. All the way along there was glacial terracing. The way the rock gently pointed up out of the ground at an angle of about fifteen degrees was so uniform that it looked man-made. It looked as though a large wall had been built to create a terrace. At the back of the house, I walked through very boggy ground and up the steep grassy incline over the front of the terrace until I got over the top.

On top were the remains of two old houses. The front entrance to one was less than three feet high and faced the steep upward slope to the final terrace. I climbed up. On the very top was empty moorland with a particularly good view. I climbed down the very slippery slope back to the two old houses. I looked through the window of one house and back at the doorway. This had obviously been built to face north, to keep the wind and rain out. I had no idea how old these houses were – they could have been anything from a few hundred to a thousand years old. There was no road and no evidence of anyone having been there for a very long time. I couldn't help wondering about the people who lived there and what a simple life they would have led. They had obviously chosen this terrace because of the advantage the distant view gave them over any visitors or invaders.

I was aware of that familiar sense of what had gone on here, of forgotten sacred space. There was a sense that this had been a peaceful spot. Even now it was a place of peaceful stillness. I imagined it to be a portal or stairway to the heavens for those who left earthly life. The Orkneys are geographically the topmost part of the British Isles, and that made it easier to get a sense that it was spiritually at the top the country too. It was not hard to imagine that five thousand years ago people had brought their dead to the northern part of the islands they knew in order to assist or offer them up to the heavens above.

It might be similar to the Maori belief the spirits of their dead leapt off the headland at Cape Reinga from the northern tip of the North Island to begin their journey to the afterlife.

Perhaps there were priests, or even a special tribe, who administered everything which went on here. Perhaps the locals were direct descendents of these ancient people, and guardians of a past unknown to them.

From my drive around the island I could now work out that nearly all of the Neolithic houses and cairns are on the south side of the island, facing the top of Mainland Orkney from where they would have been easily visible. In those days you would always be looking south.

The evening surgery was empty, so I talked with the nurse. 'So what's this about Attila the Hun dying of a nose bleed?' she asked. 'It's got to be a joke.'

'No joke. Seriously that's exactly what killed him – epistaxis. He died on the eve of his wedding. He had sex with so many women that night that it started a nose bleed.'

'How could sex start a nose bleed?'

'In the nose is a small area of tissue which becomes engorged with blood like other erectile tissue during sex. It can happen to men and women. Atilla started having a nose bleed and bled to death that evening. I'm not saying that the patient last night had a nose bleed due to sex, but it is well known to ENT specialists.'

'That's very funny. I'll have to tell my husband that, as he's had a couple of nose bleeds.'

'There you go.'

'I remember now.'

'I rest my case.'

'They never taught me that at nursing school.'

'I didn't get taught it either. It was an ENT specialist who told me about it. He worked at the old Charing Cross Hospital, and he used to look after a lot of passing trade in the sex industry in the West End of London. He came across it all the time.'

The next morning was time to be a tourist and see the most important sights on Rousay. But first I had a minor problem. My ancient phone, which I last had updated about four or five years before, abruptly stopped working. There was just one message which read, 'Insert SIM card.' From the surgery phone, I rang my cell phone provider who had, unbeknown to me, become my service provider. They said they could get a phone to me by Tuesday, which was not bad, as it

203

was only three days away. They said that I should just borrow someone's phone. Luckily the nurse had a spare phone.

Rousay is a very hilly island and has around 150 of the 1,000 Neolithic sights of the Orkney Islands. It is also one of only sixteen Orkney Islands which are inhabited and is known as 'The Egypt of the North'. The main sights are either on the shore of Rousay or on the glacial terraces, both opposite Mainland Orkney.

There were five that I thought really worth seeing. The first one was Taversoe Tuick, which was a rare, two storeyed cairn. The walk getting there was slippery, a very muddy mess created by the tracks of tractor tires. There was a very small, low door at the entrance, but when I went in I realized I was in an old tomb. It was eerie; there was no one else around and it was very quiet. It was not scary, but it inspired respect for this burial place of an ancient tribe. It was only discovered in 1898, when the landowner decided to build a lookout seat there. The two chambers were separate; you could walk freely around them; and they were connected by a ladder which is about six feet long. The tomb, where at least five people had been buried, was in almost perfect condition.

I stood outside and wondered about the wonderful, eerie feeling I was once again experiencing, which had been absent earlier on when I had been looking at the views and sites on Mainland Orkney. Perhaps it was something to do with time. If time and space were some kind of illusion and everything was not actually sequentially ordered, then the separation of myself and those buried might be partly illusory. It was as if I was more connected to these places than I was aware of. It was not that I sensed I had been there before, just that I was aware of some connection of which I knew nothing. Again, I wondered if this is what kept the descendants of those ancient people here, unconsciously, guarding the spirits their ancestors.

A short five-minute drive along the southern coastal road is Blackhammer Cairn, which is a stalled Neolithic Cairn. This is a long structure, and every yard or so on either side a sandstone slab separates the building into individual stalls for different sets of bones. This was an easy, but again a slippery walk, especially coming down the thirty- or forty-foot grassy slope.

The walk up Ward Hill to the Knowe of Yarso, also, took more than just a little skill, but it was well worth it to see the spectacular sight of the islands of Westray, Sanday, Eday Egilsay and Wyre. The first few hundred yards was simply up a farm track which ended abruptly. After a few more yards, there was a brown painted bridge which must be the most slippery structure I have ever had to negotiate. It is only safe to walk across pretending you are skating because if you lift your foot off you will almost certainly slip and slide … right into a fast flowing stream. It was good fun skating across the bridge, and I am sure that any ancient spirits who had eyes to see me were amused.

Then came a slightly difficult walk up a steep hill. The camber of the slippery path sloped at about forty-five degrees down the hill and was mainly very slippery grass. It was safer to walk on the heather that grew on either side of the path.

The Knowe of Yarsow is a much bigger cairn consisting of many stalls made by large standing sheets of rock about eight inches thick and around four feet tall. Over twenty adult bodies were found in it, which had been there from around 3300 BC, along with pottery and the bones of red deer. It is probably the highest Neolithic sight on the island, and it is a tricky walk of about half an hour each way, if you take it slowly.

It was now a tough walk, about a third of a mile down a 300-foot slippery slope made of rough coastal grass, to Midhowe Cairn on the shore facing Mainland Orkney. The walk down was as tricky but not as tiring as the walk back up the slope, but it took the prize for being the most impressive. It was a very large, grassy mound until it was excavated in 1932. It was now protected from the elements by being enclosed in what can only be described as its own hangar. You can walk around it or over it from suspended overhead gangways. It contained the remains of twenty-five adults in its twenty-four burial stalls, as well as bones of red deer, oxen, pigs and sheep. It was over thirty metres long and known locally as The Great Ship of Death.

Again, I was there on my own, and it was eerie. I had exactly the same sense of a strange connection with the place. There was nothing I could do about it; I just acknowledged it. It was as if I sensed that something had happened here which was important, and was about to be re-discovered. I began to think yet again on this island, as I had done many other times in my life, that maybe there is a plane of existence which we are only rarely aware of but with which we have some kind of connection.

The Great Ship of Death's location just above the shore line made me wonder if the whole island was used as a burial island and I wondered about the former use of the house I was staying in with its standing stone.

The last structure on my mini tour was only a hundred yards along the shore. Midhowe Broch is an impressive, very well preserved house which was built around 100 BC. There are 160 of these brochs in Orkney, and this one is supposed to be one of the best preserved. It is the central house of three. The other two nearby, Northhowe Broch and Southhowe Broch, remain unexcavated.

These brochs, or stone towers, were originally built for defense but were never used. Instead they added domestic structures to them. My theory was that maybe they heard of the threat of the Romans, who never got as far as Orkney. I also wondered if perhaps the people who lived in them were guardians of the nearby cairns, perhaps modern day graveyard workers or priests. Maybe the dead were sent to places like North Ronaldsay and Rousay and were received by a party of people who lived on the shore, who would then attend to their funeral rites. The history of the area is unknown, and its remains are only a very recent discovery. I was sure that the true story of this area would emerge, but it looked like it was going to be a very slow process and would probably not happen in my lifetime.

Midhowe Broch looked like a giant natural beehive. There were many rooms in the main central structure, with all the upright walls intact. There was a central well and a hearth. It was easy to see how this was such a good place in which to live. There were seaside views of the other islands, lots of fresh seafood, and security. On either side of the broch were two deep natural chasms, or sea inlets, which were un-crossable, and at the back to the landward side was a double ditch.

There was a difference between the attitudes of the islanders of Rousay and North Ronaldsay. The people on Rousay were much lighter of heart and not so inward looking. They had very easy access to, and, therefore, a lot more contact with, Mainland Orkney by the ferry which went every two hours to and from the mainland. It was too hilly to have a landing strip, but the ferry would go in almost all weathers, and there was always the lifeboat which would come if the weather was too rough for the air ambulance chopper. I noticed in the local papers that there was a row going on in Mainland Orkney, because most of the people were happier just using the Islander plane rather than the helicopter, and they were probably right, because the helicopter had quite narrow weather limits.

It also seemed to me that on these isles and islands a lot of patients had fallen out with their GPs, and several of these situations looked irredeemable. When a doctor lives in a community, he or she gets to know his or her patients, maybe too well, and a lot of friction in community life may prevent him or her being as objective as he or she might need to be in medical situations, particularly psychological ones. That is the most important reason why, I think, people on these isles and islands would be better served by doctors who visit regularly, but don't live there. The longest flying time to any of the islands with a strip is only fifteen minutes. Another logical reason for not having resident doctors on the island is to keep doctors' skills sharp and their experience up to date with the most common diseases. This can only happen if doctors are constantly seeing a large number of patients. It is difficult, expensive and ineffective for doctors to keep their skills sharp merely by distance learning.

Doctors have to see lots of patients to keep up to date, and if you have only between fifty and three hundred patients, it's really not enough to keep you up to date and as skilled as someone who is working with a community of fifteen hundred to fifteen thousand patients. I also believe that the anxiety of the islanders, of not having a doctor on the island, is a myth partly perpetuated by supporting doctors who want to be paid for an easy time, and who have too much power over the local population. Clearly, there needs to be access to a doctor, but it should be access to an experienced busy doctor. The list at North Ron had been fifty-seven patients, and here it was a little bigger at 256.

Just out of interest, here are the figures I came across for November 2005, for the total number of patients in each practice in Orkney:

Scapa Mainland Orkney: 5,901
Skerrymore Mainland Orkney: 4,443
Stromness West Mainland Orkney: 2,956
Dounby: 2,195
Evie: 512
South Ronaldsay and Burray Islands :1,244
Eday:123
North Ronaldsay: 57
Rousasy, Egilsay, Wyre and Gairsay Islands: 256
Stronsay: 371
Sanday: 510
Shapinsay: 300
Hoy: 381
Westray: 662

Total Number of Patients 19,991

In Orkney there are twenty-six GPs working in fourteen different practices covering seventeen islands. Nine of the practices have fewer than seven hundred patients and six had less than five hundred. The sole practitioners on the island who had to offer twenty-four hour care got seventeen weeks off a year. None of them had signed the new contract, which had expired over a year earlier. Many were in trouble, and the Orkney Health Board announced in The Orcadian newspaper that, because it failed to operate within its budget, it might lose local control and be taken over by the Scottish Executive.

The article also mentioned the salary paid to locums, and it was then that I realized that my agency was taking twenty-five percent when the usual is twelve to seventeen percent. The Health Board was paying twice the rate for locums as in England, but its own doctors were only on about half the rate in England. It is hardly surprising that they were in financial trouble, if they give doctors seventeen weeks off and then have to employ a locum at three times the cost of one of its own GPs. It was badly managed. They should have just paid the going rate for better doctors and scrapped the ridiculous holidays.

I tried to remember the official ratio of doctors to population, and I remembered that it is different in different situations. For example, at sea a container ship or any other vessel is allowed to carry up to twelve passengers on overnight trips without a doctor on board. More than that, you need a doctor. At outdoor venues for entertainment you need a stipulated number of Red Cross or St John's Ambulance personnel per one thousand people, and the same applies to doctors. I think it is one doctor per five thousand people in the crowd. But what about the UK rules on Islands? I didn't know the answer to this, and after asking anyone who I thought might know, I wasn't sure anyone else did either.

Chapter 16.

Rousay, Egilsay, Wyre and Gairsay Islands. Day 2 onwards

On my next day on my own on Rousay I decided to go to a beautiful spot called Kevaday Viewpoint. I had spotted a roadside sign on our first drive around the island and again on my subsequent circumnavigations of the island. I had told myself that, as soon as the weather was good enough, I would make the walk which just looked like a hike up a slope.

I parked half on the very narrow lane and half on the verge which was an inch away from a three-foot vertical drop into a watery ditch. I hopped over a strange kind of ladder and found myself in a field, and I walked up the tempting slope. Again, this was a very worthwhile walk, but, if you ever get to Rousay, don't do what I did and turn up in the wrong attire, which are shoes. Boots −. that's what I should have had in blindingly obvious hindsight. And this is so wonderfully characteristic of almost everything to do with Orkney, because it takes at least six weeks for it to stop surprising you with shocking reminders that you should have thought more before you made a single move.

Anyway, I was feeling particularly joyful and really positive about seeing this view on my own, so that I could lodge it in my memory and tell friends and family just what to see. It was only eleven in the morning and I had all day, until a five o'clock surgery. It is truly a great walk if you can survive it. As I carried on, the walk took interesting turns.

First, unlike the single Hilary step on Mount Everest, on Kevaday there were seven steps, which I called Kevaday Steps 1-7. You have to climb over an obstacle and then get through over a hundred yards of various challenges. But the risks on each step were not just challengingly very different, they were also surprising and worthwhile paying attention to.

Second, unlike the Hilary Step, there were no ropes from previous explorers to hold on to when there was a drop over the unusual stiles, which could present a drop of up to seven feet into very muddy ground that has been stirred by sheep's feet and other of their activities. The stiles were about two feet wide and consisted of two vertical ladders, which were five feet high, connected by a two-foot long platform to crawl or walk across. Some had a vertical continuation of a corner, which made a sort of post to hang on to. These would be difficult to negotiate in an Orkney wind.

Third, there were no aluminum ladders to get you over crevasses with fast flowing streams of brown water, which are too wide to safely negotiate in any shoes or boots, except chest high waders. You had to risk jumping.

Fourth, most of the Steps did not immediately present you with handrails to negotiate safely through the slippery, short grass which gave no traction. I did happen to use the only handrails I noticed, which began as soon as I started the first step. But there wasn't a warning of the experience until a good hundred yards later.

Fifth, immediately after I climbed over the second step, on the right hand side, underneath the end of the handrail, at the height of your knee, there was a small four-inch sign which simply says, "Attention. Electric Fence". This was the third time in my life I had had firsthand experience of electricity, which made me laugh. The sign was very difficult to see, but the wire was impossible to miss touching.

The sixth threat was on the other side of what looks like a perfect stone wall, on the right hand side of you as you walked up the Steps. For some reason there were an extraordinary number of droppings left by the sheep that shelter on that side of the windbreak wall. Slip just once and it could ruin a nice day.

Now to the seventh threat, and this was a risk to limbs. Who would ever think that a rabbit could kill you? They could. Just try crossing the seventh step at the wrong time, with no contingency plan in case something happens. For example, imagine stepping in long coastal grass which very deceivingly concealed rabbit holes. The frequent, extreme Orcadian winds cunningly concealed the Orcadian rabbit holes, because they blow the long coastal grass every which way, so it faces everywhere and covers everything. Such a single concealed deep rabbit hole could fracture your leg or foot, or injure any part of you in an extraordinary number of interestingly different ways, particularly because there was no radio or cell phone signal in that area of Rousay. So a great deal of care was needed there, and especially if you were on your own.

I am not going to attempt to describe the view at the top of the Kevaday, because it would only make it secondhand if you visit it. But, standing there, I realized that the road below me could easily be used as a runway, just like the Royal Flying Doctor Service in Australia, because it was perfectly straight. The island could have a flying doctor service.

I couldn't help noticing the graveyard facing a small loch that could not have been more than a hundred yards wide. I drove down the lane that sloped down to the loch. The graveyard looked as if it was on sea level but separated from the sea by the loch and some kind of sandbank. The graveyard had three parts to it. The modern part only had about twenty graves on the inside of two of the four walls. In the older part the gravestones all faced the loch, but I noticed that there was no evidence of any kind of church, which was unusual. Most of the people had lived until their eighties and nineties, and I noticed that there was an absence of any young people.

The old graveyard was accessed by way of an old wooden gate. Rather like the walk on the seventh step, there were concealed rabbit holes, but these ones were fearsome. At first I thought the graves and gravestones were identical to the previous graveyard, but they were much older, from around the year 1800. Instead of being buried in a box and covered over with earth and then grass, the bodies in these graves were simply lowered into the hole and a stone slab put on top. Now many of these had broken, and the long coastal grass concealed the chasms that were about six to eight feet deep. I realized that I was going to have a lot of difficulty getting back to the gate, because I couldn't see any traces of the way I had taken. I looked at my mobile phone, but there was no signal. I was in a tight spot, and the nearest of three dwellings I could see was probably a mile away. I was a little worried in case I fell through one of the broken slabs, straight onto a pile of bones. I took each step very slowly and made sure the toes had very solid ground underneath before letting my heel touch the ground. When I looked back from the closed gate I noticed that all of the graves were covered with lichen, which looked like seaweed that had learnt to survive in this harsh, coastal location.

I had two stops to make. One was to the shop to buy some presents to send to Chrisie and India, the other was to the post office to post them. I had been blessed with the best weather I had so far seen in Orkney. It was bright, low sunshine with a magnificent turquoise sea and a light blue sky.

Marian and her husband John own and run "Marian's Shop". They also grow organic vegetables and fruit, but they don't bother with labels. The Queen Mother used to, and her grandson Charles still orders, strawberries from her. She was educated at Cambridge. She and her husband had lived for a long while on the Gilbert and Ellis islands where she had run a medical clinic. He had done the paperwork for handing the island back to the locals. They had mostly lived on islands. I wandered around the shop which had everything a household would want food and drink wise, as well as being the local hardware store, the local newsagent and gift shop. I decided on the fudge. Marian and her husband John were immediately friendly.

'I saw you getting out at the surgery the other day. I used to be a physicist, then I switched to pharmacy in London.'

'Where did you work?'

'I mainly did locums in the London teaching hospitals. But then I came here in 1970 and bought a cottage. We moved up here a long time ago.'

'You must be the best person to ask about seeing the Northern Lights?' I asked.

'Not necessarily, but I've got a keen interest in them. If you look up the website of The Orcadian, and go to Skynotes and then Archives, you'll see some photographs I've taken. If you give me your number, I'll ring you if they start up. It all depends on the activity of the sun, which is a bit quiet at the moment.'

I gave John my phone number and the dates when I would be around over the next three weeks and hoped he would ring me if there was good news. I paid for the fudge and headed to the post office. Inside a woman was being served by Jackie the Postmistress, who was holding one hand above her eyes to shield them from the powerful rays from the sun coming in from the window of this old building.

'Do you think you need a curtain?' I asked her, trying only to be friendly.

'Yes. I promise myself that every year, but by the time I think about it again the sun's not a bother. We don't get much sun up here.'

'Where are you from?'

'Same parts as you - the New Forest, Fordingbridge. Marian told me in the shop.'

'How long have you been here?'

'I came up from Durham on an archeological dig nearly thirty years ago. I was digging out Viking grave boats, finding men and women who had been buried in beautiful jewelry, and I stayed. I fell in love with a local man, but he now lives on the mainland. My kids have grown up and left, and live on the mainland too.' She didn't look old enough to have been there nearly thirty years, because she had short, naturally black hair without any grey bits. She was attractive and had a friendly, pretty smile. She was chatty too.

'What's it like living here on Rousay?'

'I nearly left last winter, because the weather was so bad, and there was really no summer this year. It was the second year like that. It really gets to everyone. Sometimes the wind is so strong that it flattens the sea.'

'I think I saw that a couple of weeks ago.'

'You would have done, if you were here. The winds were 115 miles an hour and just flattened the waves. The wave is blown into the air like a spray and the sea appears a lot calmer. There are gentle rolls because the upper two thirds of the wave are missing.

'What are the people like?'

'It's fifty-fifty. Half are Orcadians and half are from south of Orkney, that's Scotland or England. If there's a vote on something, like having a swimming pool which we collected funds for, it is always fifty-fifty, and nothing gets done. The pool was abandoned and the money spent elsewhere.'

'How do you all get on?'

'Well, there have been troubles, but by and large we get on. You do have to be aware of customs. You keep on making mistakes about the local customs for the first year, then its gets easier. It was easier for me, because I married a local lad. Newcomers usually find it difficult to adjust. For example, if a boat is wrecked, there is often very good wood washed up on the shore, which is very useful here. What the newcomers do is just go and pick it up, but what they don't know is when the wood has been 'set up'.

'What does set up mean?'

'It means that someone has already put it above the high-tide mark, and that means he has a claim on it. Other things, like ordering a taxi, can land you in it and create enemies, because on some islands there are only two families who do taxis. I avoid trouble and just use a different person each time.'

'What's it like for newcomers?'

'Everyone is friendly but guarded, and you can usually tell who's going to make it or not. Often you know a couple will be gone within a year.'

'The islands really are very tiny communities, and you either fit or don't.'

'Yes. When you decide to come here you have to bring your head with you, and whatever problem you may have with yourself or others is amplified many times. Instead of there being peace there often isn't. It is like being on stage because you are more visible. You have to be a great deal more careful.'

'It must be a surprise for someone who's running away from something to discover that they've brought their baggage with them, and now it's under a spotlight.'

'Pretty much true. There are no secrets here.'

'Do you get back down to the New Forest ever?'

'Occasionally, but it's difficult to cope with the very busy traffic there. We get frequent lessons on the island radio telling islanders how to use roundabouts and to use zebra crossings; people here believe that they can just step off the road and people will stop for them. I don't miss the business of the people. I get busy here.'

'Really? It seems so quiet.'

'I've nearly run out of first class Christmas stamps. I had about 3,000 and I've only got 250 left. That is a lot of mail, and it all has to hand franked with this.' She pulled out something that looked like a salt cellar with a metal stamp on the bottom.

'That's a lot of stamping.'

'I actually had a problem with my arm last Christmas, so this year I've brought in some help.'

'And the future?'

'I'm just setting up my own small mail order silk business.'

'How come silk?'

'Well it's light and cheap to mail, and I've got all the postal facilities here that I need, so I'm just starting planning my designs.'

'What about a Rousay stamp?'

'I get hundreds of requests for items to be posted back with our hand postal stamp on them already. I want to do something a bit different.'

Before I left Rousay I had two things to do. First I had to try and find if my mobile phone had arrived. It was Friday, and I wasn't sure if there was any post or parcel post the next day, and, as I was leaving on the first boat on Monday, I thought I should see if I could track the phone's location down.

I phoned the haulier who deals with all parcels, but he hadn't seen the new phone. I phoned my cell phone provider, who were helpful and told me that it had been sent out on Monday and that it had arrived in the Kirkwall Parcel Office on Friday. They gave me a twenty digit Consignment Number, which I diligently wrote down and read back to the operator.

I got through to the Parcel line in Orkney and tapped in the number, which was automatically read back to me by their computerized operator, who said, 'The consignment number is incorrect. We have no record of that consignment number.' The computerized operator put me through to a real person and, eventually, they found the phone and put it aside for me to collect on my way through on Monday, mercifully without having to recite the long Consignment Number again. It wasn't as bad as it could have been.

I then sent this e-mail regarding the car's fuel consumption and my use of the nurse's mobile phone.

Dear Claire,
Hope you have had a nice holiday. I have.

I thought I would let you know, in advance of any questions from Orkney Health Board, about the fuel consumption of the Peugeot they lent me from their car hire firm. I had no problems with the car. However, my fuel consumption was probably unusual for this locum post as well, as I was apparently busier than most locums.

As in Kirkwall, I had no sense of the geography of this island and its various communities until I drove around with a map several times. I familiarized myself with each of the houses, so that if I was called out it would make any potential visit quicker to get to.

I also had three urgent admissions, which included one medical evacuation to Aberdeen via Kirkwall. In the other two cases I had to use my car as an ambulance and drive them on the ferry, to a waiting ambulance in Tingwall, and then bring myself and the car back on the ferry. One of these medical ferry journeys involved going to the island of Wyre on the way. In each case I left the car running, which was about an hour for each trip. This was so that the patient was warm.

There were also twice daily visits to the surgery, and I also used the car to take pathology specimens to the ferry, as well as to collect drugs from the boat for the pharmacy. I also used it to deliver drugs to patients' houses. I did several home visits all around the island.

At your suggestion, I also used my phone to make mobile calls, as there was no land line. This was from Wednesday until Saturday, when it stopped working. I borrowed the nurse's mobile phone and had to use it to order a new phone. I used it for all other calls regarding medical problems on the island.

Kind regards.

Finally, before I left, I decided to write a letter to the local newspapers about my thoughts on the Orcadian healthcare system. I wrote it tongue-in-cheek, for something to do to pass the time in an interesting way; I thought it would be put in the bin straight away as a rude letter from a locum who was too big for his boots.

I showed it to Marion and John, who run the shop. They seemed excited by the possibility that they might get young, knowledgeable doctors in the near future. Coming out of the shop, it struck me that you can get so used to 5,000 year old sights that you don't notice them anymore. I was gazing out of the front window when I noticed a standing stone right in the centre of their garden, which they had kept very well-manicured. They had done something I had not seen before with their six-foot high standing stone. They had built an ornate bench around it, rather like you would do with a tree in a particularly beautiful or peaceful spot. Their garden was in a beautiful spot. The house was on the very steep east coast of Rousay, off the steep main road. It overlooked Egilsay Island and the mainland island, as well as about four other islands. She had chosen the site for her business very well indeed.

I faxed the letter to Orkney Today but would have to hand deliver it to The Orcadian during my brief day in Kirkwall.

John Ross Scott
Editor, Orkney Today Limited
Unit 1, Kiln Corner
Kirkwall KW15 1QX
Orkney

Thursday 15 December, 2005

Sub: Scrap Isles GPs and bring in modern flying doctor service.

Sir,

I recently had the immense pleasure of serving you and your community as a GP locum on Mainland Orkney and on several of your islands, where the medical needs are, of course, the same as for people living in other parts of the British Isles.

I'm just writing to you to let you know that the services being delivered to Orcadians seem very different, in my experience, from the rest of Britain. A modern, standardised British healthcare system can only be delivered to everyone in Orkney by scrapping the archaic islands doctor service and replacing it with a flying doctor service. I would like to explain why this is so.

It is abundantly clear from the recent extraordinary cover by local newspapers that there are profoundly serious worries about the quality of doctors working in Orkney. In my time here, most local GPs and their support staff informed me that the health of Orcadians is only kept glued together by the services provided by locums. Let me explain this. Any salaried doctor thinking of working in Orkney has to take a 40-50% pay cut - the salaries in the rest of the UK are around £110,000 but only around £65,000 in Orkney. Members of the Health Board honestly need to ask themselves if the recent press coverage is evidence of the old saying, 'You pay peanuts and you get monkeys,' and if it is true for Orcadians.

Unlike most doctors, who get around only six weeks annual leave, the island doctors have seventeen weeks annual paid leave, which has to be covered by locums. These kinds of arrangements are bizarre, because they don't even happen in much more remote British parts of the world, such as St Helena. According to your Health Authority, these arrangements cost £4,000-£4,500 a week for each locum. This extra eleven weeks holiday, therefore, costs around £45,000-£50,000 for each island doctor, which for the eight islands, amounts to about £500,000 just for locum cover. If you add the island GPs' salaries, of around £65,000 for each GP, the cost comes to about £1,000, 000 for providing the whole package of GP services to the eight islands, but not including Mainland Orkney.

If the Health Authority scrapped this system and, instead, paid doctors the average British salary, not only would high quality doctors be lured to come to Orkney but the Health Board would also have a surplus of around £1,000,000 to supply a flying doctor service.

There are now so many disadvantages to having resident doctors in very small communities, that it might be seen as "good practice" not to carry this tradition into the future. Doctors who are only seeing a very small number of patients lose their clinical acumen and they de-skill quickly. Even with distant learning and video conferencing, they simply don't see the number of patients with the wide variety of illnesses that most GPs do, and they don't perform as many medical procedures.

Doctors who live in very small communities can also become too involved in their patients' lives, with the result that patients may well think the doctor can't see them objectively anymore. Fear of unskilled doctors and loss of trust in objectivity are evidenced by the fact that a highly significant number of the people on the islands refuse to see their resident GP and, instead, travel to the Mainland Orkney to use the GP services there, where they are more anonymous.

Seeing a different busy visiting doctor each time solves many problems. The doctor is working with large numbers of patients and is up to date with new methods and new drugs. The patient has the advantage of the doctor being more objective; and this method of delivery of General Practice medicine gives patients a variety of different doctors' opinions, which is usually always seen as an advantage.

One of the reasons why a doctor was first appointed to North Ronaldsay in 1914 was to stop death certificates giving the cause of death as "Unknown, no doctor in attendance". With modern medical science, there are few, if any, causes of death which can't be established after the 15 minutes it would take for a doctor to fly there. Also, modern transport by Islander planes and helicopters is not so weather sensitive as it once was, and today there is always some way of gaining access to the islands, especially with the coastguard and lifeboats in reserve. Many of the original reasons for having permanent doctors on the islands are simply no longer valid.

Rather like Londoners, who, last week, had no choice but to emotionally let go of their red Routemaster buses, it is time for the Health Board to announce to the patients of the eight islands currently being served by eight doctors that they are soon going to be served by Mainland Orkney based flying doctors, delivering modern medical practice and medicines which are not past their sell-by dates.

If the Health Board doesn't do this soon, they will be replaced by the Scottish Executive who will immediately terminate the employment of the eight doctors, who have no contracts anyway.

The future of some of your remote islands depends on tourism, founded mainly on your extraordinary, unique Neolithic sites. This future could be impaired if the medical services for visitors are perceived as being out of touch with modernity.

Lastly, which should it be? Aeroplane or helicopter? In terms of health and safety, just ask any fixed-wing pilot how many moving parts are in a helicopter and ask him to choose between a helicopter and a plane, and he will always choose an aeroplane. Even a helicopter engineer will admit that they wouldn't want to be in a helicopter when the magnet drain comes into operation, because that means the gearbox is no longer operating.

Yours sincerely,

Of the 19,991 people in Orkney, 2,660 live on eight islands with their own GPs. I happened to be the unlucky one that night when my phone went off.

'Is that you?'

'Yes, what's up?'

'Someone's fallen off the pier by the restaurant. There were two in the water.' I was already putting on my socks.

'At one o'clock?' I asked, pulling on my trousers.

'I think they're worried about drowning or hypothermia.'

'I'm dressed. Be there in a less than one minute.' A minute had not gone by before I picked up my small rucksack, when there was a knock on the door. I switched every single light on to wake me up.

There was an Orkadian voice. 'Did you get the call?'

I opened the door and a man in his late twenties stood there, shaking with worry.

'Yep. On the case.'

'You drive. I'll follow in my car,' he said quickly. He drove like he was trying to break the Rousay speed record, and as he flung and swung his car around all the corners I did too, in hot pursuit. We arrived at the pier; he ran into a house without shutting the car door; I grabbed my bag and ran after him.

There were at least ten people in the house, and I was ushered upstairs. There were two people sitting on the floor in the fetal position, with their knees tucked up under their chins. Each had a blanket around their shoulders. Their teeth were chattering, and they both had the shakes. They were still in shock from hitting the cold water at 1.00 am on a winter's night.

I checked them both over, advised them about the best way to warm up slowly and said I would see them both in the morning surgery.

I slept poorly, now that I had been woken up, and set off to Kirkwall early. I had lunch in the restful town of Stromness and squeezed in some Christmas shopping before leaving for Kirkwall.

Back in Kirkwall, I decided to buy some of the traditional music which I had not really had a chance to listen to. In the music shop I couldn't help noticing a sign which read, 'Coffee Shop Upstairs. I was really very tired from the two hours of work from 1.00 am until 3.00 am, and I needed a perk for the five hour trip back home to the Forest. When I went to the counter for a coffee I knew I had seen the young woman the before.

'Were we sitting next to each other on a plane the other

week going to North Ron?' I said.

'Yes. How did you get on there?' she said as she smiled.

'It's a very interesting place, but I couldn't live there. It really is too far out there in the ocean. Can I get a coffee?'

'Yes, no bother.'

'I want to buy some traditional Orkney music; what would you recommend?'

'Well, get one of the Wrigley Sisters. Jenny the fiddler will be up in a minute.' I suddenly realized I was in a kind of folk club as well as restaurant/bar owned by the main traditional Orcadian musicians.

Jenny duly appeared and was helpful. She gave me two CDs - one of the Wrigley Sisters and the other of a mixture of several Orcadian musicians.

At home there was an e-mail waiting for me from Orkney Today, which simply said, 'Thanks for the excellent letter.' But they didn't say if they were going to use it. I was simply glad to have given them some outside input, and writing the letter had given me something for my mind to be occupied with whilst I was there. I didn't mean to particularly upset anyone.

I was trying to switch off and plug back in to rural family life when first thing the next morning I had a phone call from BBC Radio Scotland, who wanted a telephone interview regarding my letter about getting rid of the doctors on the small islands and replacing them with flying doctors. The interviewer said at one point. 'But aren't flying doctors confined to Australia?'

'Well, you're hiring doctors from Australia to do your locum work here.' I pointed out.

'Really?' he said.

'Yes. I met this doctor from Melbourne in Kirkwall the other week. He was on his fifth locum there.'

'Does he fly?' And we both laughed as, thankfully, everyone could see the ridiculousness of having doctors only serving fifty to a hundred patients each.

The next morning after it went out on Orkney Radio, I got a phone call from BBC Scottish TV who wanted an interview when I got back to Orkney.

Chapter 17.

Locum 4. Mainland Orkney, South Ronaldsay and Burray Island

I was looking forward to doing my six nights on call covering Kirkwall and South Ronaldsay. It was a return to familiar country. It sounds odd to admit looking forward to doing twelve-hour night shifts but it wasn't busy and the people were friendly, welcoming and extremely appreciative.

My return to work began at Kirkwall airport. My early morning flight from Southampton to Edinburgh had been cancelled for operational reasons, and so I was re-routed on the Southampton to Glasgow flight. The problem was that I didn't have time to get from Glasgow to Edinburgh to catch my flight up to Inverness. I was in Glasgow at nine in the morning. Whilst waiting in Glasgow I got a call from the Balfour Hospital in Kirkwall, asking me about a patient.

'Is that the doc?'

'Sure is.'

'Can you sort out this man with dizziness?'

'No trouble, but I'm still in Glasgow.'

'How come?'

'My flight was cancelled for operational reasons, but I'm on my way.

'This one's a home visit.'

'Who's on call for the out of hours during today?'

'The young female doctor on call last night just left the bag in reception.'

'I think she was supposed to have waited until six this evening when I take over.'

'Yes, I've got you down for starting at six tonight.'

'I'll just have to field the calls by phone, and if there's

anything urgent, I'll get them to phone for an ambulance. Is that OK with you?'

'Fine. I'm a bit anxious about this, but there really isn't any other solution. Any idea when you'll be in?'

'Looks like six, but I'll call you when I get in. Can I ask you a favor?'

'Sure, go ahead.'

'I was supposed to have a car waiting for me from a car hire firm, but obviously I'm coming in later. Can you arrange for them to leave the keys at the information desk?'

'Which car hire firm is it?'

'The usual one.'

'There are several. Do you know which one?'

'Sorry, haven't got a clue.

'I'll phone the one at the airport and book a car for you.'

'Good. I'll come in and get the emergency bag at around half six.'

I ended up finally getting to see Inverness, and I spent four hours getting a feel of the place and the people. It is a small but pleasant place to see. When I landed in Kirkwall I already had two home visits booked, as I had been fielding calls from my cell phone at both Glasgow and Inverness.

'I've come for a hire car,' I said at the information desk.

'The hire car firm closed a while ago.'

'Did anyone leave some keys here for me?'

'No, but I can see that John from Tullocks is still over there chatting away to someone. I'll go and get him. Are you that doctor?'

'Which one?' I asked wondering what I had done. Had I overbooked and got two cars, or kept him waiting. Anyway, I felt guilty.

'The flying doctors problem.'

'Oh, er … yes that's me.' I was a bit surprised that the letter I had written had been published, as it was a long letter of around a thousand words.

'Glad that someone's got the nerve to mention it. We've known about these island doctors for years. They're all just taking the mickey and getting away with it. The Health Board is just impotent. They won't take these doctors on.'

'Well, it's only a bit of something for me to do up here, because it's not a very heavy workload, and I agree it needs changing sooner rather than later.'

'Clever letter.'

'Thanks. I don't usually write letters to newspapers, but I saw the situation as pretty bad.'

'It's a grey Ford, and watch the ice,' he said. It had been snowing in Kirkwall, and I eventually found the brand new hire car and set off to the hospital switchboard where I collected the maps, drugs bag, the bleep and cell phones.

But some things had changed in the last few weeks. Instead of one of the old mobile phones, there were now two new ones. Before I had left when I last did this locum, I suggested that the Health Board get a proper doctors bag. The one they had was just like an over-the-shoulder cooler bag with drugs in the bottom. A proper doctor's bag these days is really a solid box type of bag, more like a small chest of drawers, which has about twenty small drawers. Each drawer has a label so that you can quickly find any drug you want. They had responded to my suggestion by buying a plastic toolbox, with all of the drugs in the bottom part. Still, I thought it was progress and I would try and find them the telephone number of the people who make doctors bags. I liked the way they were wide open to suggestions. It meant they were open to change.

I was staying at the Commodore Apartments next to

Churchill Barrier No 1. Richard and Louise were waiting, and we had a long discussion about the letter in the papers. Both papers had printed the letter and they had saved me a copy of both The Orcadian and Orkney Today. The editor of Orkney Today, John Ross Scott, said in his editorial that I had vented my spleen about the expensive island doctor situation. This made me think even further about the situation, and I decided to write another letter ready for delivering the next morning. Again, I wrote it more tongue-in-cheek.

John Ross Scott
Editor, Orkney Today Limited
Unit 1, Kiln Corner
Kirkwall KW15 1QX
Orkney

Thursday 22nd December, 2005

Sub: Isles Doctors

Sir,

Whilst enjoying the very last of many weeks on your beautiful islands, I couldn't help noticing some rather unusual arrangements that the Health Board has with its Island GPs.

Some time ago the health Board negotiated with the Island GPs and agreed to give each Island GP seventeen weeks annual holiday. This was arranged to prevent the island GP's 24-hour on-call duty causing fatigue and exhaustion, which could interfere with the GP's performance and endanger the lives of their patients.

It, therefore, seems odd that the Health Board allows these island GPs to do their own locum work, where they can earn over £3,000-£4,000 a week, which is nearly three times their salary. If the

Health Board truly believes that these doctors really need an extra eleven weeks off every year, then it should insist that these doctors actually take the time off. If they don't believe that the Island GPs need the time off, then the Health Board should scrap the extra eleven weeks holiday and save themselves a vast amount of money. This in itself would save them around £44,000 a year for each of the eight doctors, which amounts to £352,000 per year; a large part of their current deficit.

Likewise, the island doctors who fought for these extra eleven weeks holiday should not abuse and exploit their privileged position by doing their own locums and thus creaming off the money that was set aside to bring in locums to relieve them. If they continue to work during their extra eleven weeks holiday time, which was only created to avoid fatigue and to reduce the likelihood of mistakes, then they are intentionally putting their patients' lives at risk for financial gain. They need to be responsible and should stop this, or they should be stopped.

If a mistake was made by one of these island doctors, whilst doing their own locum, and someone was hurt, the Health Authority and the doctor would medico-legally be in indefensible positions, and 'damage compensation' could cost the NHS Orkney vast sums of money. The Health Board needs to be transparent about this matter, and make a decision and assert itself in the interests of the people living on these islands.

In Chinese the word for 'crisis' is represented by two symbols: one is total destruction, the other is opportunity. Sadly, misery and suffering are all too easily perpetuated by simple inactivity and this can result in destruction and death. On the other hand, it is sometimes a duty to actually fuel a crisis in order to bring something to a head, so that things can change and be allowed to move on, which is what the Health Board should do. Yes, it can be painful having an abscess drained or a tumour removed by a surgeon, but it is healing *and brings enormous relief from further misery and suffering.*

Yours sincerely,

What I didn't write was that I strongly suspected that there was some kind of under-the-table agreement with the island doctors and the Health Board. Was this seventeen week arrangement, whereby they were allowed to do their own locums, simply a covert way of channeling extra money to the island GPs to compensate for not having time off from being on call? Was it some way around breaking a European directive on hours worked by doctors? If it was, then it was dishonest, but I thought it wise to leave someone else to work this out and make it public. I felt that I had given them enough clues.

That evening I had arranged to meet John from BBC Scottish TV at the Balflour Hospital. I had asked one of the outpatient nurses if I could borrow a room to see someone in, without mentioning that it was a TV interview.

'Was your flight OK?' John asked.

'Yes, only a few minutes late. Where are you from?'

'Northern Ireland, but I live in the Shetlands. I just want to tell the truth about this matter to get a well-rounded view.'

'That's good. With no sides is the best way to show it.

'You see, we are all nurse led. We don't have doctors on most of the islands, even on those with big populations. And we manage very well with the Air Ambulance.'

'That's what I've been saying all along. Can I get you some coffee?'

'That would help a lot, thanks,' he said as he set up his equipment. I went to the Male Ward's canteen and made some coffee and raided a good number of their best chocolate biscuits. Thankfully, this time it wasn't for a suicidal patient.

Back in the consulting room we had 10 thirty-second mini discussions.

'It's the way the whole of outside news is going.'

'How do you mean?' I asked.

'Just one person with a good digital camera, tripod and a mobile phone. No sound man or cameraman. Just one interviewer trained in all the other disciplines.'

'Must make it more challenging, but you've got more control and it's cheaper.'

'A lot easier as well, because you don't have to worry about other people, their food, transport and accommodation. I just have a producer who helps me edit all of the material. That's all I need. We could do this live, but it's still a bit in the early stages. But it works well. Should get this one out in thirty-six hours.'

The interview was for a twenty- to thirty-second clip, and all I said was that doctors naturally de-skill if they don't see enough patients, and that was it.

'Good luck with the trip back, and thanks for helping out with this situation.' And with this he had already disappeared out the door.

This short return trip proved just as challenging as the first trip, but in different ways. At seven o'clock on my second night, I was heading back home to the Commodore Apartments when I was called by Balfour switchboard to take a call from a patient's husband in South Ronaldsay.

'Is that the doctor?'

'Yes. What's up?'

'My wife's had flu a couple of days ago, and now she's being sick and she's a bit short of puff. She suffers with asthma.'

'I'm just approaching the Commodore Apartments before Churchill Barrier No 1, so I'm not very far from South

Ronaldsay. Where are you in South Ronaldsay?'

'We are right down the bottom.'

'Yes?'

'We're just opposite ...' The line cut off. I tried ringing back, but I had no signal. The signal always gets worse as you go south to South Ronaldsay, so my only choice, seeing as I didn't have a phone number or address, was to go to my apartment and use the landline. I parked in the fierce sleet storm and walked as fast as I could to the front door. For some reason, the porch light was off, and I struggled to find the keyhole in the total darkness. When I got in I slammed the door shut against the elements and discovered that the power had gone. So I couldn't use the phone. I tried my mobile again, and there was still no signal, which was unusual in the Commodore Apartments because that is one of the best places for a signal.

There was only one option, which was to backtrack and head north back towards the hospital in Kirkwall and ring Switch when I got a signal, or just go to Switch and speak to them. It was in completely the opposite direction to the house I had to visit, but I didn't even know who it was. It would add another twelve miles to the visit, but I wasn't in a rush.

Halfway back to Kirkwall I got a signal, so I called Switch. 'Where do they live?' I asked.

'It's easy, but it's a bit of a drive, and the road in South Ron is pretty bad with this weather. I mean you can get blown about a lot, so you need to be careful.' He gave me the rest of the complicated directions, telling me what to watch for at every step.

'Well, you know where I am if I disappear off the radar for a bit,' I said, as if I was venturing out into a snow storm.

'He'll be waiting for you with a red flashing torch. By the way, there's a big power cut south of here and also in South

Ronaldsay. This is their telephone number. But it may not be any use down there.'

'I'll call them and tell them I won't be long.' But when I phoned them there was no answer. They had probably lost the signal on their cell phone, and with the power cut they had lost the chance to recharge their cell phone batteries.

So, off I went on a trip of darkness and danger. On this trip I had brought a 3,000,500 candle power rechargeable torch not only to find house names in the dark but to give me a better view and chance of avoiding those areas of mud and water which looked the deepest. Probably, most importantly, I could see patients in the dark, which, because of the power cuts, was a frequent need.

The visit was straightforward, and I sent the patient and her husband off to hospital. She was being very sick indeed, and she had a pretty bad chest infection. If the weather got any worse, she might be stranded here for a while and deteriorate, and it would be no fun without any power. It was the safe option; there were some available beds in the hospital, and she was happier with this than staying at home. The problem was that, by the time I wrote a letter and helped him get his wife to the car, my 3,000.500 candle power torch was dim and needed recharging. I followed the patient's car and thought about my options. It was totally dark, and the power cut was now two hours long. I spotted three teams of electrical power engineers trying to fix large transformers on the top of high posts, and it didn't look optimistic.

When I crossed Barrier No 1 I decided to swing a right to the Commodore Apartments and see if the power was back on, but it was still down. I lit one of two night lights I had spotted earlier and realized that I didn't have enough light to take messages down. I had no electricity to cook by and no landline. My cell phone still had no signal. My only choice was a comfortable one – The Kirkwall Hotel. I collected the battery chargers for the phones and torch and merrily got in the car. When I got a signal I was nearly in Kirkwall, so I dropped into Switch to phone the hotel. They had no idea of how long the power cut was going to be, but they had heard it was a bad one, which reinforced my decision to have a night of comfort.

In the morning, the practice manager, who was the person I handed over my night notes to, had the day off, so I left the notes on her desk. As I was leaving one of the secretaries asked me if I would like to do the on-call work during the day, as the doctor who was supposed to do the shift had just called in sick. I hadn't been woken during the night and I had a free day, and so I volunteered.

My first call was in St Mary's Hope, just around the corner from where I was staying. On the way down the six-mile stretch, which is more or less straight for up to a mile and a half at a time where I could usually speed, I did not today because of the ice. A collie dog jumped out of a gateway and barked at me, but I carried on. I did the visit and came past the same spot where the dog had barked at me.

There was an ambulance there, and as I cautiously approached in the icy conditions I could see to my right, about three hundred yards down a track, the yellow jackets of two ambulance personnel. They seemed to be bending down as if someone or something was in a ditch. I thought they might be in a real jam, especially so far down a muddy, uneven path. I pulled up in front of the ambulance, and put my warning lights on. I now felt terrible guilty for not stopping for the dog. The dog had been trying to stop me and warn me there was a sick person somewhere. Now I was here, I rapidly tried to find out where the problem was.

The path I had to take was very boggy, and my boots went down five inches with each step. Some of the steps filled my boots with water and some with mud. It was a yucky attempt at a fast walk. As I got close I spotted the dog, the two ambulance personnel and three farmers. On the left in the ditch was a person face down, half in the ditch. They had a red sailing/walking jacket on, yellow wellies and brown cord trousers.

'Are they OK?'

'Hi there. How are you? He's got a glucose of 2.3, which is low.'

'Any pulse?' I asked, bending down with my knee in two inches of mud.'

'Yes, but weak.' I then felt the man's pulse which was fine. It was around seventy per minute and regular.

'Any ID, or do you know who he is?' I said looking at the farmers.

'No, none. The dog came over to us, barking and pulling at my wellies.'

'That's a very clever dog,' I said, deeply regretting I hadn't stopped earlier. I stroked the dog which was pacing and looking worried, as if trying to say, 'Get him out of there!'

'A very clever and very good dog,' said the male paramedic.

'I thought she was just barking at the car. How I wish I had stopped and taken notice - a barking dog in the middle of nowhere. Next time I'll stop for every dog.'

We couldn't find the spot easily, even with the farmers there,' the paramedic said.

'Better get a space blanket and get him in the ambulance, but I'm not sure how to get him there,' I said.

'I can get my tractor trailer from the farm. I'll be five

to ten minutes, mind,' said the burly farmer in padded, blue Orcadian overalls.

'Go now,' I said to Caroline, the blond haired forty year old paramedic whom I had met a couple of times at Tingness ferry to transfer patients to the mainland Orkney from Rousay.

'Have you got a space blanket handy? I haven't got one, but I usually carry two in my other winter jacket at home.'

'Got one in the truck,' she said and walked as fast as she could down the path to get the jacket.

'That dog saved this man's life. The ditch is too far for anyone to see.'

'Let's try and wake him,' said Fred, the male paramedic.

'Can you turn his face around?' I asked, and he turned him around and I removed the oxygen mask for a moment. 'Wakey! It's the ambulance and doctor. Can you open your eyes?' I shouted, and he grabbed at the mask and my hand.

'That's good,' said the paramedic.

'Yes, at least he can grip with both hands, so it's less likely a stroke.'

'Let's go through his pockets.' I found a packet of gum and some Vaseline.

'Here's a letter from some friends on the Shetlands. It says ... Dear Billy.'

'Could be him,' I said.

'Hello Billy! Billy hello!' shouted the paramedic loudly. There was only a glimmer of a response, but there was some. The female paramedic arrived just before the tractor did. A young woman with blonde hair came down the path and it turned out to be the man's daughter.

'He's OK, got a pulse, breathing OK and is responding. Ever happened before?' I said.

'Yes, a year ago on another walk. But he came around

and walked home.'

'On any medication?' I asked.

'Just a beta blocker for high blood pressure.'

'Sounds more like some kind of seizure,' said the female paramedic.

'I agree,' I said as we all helped lift him into the massive metal digger bucket on the back of the tractor. This was a slightly unconventional way to move a patient, and it looked very strange, but it was the only way of moving him. The ground conditions were too severe for a safe ride in a four-wheel drive.

His wife then arrived and I reassured her. She and her daughter, as well as the two paramedics, lifted him into the bucket and stayed in it with him until they got to the road. The two farmers and I walked behind this strange sight to the ambulance. As I was following the bucket with the family at either end of a man on an ambulance stretcher in it, I wondered, if there was a photograph of this, could anyone guess what the situation was. It was a slow and careful walk back to the ambulance. He was gently removed from the bucket and put in the warm ambulance.

'I'm on my way back to the practice, so I'll let the on-call doctor know,' I said to the ambulance crew. They looked happy and very satisfied with the work they had just accomplished. 'Thanks.' I said.

'Have a quiet day,' said the male paramedic. And with that I was off to clean up, as I was covered up to the middle of my thighs in mud. I had a rapid shower and changed into some fresh, warm clothes. It wasn't fashionable, but it was certainly OK in Orkney to dress very unconventionally as a doctor, compared with other parts of the British Isles. There was no dress code, and I hadn't seen a doctor in a tie in two months.

Wrong … the Australian always sported one.

The rest of the day at the practice was quiet, so I took the opportunity to take my second letter to the editors of the Orcadian and Orkney Today. They were both receptive, and I liked them both, but John Scott at Orkney Today was particularly happy that the last letter had been published.

He was an enthused man and opened by saying, 'You've won the Letter of the Month award, which is a watch,' I liked his enthusiasm and his genuine smile.

'What! Really?'

'Can we present the watch to you at three tomorrow?' He smiled with glee.

'Well, yes. Sorry, I'm a bit surprised. I wasn't expecting this. It was just a letter.'

'You can never tell what's going to happen next on these islands.' I think he was the most cheerful Orcadian I had met so far. I could tell he was planning something a bit more long range than just my letter, but I didn't ask him. I didn't want to get any more involved than I had already done in local politics, as I would out of there in a few days. However, I sensed there was something cheerful and optimistic about his response to my letter, but I wasn't quite sure what it was.

'I have to agree. There's nothing boring about this place at all.'

'If we present the watch to you and take a photograph, the newspaper can use it in the first week of January to keep the story alive. Not that the story will be dead, but it will just stoke up the fires a little.'

'Sounds fine with me, because things really need to move on here.'

I also dropped in to meet John Ferguson, who had interviewed me for BBC Radio Scotland. He suggested I call the Chief Executive, for, he said, he needed allies. I called but got an answer machine. No response came. They must have been extremely angry with me.

I believed I had done enough, and it was time again to move on. I thought I had seen the bigger picture of what was going on in the health system in Orkney and shown it to Orcadians. It was now nearly time for the locals to see the bigger picture themselves and take up the challenge of changing what they could, if they really wanted to. I felt good about what I had done and I believed that was the end of it.

The rest of the day was the busiest I had had in two months - twelve phone consultations, with six visits ending in six serious admissions, and there was the stop for the man whose dog had saved his life. As well as endless conversations with staff at the practice asking advice about everything from cats, sheep, cows, car mechanics and computers, they were interested in how I thought things could change in the future for patients and for GPs and their staff. I said that amongst them there were some individuals who were enthusiastic and honest about sorting it out, and so they should trust them.

As I was sorting paperwork out there was only one odd thing. A member of the Health Board's Primary Care Group came and very formally said, 'I have come to say thank you for helping out and covering as a locum today, but we don't need you tomorrow.' This was a planned announcement that she had checked over with someone else.

'Fine. If the person calls in sick let me know.'

'No. We've got someone else, another locum.' She was stern voiced with an unmoving face. The way she was talking, I thought I was being dismissed, and so I was careful.

'And the next day?'

'We won't be requiring your locum services anymore.'

I thought this was really the end, or she was being aggressive in her rather awkward over-formal way of presenting things. There was no informal reassurance that things were ok. So I gave it one more go.

'And what about the evenings?'

'What about them?' She was ice cold, as if dealing with a piece of kit.

'Well, the way you're putting this, it seems to me that you have someone else to do the evenings.'

'What makes you think that?' I thought she was guarded, as if she was on a short lead and could easily pounce given the opportunity.

'Well, you're not saying that I am still doing the evenings.'

'Yes, you are still doing the evening.' The first thought that crossed my mind was that there was clearly a communications problem here. My eyes were even more open than usual, and I knew I had to tread very gently over the next few days and keep my mouth shut. I had just witnessed a display of either extremely poor communication skills or of power in the form of passive aggression. I was really lost as to which it was. I was aware that people in these sorts of committee jobs can usually instantly quote medico-legal acts or health and safety legislation at the first opportunity. So, with difficulty, I withdrew my reaction to our conversation, plucked up the skills of an actor, gave her my best effort at a sincere smile and walked away. I was not drawn in, and I felt happy that I hadn't let her engage me in challenging her. I could see how easy it would have been to give the wrong response to what she said and how she said it.

I can't remember going to sleep that night, it came so fast. I was woken just as quickly just after midnight by a request for a home visit from a person with a dislocated knee. Within an hour I had met the ambulance and borrowed their laughing gas which is a good anesthetic. I whacked his knee cap gently with my hand and the knee was back to normal.

In the morning I watched the BBC Scotland News, and I was relieved not to have appeared on it. Instead, they said that NHS Orkney was considering replacing their island doctors with a flying doctor service backed up on some islands by nurses, as it was costing a million pounds to keep the doctors on the islands. At last I had managed to persuade the Health Board to come out and air their opinion on the subject along the lines I thought were their only alternative to going belly up, such as NHS Argyle and Clyde, who had run a similar locum based service for GPs in remote areas, after facing debts of £100 million.

As the morning news progressed the slot expanded to include the opinions of the Island doctors, who said that bringing in flying doctors would bring in less skilled doctors. I was very pleased they said that, because everyone on the islands and the mainland knew that the opposite is true and that was why the whole debate had arisen.

I had a leisurely day off and spent most of it walking around Kirkwall, looking in the shops. I bumped into a few patients, even the one I had attended to at one in the morning to reduce the dislocated knee. They were now back to normal. I was phoned by the head of Primary Care and told to take my hire car back to the hire car company and downgrade it to a model from the company they have a contract with. This was expected but slightly odd, as they were not interested in a refund. They knew I had paid for the car and would be claiming it back off them, but as they were paying another company as well, with whom they had a contract, they felt obliged to take the more luxurious Ford off me, although it was paid for. I filled the Ford with forty litres of fuel and dropped it around to the dealer I had hired it from.

'I was talking to John Ferguson about what you said on the radio the other day. You are very right about all this. It's time to end it. They have to go or we'll all suffer,' said the car hire manager.

'Thanks for that,' I said. 'It will be worth the effort in the end.'

In the car hire shop, I signed the document and put forty litres of fuel in the blue Peugeot 306 and set off. But one of the rear wheels was completely jammed. The mechanic couldn't unfreeze it, so they ended up having to give me a large Vauxhall, which was more expensive than the Ford which I had already fully paid for and had to give back. This was madness. I put forty litres of fuel in the Vauxhall and went back into the shop to sign for it. I wondered what the Health Authority would say now that I had put 120 litres of fuel in three hire cars in less than an hour. What would they say in retrospect about someone's decision to make me take a smaller car which had to be replaced by a more expensive car? I was only doing as instructed.

As I signed the fuel bill the woman said to me, 'You'd better change the paperwork to the Vauxhall. Someone like you had better have the proper paperwork, so let me change it.'

'I don't understand.'

'I heard you on the radio and read your letter. You won't want to get found or stopped with the wrong paperwork.'

'I suppose not,' I said. 'Is it that bad?'

'Yes.'

'How bad is it?'

'People are falling out over this – families, friends,

other groups of people. There are two sides, and they are at each other's throats. You must feel secure in yourself. Any other doctor or person would be so scared of these people.'

'Thanks for letting me know.'

'Be careful until you go.' I heard this loud and clear.

'They'll try and get me for anything, I suppose. If it's not what I write, it'll be the fuel bill again.'

She laughed as she said, 'I had to deal with the Health Board questioning our fuel bills to them for your fuel consumption of about 198 litres in two weeks. Your letter was so funny. I laughed all afternoon.'

'Thanks. It was fun writing it. Thanks for supporting what I said about fuel consumption. It was busy, and I did see a good bit of Mainland Orkney.' She laughed again and I started laughing. And that is how I left her and went back into the town.

At three I was to meet John Ross Scott and the owner of the only jewellery stop in Kirkwall. I got into the city early and realised I should look smart, as they wanted to take a photograph of me being presented with a watch, which might help their cause. I went to the dry cleaners to ask where I could buy a tie, and they gave me one someone had failed to collect and told me to keep it.

The presentation and photograph was very light-hearted. 'This should keep the dialogue going for a while longer after you've gone,' said John Ross Scott. He was light of heart and good fun, even as he pursued a very serious issue.

'I'm sure it will,' I had to agree.

'Is there anything you'd like to say about receiving the award?'

'Seriously?'

'Yes.'

'Well, I hope this watch is a symbol for the island doctors to bear in mind when they think of how much time they have got left on the islands, because they should stop looking at their diaries and look at their watches.'

'Oh, that's a good one,' said John, smiling.

'But it's true.' We exchanged phone numbers and e-mails, and knew we would most likely be in touch.

In the afternoon I got a call from the Deputy Director of the Health Board in charge of Primary Care.

'We are looking for the paperwork for the patient you saw on Sunday night.'

'I gave one copy to the husband to take to the ward where he was being admitted, and I put one copy on the practice manager's desk the next morning as usual, as she had the day off.' I very much suspected that they were trying to find a fault with me to report me for some error. The gloves were off, and their guns were out.

When I turned the BBC Scotland six o'clock news on, the slot about Orkney flying doctors had got even bigger. This time there was an island doctor and a patient who said he owed his life to this doctor. But then they introduced another doctor who didn't agree with this. Then, to my surprise, I came on and said that it was just a natural thing that doctors' skills decline with time if they haven't got many patients.'

This had been an interesting day, and I knew that when my next letter came out in two days' time I might not be the most popular man in town. I thought about it for a while and then decided not to spend my last night on call staying at the Commodore Apartments, just in case any of these eight doctors might be offended at what I said. I was hoping that I had not created eight assassins hiding independently in the bushes. I would simply stay in the Kirkwall Hotel again and say that I was staying with a friend, if anyone asked. I would book in late so there was less chance of anyone knowing where I was. I would book in under a different name.

The weather changed overnight, and a couple of barking wild dogs unnerved me just a little at around midnight. I woke at about five to gale force wind, like it had been several weeks earlier. The TV said the winds were eighty miles per hour, which meant that they were more likely over a hundred mph in very exposed oceanic places like this. I knew from my limited experience that I would get a better night's sleep in the hotel, so I resigned myself to spending my last two nights in the hotel. Also, this would give me more security from any disgruntled doctors. I packed up my things and was out of the Commodore Apartments, into the car and on my way to Kirkwall.

The next morning at the practice, the GP who was under supervision for unknown reasons and who accosted me every day said, 'You were on the television last night.'

'Yes.'

'Didn't see it myself. It was on the same time as The Simpsons.'

'That's a priority is it?'

'I never ever miss an episode no matter what, pal.'

'Oh well,' I said leaving the communication space open.

'So, were you filmed whilst you were on call last night?'

I guessed where this was coming from and where it was going, so I said, 'No, I recorded it at the weekend when I was off duty.' He was clearly going to communicate this up his own power ladder.

'I've never watched it,' I said.

'What?' he asked.

'This program you call The Simpsons.' And thankfully that made him exit my visual field. Like the old office gossip, who hung around all the time to grasp at any information which might increase his sense of his self-importance, I thought he was best avoided.

As usual, I was supposed to hand over at nine in the morning, but this time there was no one there, not even the doctor who was supposed to take over from me and take all the maps, the tool kit/drug bag, the defibrillator and another bag of junk. At nine thirty one of the secretaries said that the Health Board had booked the wrong doctor to take over from me. He had covered the day before but was now working in the hospital. So there was no one.

I offered to carry on, but she said, 'I wouldn't bother. The weather's bad now, but it's going to get really awful later. I'd stay in and chill out.'

I thought about this for less than a second. 'Do you know, that's really good advice. I can actually have a whole day to myself, and this doesn't come up as a choice for me very often, so I'll take it. Thank you. I'm going to do what you suggested, and I'll be back at six tonight instead of working through the day.'

Back in the car I looked at my watch and realized that it was the 21st - the winter solstice and the shortest day of the year. I had booked in a month ago to be at Maes Howe at 2.00 pm to see the sun go down. You had to book well in advance, because only a small number of people can fit in the space.

I made a reservation at The Kirkwall Hotel in the name of Smith and set off for a leisurely amble around the town and around the northern part of the Rousay Island. I drove to Tingwall Harbor and sat there in the car, looking at the island. I could see the white house I had stayed in for those twelve days. It was in the past now, and I was looking back on it without re-visiting it. It was over with.

There were eighteen people booked in to see the sunset from within the thick walls of Maes Howe. All of us got there about ten minutes early to wait for the guide. There were cameras outside and inside, broadcasting the scenes on the internet. As we waited I heard someone from a group of four people say, 'That doctor doesn't know what he was talking about. It was actually a payment called an Inducement Payment for small practices. They will never replace us with flying doctors.'

Mercifully, my phone rang, and as I answered it I stepped away so that they couldn't hear what I was saying. If they hadn't recognized me from the television, then they probably just saw my name on the list of people on the visit, which I had forgotten about. I was particularly glad that I had put my address down as the Commodore Apartments on the list and that I had already gone underground and moved into a hotel. I had a feeling that it might prove to be a slightly difficult departure from these islands, and I was trying to play it as cautiously as I could. But this was all blown away, not by the wind but by the Maes Howe's staggering physical presence and history.

Maes Howe is probably the same age as the village of Skara Brae at five thousand years old. From the outside you wonder if it's worth paying the entrance fee; it looks like a mound of grass. Nothing could be more surprising. You can only get into it by a low stone passage over thirty feet long. You don't have to go down on your haunches like a Cossack dancer, but you certainly have to bend right over for the thirty-foot walk. As you walk along you are very aware of the solid stone roof just skimming the top of your head. It is made of massive slabs of granite. But there is one immediate thing which, by any engineering standards, is staggering and stops you in your tracks. It is the wall on the left hand side of the passage. It is a single slab of stone over thirty feet long. The passage slopes up, and suddenly you find yourself in what you could call a stone igloo; it is like being in a domed structure, but it is very different.

The chamber is nearly five metres square and nearly seven metres tall. The whole structure is not made of bricks but of horizontal stone slabs which are about eight inches thick, twenty feet long and weighing thirty tons each. You stand there wondering how they moved hundreds of these thirty-ton horizontal slabs. In each corner is a stone buttress flanked by the thirty-ton stone slabs which lap over each other, rising vertically and inwards until they all meet at the top of the ceiling that is nearly seven metres high. There are three very large alcove chambers, one in each wall excepting the wall which has the entrance chamber. Under each entrance lies the stone which originally plugged the entrances. These three stones are roughly two-third metres square but are tapered so that they could be inserted into the entrances to plug them up. If the tomb ever had bones in it, this is almost certainly where they were kept.

Apparently the Vikings came here in the twelfth century hoping to raid it, but it was already empty. They left all sort of runes, which are early graffiti, like 'Benedict made this cross,' or 'Ingigerth is the most beautiful of women.'

The winter solstice sunset was at 2.52 pm but the sun was hidden by a small cloud that day. However, the light was very good. Inside the chamber, the light from the passageway was very impressive - you could read a book by it. I was surprised at how sharp the light seemed to be. Interestingly, I noticed that most of the floor of the passage seemed to collect just a very small depth of water, perhaps two to five millimetres so that the sun bounced all over the walls and ceilings. I wondered if this was part of the planning, as the inside of the rest of the chamber seemed perfectly dry. This might have partly accounted for the quite surprising brightness of the light.

Standing there encased in thirty-foot thick walls under a domed stone ceiling in such natural light felt very unusual. The chamber had not been open many years and had been closed for thousands of years, so only a few people had witnessed this winter solstice from inside the chamber. The Neolithic people must have used the positioning of the passage and light to mark this time of year. Otherwise, why would they go to all the effort? Even today, you wouldn't waste that much energy moving so many tons of rock to form a passage aligned to the sun unless you were actually going to use it.

I wondered how many people used it five thousand years ago and what exactly they did on the winter solstice. Did they worship gods, dance, have sex or even sacrifices, or were they just quietly celebrating the shortest day in anticipation of spring and the renewal of life. It is just too long ago to know, and with the resources we have, the woman at the Tomb of the Eagles was probably right – it will probably be a hundred years or more until technology progresses so that we can gain more knowledge from these ancient sites.

I felt very privileged standing there. I remembered that Christmas was two days away and that the winter solstice used to be a major Pagan festival until Christianity overpowered it. I was acutely aware that I was probably standing in the oldest remaining intact Neolithic structure where a winter solstice festival took place. For those early farmers the end of the longest day must have been a time of great relief, as they could look forward to six to nine months of good weather. I thought about what we had lost in our pursuit of what we regarded as

progress.

I see Paganism as having a great deal of significance in the materialistically turbulent times we seem to be in at the present moment. In particular, it is a significant step in mankind's search for the significance and meaning of life, which organized religions have failed to successfully provide. Destruction of the druids began with the Romans and has continued since, largely by the Christian church. In replacing Paganism with Christianity, the Christian church was opportune in seizing dates of Pagan festivals for their own use. They not only seized the major festival dates, but also Pagan symbols and rituals.

If we want to see what spirituality is, fundamentally, then it is worth looking at Paganism, because Paganism has been around longer than any of the official religions of the last four thousand years. It is very likely many thousands of years older. However old Paganism proves to be, it is important to help us understand the meaning of life, because it consists of the core elements of spirituality which later religions borrowed for their own use. Spirituality refers to the "ultimate reality" of a person's inner path, which consists of the deepest values by which they live and feel connected to others, the wider world and the Universe. Traditionally, spiritual experience was part of religious experience, but this is not necessarily the case anymore because of the recent decline of organized religions which rely on doctrinal faith and ritual.

Pagans essentially worshipped nature and, in particular, the Sun and the Earth. Rather like Aboriginals, they believed that certain types of places, like hills and rivers, have spirits. We know that fire was first used as long ago as 957,000 AD. Ancient Celtic Pagans had four fire festivals a year, which are still celebrated. Modern Pagans have accumulated

253

more festivals from Norse and Germanic Pagans and have incorporated these into eight major festivals each year. These eight festivals celebrate the passage of a year, or what is known in paganism as the 'Wheel of Life'.

The word pagan originally meant 'country dweller', and the original Celtic Pagans spread over Europe around five thousand years ago. The winter solstice was probably celebrated long before the Celts' migration. Paganism as a religion almost certainly predates any other religion. The male pagan God dies at Samhain (Halloween) which is the Pagan New Year's Day, but he is reborn as Yule to a Virgin Goddess at the winter solstice, where he is seen as the newborn solstice sun. Only then does the sun begin to return on this darkest night of the year to bring light and warmth, and fertilise Mother Earth so that she is full of life once again. This was represented by having lights around the house and on trees.

Interestingly, Christianity has borrowed many Pagan traditions. At the time when Christianity began, it was not unusual for religions around the Mediterranean to combine beliefs from different traditions. The practice of having a festival where lights are placed around the house and on trees has been borrowed from Pagans by Christianity with its Christmas lights and lights on Christmas trees.

The Christian idea of Mary the Virgin being the mother of God is borrowed from the Pagan idea of the male god dying at Samhain and being reborn to a virgin goddess as Yule on the Winter Solstice. It is a Norse tradition that the winter solstice is a twelve-day celebration, and it is not by chance that we have the popular song The Twelve Days of Christmas. In ancient Egypt the winter solstice was the time when the rebirth of their male Sun God was celebrated, and it marked the beginning of the rainy season. In Norse, Yule actually means 'wheel', and

wreaths, which many put on their front doors, are older than the four thousand year old pre-Christian symbols of The Wheel of the Year, which represents the annual cycle of the Earth's seasons. Apart from the Pagan importance of mistletoe, natural materials like holly, ivy and pine cones which are used to make Christmas decorations are all based on the Pagan wreath. These decorate Christian homes now and decorated Pagan altars in ancient times.

The tradition of giving presents at Christmas comes from Roman Pagans who worshipped Saturn. They gave presents to honour all those who had died that year. Decorating an evergreen tree was an old Pagan tradition. Celtic druids adorned the tree with symbols of things they wanted in the coming year. Hence, their evergreen trees had candles for warmth and light; coins for wealth; and symbols of fertility, such as nuts, which are still used to decorate modern Christmas trees. The song Jingle Bells comes from the use by the Norse of bells on sleighs to frighten off evil spirits at Yule. Lastly the Yule log was traditionally a Celtic symbol of Yule. The log was cut from an oak tree and brought inside. People danced around it and then burnt in the fire. This later became a log with three candles, symbols of fire, inserted into it.

Ten minutes after sunset, although the other seventeen paying guests stayed on to look at the light projected on to the wall, I decided to leave, as there was no more to see, and I was beginning to feel the cold air on the inside of my jacket.

I would probably be permitted to come back to these islands to work, but I don't think it would be wise for me, given my reputation, simply because my stay there would keep on coming up to haunt me. It was time to think about the next job after a holiday in the first two weeks of January. Nothing leaped to the front of my mind. I had had enough excitement and had already asked the locum agency to look out for something simple, dull and boring. I knew, of course, that was unlikely to happen, and I would probably end up somewhere very odd indeed.

I suppose it is the administrators that created the problems. Of course, they had to know about health and safety regulations and various laws, British and European, but why did they have to confine themselves to rationality and forget the human side of things? Healthcare is all about being human, and the ever rising tide of officiousness needed to be stemmed. Perhaps the local doctors in the Orkneys had merely taken advantage of this businesslike approach to make money. The Health Board needed to be sacked and replaced with people who looked at things from the patient's perspective, and not just in legal terms of cover. Why pay doctors to be on islands if the locals don't use them?

This problem should have been sorted out a long time ago. But how do you get rid of administrators, who have made the regulations that make it nearly impossible, and very expensive, to get rid of them, without either going to court or paying them off with outrageous sums of money. One thing is certain: these administrators look after themselves better than the patients they are supposed to be serving. And where do you find people who have a human touch? I was lost for an answer.

I had walked into this problem, which was not mine, but I could not simply ignore it. I would not like to look back and know I had said nothing, done nothing and contributed nothing.

I had no calls that night; and I rested and enjoyed the comforts of the Kirkwall Hotel. It is a really good hotel, and I assumed that they were ahead of their time, like other Northern hotels, in the awareness of the need to conserve energy by cutting down on gas emissions, in an effort to save the planet. I noticed that the heating was switched off at around eleven at night. I was up at five, and the heating didn't come on until six, and this meant a cold shower in a very cold room. However, I felt satisfaction that I had contributed in some small way, to saving energy and counterbalancing our wasteful lives. In our current ecological crisis, to openly display your ability to endure financial wastage is just as wrong as an adult dropping litter, because somebody else has to use a lot more energy to pick it up.

From my chilly room, I had a good view of the harbour, and I could see what I thought was the distant ferry to North Ronaldsay, which would arrive there three hours later at eight.

It was my last day in Orkney, my last night on call, and I had a blank day ahead of me to recharge my batteries for the next day's flights down south. I was interested in any replies to my letter in the paper last week, and to see whether they would print my second letter, but if there were none and they didn't follow up with my second letter, as the Orcadians say, 'No bother.' I would still be happy with the response from the Health Board and the public.

Over breakfast I talked with the waiter, who had lost his wife just before Christmas two years ago. He and his wife had come up here to live, because she was from Mainland Orkney. When she died, he continued to live here, as he had a mother-in-law and two brothers-in-law, but no other relatives anywhere else, and so it was home. He talked about how kids were being misled by the Government and how the values in Orkney were different from those down south. He reiterated what I had heard many times, which was that Orkney is a great place to bring up children. I agreed with that, but I still thought that there were two drawbacks. The first is that it was three flights and a journey of least five hours to go anywhere south. The second is that most children would eventually want to leave and experience life down south, which means they would be a very long way away.

The waiter was cheerful despite the recent anniversary of his loss. 'I now know one thing about loss. Life goes on. You think it won't, but it does. Where she has gone, I must follow. She would want me to be happy and still telling the odd joke, so I carry on with life as cheerfully as I can.' He was still grieving but in a healthy way.

After breakfast, I walked down Main Street to get The Orcadian which is published on a Thursday. I was surprised to see that Orkney Today was also available, probably because it was Christmas week. I picked up one copy of each and handed them to the woman behind the counter. I was handing her my money when I saw my picture on the front page. I quickly flipped the paper over so the back page was facing upwards. I didn't want her or anyone to say 'Is that you?' I was trying to keep a low profile and leave, not just the shop but the job and the islands, without being recognized.

When I got back to the hotel room, I looked at the two papers which had both printed my letter. The Orcadian had an amusing letter from the wife an isle GP, saying that she was fairly sure she was not living with a monkey even though he was currently in a Christmas pantomime. She had taken my quote, 'If you pay peanuts you get monkeys,' literally, and I suppose it was a bit sad really. Both papers had an article about my letter, and Orkney Today dedicated its editorial to the letter's topics. I decided that I should write one last letter before leaving, most likely, if not certainly, for good. I wrote it to try and show these rather special people that, even though they were geographically isolated, they did not have to simply accept that they had to be isolated from modern medical standards, which everyone else in the UK expected and had been receiving.

John Ross Scott
Editor, Orkney Today Limited
Unit 1, Kiln Corner
Kirkwall KW15 1QX
Orkney

Thursday 29 December, 2005

Sub: Gypsies would make the health service run more smoothly

Sir,
During my very happy stay on your islands, I have aimed at trying to get the Health Board, the patients and, with considerably more difficulty, the doctors to become aware that by now that you should really have had a much better healthcare system in place.

When you are able to put all of your personal and emotional attachments aside, you will see that you do have serious problems, as every healthcare system does. However, you may not be fully aware of them nor, because of your isolation, of what nearly everyone else is already enjoying in the NHS in most of the British Isles. Let me show you.

In most of the UK, each area has GPs who are known as Gypsies, but spelt GPSIs. This acronym stands for General Practitioners with Special Interests. They enable the whole system to tick over and run smoothly, and also save the NHS millions of pounds each month. GPSIs are regular practicing GPs who have also spent years training in another specialty as well. They have been accredited with specialist status by the Royal Colleges and are subject to governance, review and audit. They specialize in some field, such as Pediatrics, Care of the Elderly, Diabetes, Cardiology, Obstetrics & Gynecology, Orthopaedics, Psychological Medicine, Dermatology, Ear Nose and Throat, Ophthalmology, Gastrointestinal Medicine, Respiratory Medicine, Nephrology, Hepatology and other fields.

These women and men GPSIs, who spend three to four days working as regular GPs, also spend one day a week seeing patients who have problems within their specialty. Nearly all the patients they see are referred by other GPs. This system has been in place for a long time in the UK and is a standard way of referring patients to a specialist these days.

With GPSIs, the waiting list to see a specialist is reduced from three to six months down to one to three weeks. Patients don't have to travel to see the specialist in a distant hospital, because GPSIs usually work within a General Practice setting, and they will sometimes work in a different practice each week as a specialist to save patients having to travel. Imagine the convenience of not having to ferry specialists and patients to and from Aberdeen, and also the savings. GPSIs can also provide expert backup to hospital patients, when cross referrals are made to other specialties, when a patient has more than one illness, a practice which is always welcomed by hospital doctors.

The formal framework for GPSIs is going to be presented to your GPs over the coming months by the Department of Post Graduate General Practice Education in Aberdeen; and in your current state of crisis, it would not be seen as opportunistic to start recruiting only GPSIs now from elsewhere in the UK. It is much less expensive to poach already accredited GPSIs than to spend years training them. One or two of your current mainland GPs already fit nearly all of the criteria.

Flying doctors or not, locums or not, this is where you really should be going, now, not in the future. If you aim for this now and *adopt the mantra of the best fighter pilots, 'Keep the main aim the main aim,' you can achieve this within months, be on a par with the rest of the UK and be part of setting some of the highest standards of healthcare. Recruiting GPSIs now would be perceived as having foresight, being futuristic and being a leading light in Scotland.*

How do you do it? Get the Chief Executive and the Health Board to say 'yes' to this and advertise for GPSIs. It's not difficult or complicated. This is where the Scottish Executive would wholeheartedly back you. They would almost certainly bend over backwards to bring GPSIs to Orkney.

Yours sincerely,

There were no calls during the whole shift, and I started the day refreshed and keen to leave Orkney. I dropped the medical gear at the surgery and then gave the letter to John Ross Scott and bade him farewell. He asked me to keep an eye on my e-mail; he would mail me any interesting replies when I was away in Spain with the family for a short break.

John Ross Scott was not only genuinely interested in improving the community's health care system, but he had a wonderful sense of humour about the community. In tandem with his award winning career as a journalist, he had been a spokesman for the Scottish Liberal Democrats and leader of the Scottish Borders Council. I agreed I would look at my e-mails and said that I hadn't had time to give the article to The Orcadian. I said I would be in touch if I felt I could help further in any way.

Soon I was back at the Commodore Apartments, and I said farewell to Richard and Louise and then checked my luggage in at the airport. I had the car and I was free, but I was toured out in terms of sightseeing. I spent the morning buying stocking fillers for India's Christmas stocking and then went to the airport, as there really was nothing else to do. The job was done.

When I had arrived in Orkney I had no intention of doing anything other than my job as a doctor ... well, perhaps also seeing the people, the islands and the sights. I didn't anticipate the things I would see or the experiences I would have, both as a person and as a doctor. I didn't come here to write about these, but I felt better for having done so. Most of my interactions with people showed me that Orcadians are very relaxed, and have genuine, friendly smiles, not just polite smiles. They will stop you and want to talk and listen to you. They are a very warm reminder that it is so easy to have a good quality life. I knew I could fly away later that day with a happy heart, a clear mind and a sense of completeness that I had done my job happily. I couldn't have wanted more than this.

Postscript. January

Just before leaving Orkney, I had begun a year-long subscription to The Orcadian and Orkney Today... just to keep my eye on them! I seriously cared about what was going to happen to them as as result of my being there. I felt responsible. Taking such distant, local papers was partly out of interest in the local community and partly to see if, with time, Orcadians would take on board any of the changes I had suggested to them. I really wasn't sure.

On my return home from a short break in Spain, I opened a copy of Orkney Today. In its last edition of the year there had been a couple of negative responses to my first two letters. I thought these attacks on a visitor were a shame, because my letters were tongue-in-cheek and were meant to stimulate Orcadians' thinking. However, there were two pleasant surprises. There was a photograph of John Ross Scott giving me the present of a watch - so that the matter would not be forgotten - and he had printed my third letter, to which there was not yet a response.

I decided to write, not a fourth letter to him but reply to a letter written by an elderly retired GP who used to do some locum work on the islands. This GP had quite rightly questioned the integrity of doctors on the Isles and said that it is not ideal to have GPs as community leaders; it was not necessarily the best choice for people on the islands. I thought I would give it just a little while before I decided whether to send my response or not. However, sometimes putting your thoughts on paper clarifies things, and it took me only about two paragraphs to make me decide to send it. This, I thought, would be my last contribution to Orcadian life.

John Ross Scott
Editor, Orkney Today Limited
Unit 1, Kiln Corner
Kirkwall KW15 1QX
Orkney

Thursday 19 January, 2006

Sub: Doctors as leaders

Sir,

I would like to reply to a letter of 2nd December, 2005, from Dr Olaf Cuthbert, a GP who, like myself, had many years of experience in General Practice before doing locum work in Orkney.

Dr Cuthbert raised an important point about island doctors acting as leaders of the community in which they live and work. Like myself, he seems to have some rather grave doubts about GPs being the best choice as leaders on the islands.

On an Orkney island where I recently worked I was slightly aghast to discover that the local GP was also chairman of the local Community Council for that island. I was greatly saddened to hear from many patients on the islands that they frequently feel intimidated and overshadowed by these very powerful Island doctors. I listened time and time again to reports from patients about doctors who appeared to become agitated when patients normal questions regarding medication or treatment plans. These days, in the rest of the UK, patients are actively encouraged by GPs to be involved and discuss management plans. Many of the patients asked me if these older doctors had any psychological training, because they found these GPs very difficult to get on with.

Doctors are often the highest earners in these small communities, which of course can create a 'them and us' situation, *where patients may often feel inferior. But the fact is that island doctors often get over-involved in other, non-medical, duties, such as lifeboats, firefighting, crofting, council activities and trades, which can deprive native islanders the chance to run their own communities and profit from them, thus remaining autonomous and, therefore, able to survive.*

In a small, and dwindling, population, a doctor who is also a community leader is, by occupying leadership positions, preventing native members of the community from being appointed to such positions and benefiting financially from the appointment, and also disouraging native involvement in local affairs. This works against the islands' future security and survival.

The above facts may go a long way to explain just why, on these particular islands, so many of the patients see doctors on Mainland Orkney.

Perhaps you should challenge your Health Board to not only reveal the number of patients on each island, as they have already done, but also to reveal the exact numbers and percentage of patients on each island who choose to use the Mainland GP services instead of their local GP.

Orkney Today, in highlighting such anomalies, will do the islands' inhabitants a massive favour in initiating a change, and also put Orkney first by serving the whole community of Orkney and its future.

I would like to make one last, small, positive comment. Rather than criticizing a visitor, such as me, and appearing to be defensive and negative, a small minority of your readers, and most particularly your doctors, may like to look into themselves and ask just what they are going to do about the situation I have laboured to highlight. This is especially urgent on these islands, which are slowly depopulating and on the decline.

These are your islands, and you are in a position to secure their future. So get on and help these people as you're supposed to, and accept change. And don't shoot the messenger.

Yours sincerely,

But just as I was about to send it I received an e-mail from John Ross Scott.

Doc,

I hope you are well. Here is my latest story on the GP situation in Orkney (an exclusive):

GP Number In Orkney Could Be Cut To Ten.

SECRET plans are in place to reduce the number of doctors serving Orkney to ten. Orkney Today can exclusively reveal that, in a bid to reduce the amount of money spent on locum GPs and balance its budget, NHS Orkney aims to urge each local GP to take a patient roll of 1200. The proposals form part of the emergency measures worked up by health chiefs and sold to the Scottish Executive as a means of curbing escalating costs.

A private internal consultation document, leaked to Orkney Today, states that at present there are 14 GP practices in Orkney, with an average list size of 776. Eight doctors currently operate as single-handed practitioners, while Westray and Shapinsay are each covered by three part-time GPs. Plans suggest that a change is required in areas where GPs serve on their own, and a more flexible approach introduced so that GPs in their spare time can cover the absences of other GPs or as GPs with special interests (GPwSPs), and contribute to GP led services across the country. As reported recently in Orkney Today, single-practice GPs have also been granted 17 weeks leave each year on grounds that they undertake their own out-of-hours cover.

This has resulted in a bill of £994,000 for locum GPs in Orkney in the last year alone.

Acknowledging on Tuesday that the plans are part of the money saving measure, NHS Orkney Chief Executive, Steve Conway, said, "By working in a different way, and getting Isles doctors with low patient rolls to free up a bit of their day to provide medical cover to other parts of Orkney, we could greatly reduce the need for locums. We estimate that as much as £500,000 could be saved through cutting out locum costs involved in the 17-week leave pattern, although some of that would have to go back to the GPs undertaking additional duties." He added: "It is our aspiration to establish patient list sizes to the national average of 1200 per doctor. When you get to that figure, practices become sustainable and don't need additional funding. It would mean that all GPs would have balanced, if fairly full, workloads which is the way we would like it to be"

At present GPs' workloads vary, with recent figures showing practice sizes ranging from 5,901 at Scapa, 4,443 at Skerrymore and 2,956 at Stromness, to 371 in Stronsay, 300 in Shapinsay, 256 in Rousay, 123 in Eday and only 57 in North Ronaldsay.

The internal consultation paper also stipulates that more use be made of tele-medicine facilities, with a new link provided to Flotta, and that Primary Care teams of visiting consultants, nurses with extended skills and GPs with special interests be established. NHS Orkney has also given a commitment to provide transport links, where existing services do not exist, to enable the workforce to travel to remote locations. It adds: "If successful, this could largely negate the need for further resident practitioners in the smaller communities, but will have to be flexible to cater for adverse weather and sea states."

Prescribing is also listed for savings, with plans to make up repeat prescriptions in Mainland Orkney for transportation to the Isles. Following on from last month's story in Orkney Today, which revealed that Isles doctors were undertaking their own locum work, it *is hoped that Isles GPs will share locum work in future, and Mainland doctors will not be expected to provide their own out-of-hours service. In future, the internal document states, an opt-out on out-of-hours could be possible also in the isles, when multi-professional teams have been developed. Isles Community Nurses have already, over recent months, been trained in BASICS standard for emergency care. Mr. Conway also confirmed this week that, although the GPs in Rousay, Eday, North Ronaldsay, Stronsay, Hoy and Eday were still without contracts, their employment would not be terminated. Negotiations to draw up new contracts with the GPs involved were continuing.*

I was proud that this newspaper editor had genuinely acted on behalf of the people, and that he had managed to get them to change things and start to move forwards. I sent John a note.

Hi John,

Thanks for the latest lead story. It was very much appreciated. I think you've done a great job by keeping the change process going, and it's a really important contribution to the Orkney community.

Hope all is well with you.

Best Wishes,

After this, it all went very quiet for nearly six months whilst I continued my locum work in the south-west of England, happily uninterrupted. Each edition of Orkney Today and The Orcadian I read was strangely dull, as the issues of the Outer Isles doctors and their expensive presence on the isles seemed to have been forgotten … that is, until on the 25th of

May, when I noticed that there was a short, unusual letter in Orkney Today. It concerned not only a locum Outer Isles GP, but it was written by the member of a lifeboat crew about how, in one of the worst cases of the bends they had seen in a diver, the locum GP had managed to save this person's life. I was surprised and knew that this was almost certainly not the case, but merely a chance to say how valuable Outer Isles GPs were to the local communities. My reply was of course tongue-in-cheek and as follows.

John Ross Scott
Editor, Orkney Today Limited
Unit 1, Kiln Corner
Kirkwall KW15 1QX
Orkney

Thursday 1 June, 2006

Sub: Replace the outer isles GPs with physician assistants.

Sir,

It was with great pleasure that I read the letter from the crew of the Longhope lifeboat, who, together with a locum GP, managed to successfully transport a critically ill diver on his way to Houton.

The reporting of this incident may not at first seem unusual, but it is, for it is neither insignificant nor just simple hagiography. It was, of course, particularly interesting to learn that the GP involved was a genuine locum GP and not an Outer Isles GP doing his own locum. This is encouraging, and I hope this incident reflects that the local GPs are not doing their own locums anymore.

I was especially pleased because the letter from the Longhope lifeboat crew seemed to indicate that there is still a lively interest in the issues regarding the continued presence of resident doctors on the Outer Isles. To take this a little further, if the presence of the Outer Isles doctors needs to be continually justified by public medical anecdotes, then this is worrying, because this certainly isn't how the existence of GPs is justified in the rest of the British Isles.

Most British GPs would be highly embarrassed if, every time they successfully treated a critically ill patient, it was made public. To permit this, these Outer Isles doctors must be acutely aware that their presence on the Isles is very questionable and is probably coming to an end. I can't believe that they would allow the use of these tactics to simply massage their egos in public.

Professionally, I have recently lived and worked on several of your Outer Isles as a GP, so I have direct privileged knowledge and experience of some of these archaic systems. When I relate the workload of the Outer Isles doctors and the number of patients they have on their lists to medical colleagues, I always receive comments indicating that in these dark times of the NHS, this is only an outrageous waste of precious resources, but also an unnecessary, selfish luxury. Of dozens of GPs I have spoken with, every single one says the Outer Isles GPs should be replaced with a more modern service.

If Orkney wants to bring itself up to date and in keeping with modern medical thinking and modern medical practice, it might want to take a look at what other parts of the British Isles are doing to improve their services to deliver the best, cost effective primary medical care. For example, in Weston-Super-Mare three GPs have recently returned from the USA after having interviewed and recruited eight Physician Assistants. These will be working in GP surgeries, performing almost all GP functions and, of course, much more economically. Would Orcadians welcome American Physician Assistants? I hope so.

I sincerely hope that this information helps to enlighten Orcadians further, so that you can join the rest of us in striving to *continually update and improve primary medical care in the British Isles.*

Finally, as I am sure your lifeboat crews know, the only known medical treatment for Caisson Disease, also known as decompression sickness or the bends, is immediate recompression in a high pressure oxygen chamber. Rapid transport to a recompression chamber is absolutely paramount, and so, by rapidly getting the diver to Houton, the lifeboat crew actually needs to take the credit, which it has misplaced onto the locum GP, as nothing else but speed could have helped this man. Any delay in getting to a recompression chamber, such as waiting for a GP, who in these circumstances would be useless anyway, would have been brought to your attention by the coroner if the outcome was less fortunate, and this could have resulted in disciplinary action, compulsory re-training and possibly expensive litigation for the Longhope lifeboat crew.

Yours sincerely,

The letter was published in Orkney Today but the front page lead article was titled "Nurses To Fill In For Absent Island GPs". It was all about how NHS Orkney announced that locums were no longer going to be used for a lot of the islands. This clearly implied that if nurses could stand in for GPs then they could eventually replace them.

I thought this was a mere coincidence, until a couple of weeks later, whilst reading a medical weekly newspaper for GPs called PULSE, I couldn't help noticing a small but significant article which mentioned that Scottish Executive officials had been flown to America to recruit Physician Assistants. Curiously, the article said that these assistants would be working in the Western Isles, Lanarkshire, Grampian, Highlands, Lothian and Tayside areas, but Orkney was not mentioned. I had not spoken to anyone from NHS Orkney or to anyone from the Scottish Executive, so I could take no credit for this, nor did I want to, but I did have a moment smiling to myself about how change sometimes happens.

I sat back, continued doing my locum work in South Gloucestershire and waited for another backlash against me from Orcadians. And sure enough it came in the form of several letters from GPs, saying I had over-stepped the mark this time and gone too far. I couldn't take this personally and didn't want to bother engaging in a bun fight. But I nevertheless felt inclined to repeat the whistle blowing I had done on them some months before, and so I wrote another, final, letter.

John Ross Scott
Editor, Orkney Today Limited
Unit 1, Kiln Corner
Kirkwall KW15 1QX
Orkney

Thursday 10 June, 2006

Sub: Honesty from GPs must be a priority

Dear John,
It was with great pleasure that I read that NHS Orkney was able to balance its budget and realise nearly £2 million. Congratulations are in order. Obviously, like everyone else in the UK, NHS Orkney will need to continue to find more ways of making similar savings in the coming year, and I wish them every success in this difficult task.
With this in mind, if, in trying to improve health care delivery, journalists and doctors find that their integrity is being questioned, it becomes quite a serious matter. Journalists and doctors still have

a duty to report important facts which can result in enquiry and change. Freedom of speech is paramount to change and development, even if it is sometimes done without taking sides, or in tongue-in-cheek manner.

Last year, when I worked in Orkney, there were so many weekly reports of amusing anomalies, such as GPs working under supervision, GPs being investigated by the General Medical Council, and heroin was mentioned in one case. The Health Board was even being investigated by the police. Local GPs were doing their own locums, and locum GPs were coming from Southampton and even Australia to dip into the unusually high locum salaries being paid by NHS Orkney; and it was jolly unusual.

There are, however, two other factual anomalies about NHS Orkney which are unique in the British Isles. Both concern the Outer Isles doctors, and I am duty bound to report these. But let me first say why. Being painfully truthful is actively encouraged throughout the NHS as a form of self and peer appraisal, as well as an informal method of regulation. Fundamentally, all doctors have a duty to protect patients, and I would encourage the Outer Isles doctors to think long and hard about what I am about to say, as I have done.

Whilst NHS Orkney, along with the rest of the UK, are trying to help people by spending millions of pounds on smoking cessation clinics and providing expensive nicotine replacement therapy and expensive drugs to help smokers to stop smoking, I find it almost unbelievable that at least one Outer Isles doctor is allowed to sell tobacco and cigarettes to his patients in bulk for profit. This is not only improper but an abuse of a doctor's privileged position on these Isles, because he is actually working against the very basic principles of the provision of medical care which NHS Orkney pays him to provide.

In carrying on this activity, the Outer Isles doctor is certainly not upholding the duties of doctors registered with the General

Medical Council. The GMC clearly states that, because patients must be able to trust doctors with their lives and wellbeing, doctors have to respect human life. The duties of doctors described by the GMC begin with, "As a doctor you must make the care of your patient your first concern." The last two of the fourteen duties are, "As a doctor you must avoid abusing your position as a doctor, and you must work with colleagues in the ways that best serve patients interests." I find it very hard to believe that the Outer Isles doctors honour this, especially if they collude with medical colleagues in selling tobacco and cigarettes to patients for profit. They may have to question their soundness and whether or not they are actually upholding moral principles, which is the simplest definition of integrity.

The second bizarre anomaly of Orcadians, which is unique in the UK, concerns the fact that a significant number of patients from the Outer Isles are able to have regular routine primary medical care from GPs on Mainland Orkney. In the rest of the UK, patients who live in one area are not allowed to regularly use the primary medical services in another area simply out of choice, unless they are temporary residents. It is obviously more expensive for the NHS, as the patients are using services meant for others and not the local services which are being provided for them by NHS Orkney.

Therefore, without at all questioning why patients do not want to use the Outer Isles GP services, would all of the Mainland Orkney GPs who are colluding in providing "duplicate care" to Outer Isles patients please come clean about this matter; be honest, put everyone out of their misery and let everyone know exactly how many people are being seen this way, so that NHS Orkney can rationalize this and improve its delivery of services. A little honesty may help to restore some integrity to the GPs in the Outer Isles and indeed in all of Orkney.

If integrity is the yardstick by which we will all be judged, then the Outer Isles doctors and Mainland Orkney GPs may need *to think about these matters and consider making some very basic adjustments before they are forced to do so by outside agencies.*

Yours sincerely,

Once again there was a rather caustic reply, criticizing me. Sadly, there was no reflective thinking about what I had said, so I decided to let it all rest again and see what the papers announced next. I also knew I probably had another long wait.

In February we moved to South Gloucestershire in the west of England, just north of Bristol. A couple of weeks after arriving, I wrote to twenty-five practices in the area. The only replies which I received, offered shocking rates of pay and archaic hours. The work was from 8.30 am until 10.30 am and then from 4.30 pm until 6.30 pm. This would have meant a six-hour gap in the day, with no possibility of doing any other work. The drive to and from work sites was thirty to forty-five minutes each way, which would have meant two to three hours in the car every day, or just hanging around. It dawned on me that British locum GPs were working abnormal hours unlike everyone else.

What I really mean is that the way they work is almost bound to cause inner conflict, because British GPs can't simply just go and do a job with an ordinary lunch break. Instead, they have to do fill a two- to six-hour unpaid stretch of time in the middle of the day. Most people would not agree to this way of life.

I did fourteen locums in thirty-one days, and I also did the out-of-hours evening shifts from seven to eleven from a building in the Old Market of Bristol, which is the red light district. Anyone visiting would be given instructions to turn left at the large converted pub, which was a very busy lap dancing club. The advertising on the outside walls left little to the imagination. However, problems often arose here, because there were about fifteen lap dancing clubs in the Old Market, so patients would ring back and ask which lap dancing club we meant. Bristol is an earthy city with busy docks and all the services that this requires, including doctors working in the red light district.

So Orkney was not as bad as I thought. However, there was not a ripple of thought about going back there to work. Maybe, if there are new findings of ancient things, I would go back to look, but not to work. It is a loss to live in Britain and not visit those isles and islands at least once.

The effectiveness of the organization and delivery of medical care in Orkney has vastly improved since I was there, thanks largely to the insight and courage of one man - John Ross Scott; former editor of Orkney Today, and now Chairman of NHS Orkney. General Practice in North Ronaldsay was taken over by a GP who works on Mainland Orkney and only visits North Ronaldsay.

Hours, months and years passed, and I noticed that my time in Orkney had quietly re-stimulated in me an enquiry which took me on many other journeys. One of these was an archaeological dig. This dig, just like the mystery of the archaeology of Orkney, was full of inconclusiveness, and it left me wondering about the past. If we understood time and space better, it could just as well be yesterday or right now. There was that unifying sense in Orkney which I sensed acutely on this archaeological dig. It was a sense of stillness, of silence. It is raw spirituality. The place had an eeriness to it, just like Uluru, which when listened to seems more like an inner demand for solemnity. There was something overwhelmingly unearthly there.

Just like Uluru, it had a clear sense of the past and particularly of the ancient ancestors, mine as well. The only place I had ever been before where the sense of my ancestors and my own inevitable fate was so amplified was in India. It reminded me almost exactly of the power of the Red Hill in South India where we had lived for several months.

The time in Orkney was the catalyst which made me rip away the final shreds of religious and spiritual conditioning which is forced upon us. Since the existence of human consciousness, in searching for happiness mankind has probably always wondered and tried to understand the meaning of human life. This has been man's search to understand himself, his soul, the atman, the Self. It is the search to understand himself in relation to what he regards as the sacred. Why he looked, how he looked, where he looked and what he found over many millennia may have seemed like progress, but modern archaeology and psychology indicate that he might actually have been indulging in several millennia of delusional searching and belief.

The sense I had in Orkney was acutely brought back to me during an archaeological dig on Salisbury Plain. The site was East Chisenbury Midden, a massive five hectare, 2,700 year old, three-metre deep Feast Midden (rubbish tip) which was formed at the cusp of the end of the Bronze Age and the beginning of the Iron Age, over a period of between eighty and a hundred years. The reason for their feasting on a massive scale remains unknown, but it is estimated that, because of the large size of the site, a large proportion of the population of Southern Britain would have participated over that period of time.

Standing at the centre of the 2,700 year old Feast Midden, I was aware of the old warriors buried in the barrow type graves I could see in the distance on Salisbury Plain. At the same time I was aware that I was at the very centre of a massive circular area a few miles in circumference. Geographically, it was exactly as though I was at the centre of a giant saucer, because all of the hills around the site were slightly higher and looked down on this area that was about the size of a sports pitch. On the ground around me were thousands of pieces of broken pottery and large animal bones which had been dug up by a colony of badgers. A small, three-metre bore hole under my feet revealed thousands of pieces of bone and pottery.

Whilst wondering what this had all been about I felt very privileged to be there, and I felt in awe of what had gone on here. We don't know why around 2,700 years ago the culture of feasting went on for eighty years, but what we do know is that 2,600 years ago, during the hundred-year period at the end of that, many of the most profound forms of spirituality were born simultaneously around the world.

I was doing a research project to see if an archaeological dig could help early returned soldiers from Afghanistan with their psychological decompression. These were modern day warriors excavating the feasting ground of their forefathers. Poignantly their sense of time was given a heightened experience because they were the first to see the fingerprints of the potters on 2,700-year old pottery which they unearthed with their own hands.

During these one hundred years, the Buddha and Mahavir were alive in India, whilst Confucius and Lao Tsu were in China. The Ancient Greek civilisation was finished whilst the new Roman Republic was taking over from the Pagans; and Zoroaster was most likely beginning his work in Persia. This means that over this period Buddhism, Jainism, Confucianism, Taoism and Zoroastrianism all came into being. This is too unlikely to be just coincidence. The world must have been particularly ripe for the development of spirituality. How had the different civilisations arrived at this need at the same time?

Recent findings in a temple complex in Southern Turkey, known as Gobekli Tepe, have confirmed that the temple and religion there were established by hunter gatherers. The huge complex of Gobekli Tepe is 11,600 years old, and it appears to be the world's oldest temple. Before man was civilised, before he developed language, he built an ornate temple with eighteen-foot tall pillars covered with carvings of dangerous creatures, such as scorpions, wild boars and lions. This tall temple was built skywards, in keeping with the basic architecture of almost all buildings to heavenly deities. Why would a group of hunter gatherers portray these wild animals, that lived in the dangerous land beyond the safety of the campfire, in a temple reaching for the sky? Maybe in gaining mastery over the known world, including these animals, man turned his attention elsewhere in search of something more profound. Maybe he had a sense that there was something more important than himself, "the sacred", and this was a way of worshiping it. Perhaps he saw these dangerous animals as guardians of the primitive spirit world, and to outwardly respect them in a temple might gain favor with the sacred. We may not know until archaeology has given up more of its secrets. The temple not only pre-dates writing by six thousand years, but it predates settled human life. However, the most important thing this temple and its religion have shown us is that having a sense of something sacred in ourselves first and then worshiping what is considered sacred is a primitive impulse which preceded civilised life as we know it.

Over the last three thousand years or so, the traditional religions attempted to displace Pagan practices – these were based on the natural seasons and had sophisticated customs – in order to gain supremacy by claiming to be the authority on the soul, the atman, the Self. Imagine for a moment that all the religions of the modern era suddenly disappeared. We would be left with the winter and summer solstices and the two equinoxes, and they would still weave their magic. Just how do they do it, and where in us does it resonate so profoundly?

Religions can be seen as externalised representations of man's inner spiritual sense, and, basically, there are two types of religion. The western religions, such as Christianity, Islam and Judaism, look outwards (extraverted) to the outside world for how we relate to each other and to God; and, essentially, prayer and worship are community based. However, the religions of the east, like Hinduism and Buddhism, encourage looking inwards (introverted) to find liberation or enlightenment by the practice of meditation and detachment.

For many people today the sense of spirituality is no longer based on doctrinal-based, organised religions. And so, it may be useful to look at what was around before organised religions seized the most central aspects of previous forms of worship to opportunistically promote themselves. Pagans respected the Earth and, like Native American Indians, Aboriginals and Maoris, they believed that certain types of places like hills and rivers had spirits and were sacred. We know that fire was first used as long ago as 957,000 AD, and ancient Celtic Pagans had four fire festivals a year, which they still celebrate. So why are the religions which displaced the more Paganistic religions now in decline themselves? It is worth looking at why they have declined and what has at tried to replace them.

Religions seek to explain all of creation, and seek to be all-giving, all-loving and, in times of desolation, despair, grief and pain, the source of hope. But their keepers decided that religious knowledge and power needed protecting – sometimes by whatever means – and that is their major fault, which reveals their darker side. Essentially, religion encourages differences and separatism in the form of neighborhood, national and global tribalism, which has bought out religion's darkest side, resulting in some of the most terrible wars. Perhaps man's consciousness and knowledge have acquired wisdom, for we now see that we are actually more similar than different. The need for unification of mankind may be part of the reason why so many people are turning away from any thinking which encourages people to separate into opposing groups, each arrogantly claiming an exclusive right to truth.

Until recently, many people looked to priests of organised religions for the answers to problems of the spirit or soul. But trust and belief in these religions and their local religious leaders has almost gone. This has partly been due to the negative picture the media has given of religious organisations. For many Christians, Buddhists, Jews and Muslims, the slaughter of thousands of innocent people in recent wars, even as their religions propagate the messages of 'thou shalt not kill' and 'love thy neighbor', has confirmed to many that these rules of conduct are hypocritical.

To claim a monopoly on truth could be seen as arrogant exclusiveness and also as extraordinarily irrational. Perhaps this is why atheists believe all religions to be untrue. This trend of rational assessment of faith based belief systems may also partly explain why interest in religions has recently drastically fallen. At the same time, religion has also been eclipsed by seemingly brighter ideas on the horizon. The current unpopularity of many organised religions indicates that we may have lost a lot of our beliefs which we acquired over thousands of years. But are they really lost?

For the last hundred years there have been surges of interest in other ways to understand the soul, the atman, the Self, first in psychoanalysis and then in the more recent schools of psychology and psychotherapy. From Maslow who emphasized self actualisation, and Assagioli who emphasized psychosynthesis to Jung who emphasized individuation, there is little doubt they can help us to understand ourselves.

The last psychological attempt to understand the soul was a form of psychology called Transpersonal Psychology. It is an attempt at personal transcendence, also known in psychology as the fourth force. It attempts to go beyond the ego, or the mind, and is concerned with the journey of man's soul. It is an umbrella term for a spectrum of approaches to understand and know the soul, the atman, the Self, and includes psychoanalysis, humanistic psychology and psychosynthesis.

But it also includes various types of meditation and yoga, and the contemplative aspects of Buddhism and Hinduism, and Sufi, Christian and Judaic mysticism.

Modern psychology has shown us that spiritual experience may involve meditation, mindfulness, contemplation, just being, chanting, singing or prayer. Spirituality can also involve participation in rituals, as well as the celebration of festivals, which may include periods of abstinence or indulgence. We understand that spirituality may not necessarily involve a belief in supernatural gods or goddesses. It may simply be a person's own path, or absence of one. But even this has to a large extent been left behind or ignored, and has been superseded by interest in New Age astrology, music and technology.

Scientists and researchers have looked with extraordinary telescopes, visualizing the ancient light in our skies, to see if the hand of a maker of the universe can be identified in its creation process. Science has also used vast machines, like the Hadron Collider, to try and single out and identify the smallest God particle. One thing which both instruments highlight is that man's search in understanding his relationship to the wider universe and to God is still external. Curiously, mankind is still using his most modern tools to understand himself and understand God, forgetting that they are just tools, just as the tools he used to build Stonehenge. Although these modern tools explore things in more detail, they are still only exploring the external world, not the internal world, and cannot be thought of as progress. Churches and temples have been slowly emptying over the last hundred years, and many have been bulldozed or converted for other use. In the remaining ones, where congregations once numbered in their hundreds, there are now frequently less than half a dozen people at their main services. Their time has come and gone rather like the finite life of a man. God does not return to a church he has left; and neither does man. Religions have come and gone, and the major ones have gone past their peak. Religion cannot be resuscitated.

For a time, it looked like psychology, in the form of psychoanalysis and therapy, would replace religions, but this has not been the case. Belief in something greater than man, that can save mankind, currently seems to be firmly in the hands of technology. It seems for the moment as if technology is modern man's religion.

In the early 1980s I was privileged to be asked by Rank Xerox to look at the effects of future technology on levels of stress in women. I asked John Heron, who was an avant-garde research psychologist, to work with me. Xerox was using the Xerox Star, which was the first machine of its kind to incorporate various technologies that have become standard in all personal computers today. The Star had window-based graphical display, bitmapped display, a mouse, icons, folders, file servers, print servers, Ethernet networking and e-mail. Our research was very thorough, and we found no adverse effects of the new future technology.

However, this was very early on, when very few people even knew about this technology, and we were not looking at the extent to which people, as they do now, would interact with that technology. Today a person may use a laptop, smart-phone, wrist watch, eyeglasses, contact lenses or heads up display to communicate with hundreds to millions of people by e-mail, Facebook, Twitter, podcasts or other electronic formats. They may use these through all waking hours, at work, in education, at home, in intimate relationships, for sex, for religion, for entertainment, as leisure, as therapy or in criminal ways.

With these devices a funeral can be relayed to absent relatives who may not be able to travel, wherever they may be in the world. And although this may be seen as development, it comes with the loss of many things and can give only a second rate reality to life. A person has not travelled and thought about the journey to the deceased and loved ones. You cannot meet, greet and hold the people in mourning and give them your warmth. You cannot share the experience of being there as much as you cannot smell the flowers or be with the deceased on their last journey. You cannot throw that rose onto the coffin.

The loss of basic experiences is a serious challenge and a threat to mankind, because, by permitting the entry of technology into our lives to help us we may have removed experiences; and this reduces not only our understanding but also our feelings about people, places and things. It may be making us behave less autonomously and more like automated machines.

In their advanced training, members of the armed forces, such as air crew and special forces, who are at the highest risk of falling into enemy hands, have to re-learn basic survival skills, such as how to find water, food and shelter, and learn to live whilst hiding and evading capture. To primitive man the use of these skills were automatic, everyday experiences. In the world's most advanced countries air crew and Special Forces now have to spend weeks learning these essential skills on specialist Survival, Escape, Resistance and Escape (SERE) courses. That it is only the most advanced countries that have to do this is indicative of the fact that technological advance is often accompanied by a loss of fundamental self-reliance.

It is common to overindulge in the use of technology to the point of binge use. We are already at a point where technology substitutes everyday experiences. We may have to go on specialised courses to learn how to be in a room with family or friends for prolonged periods without resorting to technology. We might have to go on courses to learn how to be able to have a meaningful intimate relationship. We may have to go on courses to learn how to spend leisure time without technology so that we are relaxed by it and psychologically decompressed. Perhaps this is why mindfulness courses are currently so popular.

If we have to go back to classes to re-learn how to be friends, how to relate to people, how to be gentle and kind and how to enjoy life, then what have we become? We just haven't realised the position we are in because the consequences have not been seen or felt on a large enough scale nor made a significant impact to make us want to do something about it.

Technology, in the form of simple tools, originally helped man to survive. A rock could help fight off an assailant, whether another man or a beast. A rock could also be used in the form of an arrowhead to kill an animal for food. A rock could be used to cut wood for a timber shelter. Technology might one day be able transport us to distant planets to set up new civilisations. It may even let us preserve the ways our brains think in a memory device. But it won't be able to preserve our sense consciousness of the soul, the atman, the Self or God.

Early conclusions about the worship at the Gobekli Tepe temple seem to indicate that searching for the sacred and then worshiping it is a primitive impulse, which seems to have preceded civilised life as we know it. Whenever man first had this sense of the soul, the atman, the Self or God it was due to a sense of something else – the sacred – other than himself, which he perceived as more important and more powerful. What made him have this sense of the sacred? Was it something about the Sun or the Earth, about an event, or just an awareness, which came with the consciousness of self that he alone had in the animal kingdom?

It could be argued that if the Sun, the Earth or an event initially prompted him to have this sense of the sacred, then it would be easy to understand how man projected his sense of the sacred externally onto whatever it was that had prompted him, creating the idea of a Heavenly God, which he then worshiped and which evolved into a belief system. Identification with and devotion to the sun or a holy site can take man deep into the soul, the atman, the Self, producing a profound sense of the self in relation to others and the wider world. This may have enabled man to see the transience and futility of his ego. This dynamic is possibly the essence of the origins of spirituality.

For this identification with the sun or a holy site to happen, man had to realise something sacred in himself – the soul, the atman, the Self – which he thinks he sees in the sun or in the holy site. From here man could have conjured up rituals to support his belief in identity of the sacred. From here any religious belief system could have begun, whether it was the religious worship at Gobekli Tepe, Paganism or Aboriginal beliefs. The point is that this would mean that the origins of the sacred or of religious belief may have been through projection, or externalisation, of one's soul, the atman, the Self.

Perhaps, whatever the origin of the prompt that gave him his inner sense of the sacred, man chose to separate it from himself and see it externally rather than as originating from inside him. The worship at the Gobekli Tepe temple seems to evince this externalisation. This may have been because it was perceived as easier to see this inner sense in a physical form than to seek it as an amorphous inner sense. It may be that it took many more millennia for Buddhism and Hinduism to consider that the origins of the sacred could be within.

We seem to have an inner, intuitive sense of what we could be, and, maybe, because this has not been met, we are disappointed and left searching. If happiness is to be found inside, then looking outwards will lead to a never ending search because it is in the wrong direction. Man follows the easier path of least resistance and projects his sense of the sacred externally, but if he could recognise it as a projection, he could blank it out. And this might set him on the path to discover the true relationship between his mind and his inner self. He might see that the mind, though powerful and clever, can be deceptive and project the needs of the soul, the atman, the Self externally. Maybe man's error has been to rely on the mind using external means to make him happy and, consequently, feeding the ego's desires whilst ignoring food for the soul, the atman, the Self.

Maybe the reason why none of man's tools seem to have worked and made him truly happy is that he chose to develop his mind at the expense of the soul, the atman, the Self, the sacred. Perhaps, following the desires of the mind to use tools to externally understand the sacred has for millennia been an unfortunate delusional movement away from connecting with his soul, the atman, the Self. Maybe we need to challenge the belief that happiness lies outside of us. If we accept our externalised culture, then to turn around and go inwards, or to be internalised, seems to go against the grain of modern society's view of man. To be a nerd, a geek, a loner or a recluse is generally regarded as eccentric behaviour. Perhaps these types of people have already dropped out and care not what others think about them, simply because they are happy with themselves. Although they appear to be at odds with the normal, modern society may have got them completely wrong. After all, these odd people are happy in themselves, which is exactly what we actually want to be.

It seems that society does not want us to nurture ourselves in this way and instead wants us to conform and be compliant so that we can be organised and civilised. Part of the solution lies in understanding that we are much more divergent than we imagine, that no single answer is going to fit all, and that all answers are not going to fit a single person.

So, where do we go next? If religion, science, astrology, psychology, psychoanalysis, self actualisation, psychosynthesis, individuation, transpersonal psychology, science and technology have failed to come up with a reasonable answer, then it seems that, although all of these have been part of an extraordinary journey or process, they have not been progress at all but have merely been a lesson in finding out what doesn't make us happy. So where should we go now?

Spirituality refers to the ultimate reality of a person's inner path which consists of the deepest values by which we live and feel connected to others, the wider world and the Universe. For a very long time man has identified his sense of his soul, the atman, the Self with external objects which can actually be observed, primarily the sun but also sacred sites such as mountains. Almost every religion subscribes to this practice. Buddhism has Bodh Gaya in India and Mount Kailash with Hinduism in Tibet. Hinduism has Varanasi and Arunachala in India. Islam has Mecca in Saudi Arabia. Judaism has Mount Sinai in Egypt. Christianity has The Church of the Holy Sepulchre. Paganism has New Grange in Ireland, Maes Howe and the Tomb of the Eagles in Orkney, and Stonehenge in England. In fact every country has its own sacred sites. To name just a few, the Aboriginals have Uluru and Kata Tjuta in Australia; the Maori have Tongariro and Cape Reinga in New Zealand; the Cheyenne - North American Indians - have Bear Butte in South Dakota; and there is Mount Fuji in Japan, Mount

Kilimanjaro in South Africa and the Temple of Delphi in Greece.

Each sacred site would have been designated sacred because of some special feature. Orkney has tombs and stone circles, but these were put there by man in response to the presence of something else there. But what was there in Orkney that made man regard it as a sacred place? Whatever it was is likely to be still there, and I think it is right in front of our eyes, or above them. I think the most likely candidate for making it a sacred place, so that people made stone circles there and buried their dead there, is the Aurora Borealis. This is the spectacular colour-light show which is frequently seen in Orkney.

Our ancestors could not have failed to have noticed the Aurora and would have given it special significance. The Romans called the Aurora the Goddess of Dawn; Shakespeare wrote about it. However, most significantly, five thousand years ago the inhabitants of Orkney were almost certainly not the only people to give the Aurora sacred significance. The South Australian Aboriginal Ngarrindjeri tribe regards the Aurora as the campfires of the spirits in the land of the dead, and the Queensland Aboriginals regard the Aurora as fires through which spirits speak to people. The Aurora could be the reason why the places where it was seen were regarded as sacred.

When we see and wonder at the sunset on the winter solstice or the sunrise on the summer solstice, or walk around a sacred mountain, we seem to witness it as individuals, each person experiencing it differently. But it is still the same moment, the same sun, the same mountain symbolising and mirroring the same soul – the atman, the Self – that exists in all of us.

Man is now very technologically sophisticated and less aware of the importance of the sun and the sacred sites associated with pilgrimages, retreats, meditation and contemplation. He is in danger of being out of touch with his soul, the atman, the Self, the sacred. He is still too externalised in what he perceives as important. To progress forwards is to go back to the basics and see the sun and the sacred sites as a way to begin our search, to use them for pilgrimages, retreats, meditation and contemplation simply to help us to journey inwards.

More than 11,000 years ago, hunter gatherers built large stone temples with elaborately carved, stone pillars, even before they had written language. We have to assume that this was a result of an impulse to seek their sense of God or the Self. Ancient and modern spiritual disciplines recognise this as none other than outward display of a search for the soul, the atman, the Self/God.

Today, what does going back to basics involve in terms of man's impulse to spend time seeking his sense of the Self/God? Maybe it is no different from thousands of years ago. What has changed about man that it should be any different?   All religious denominations are in crisis with dwindling numbers of followers. The ancient Chinese term for 'crisis' has no single word. Instead, it is represented by two symbols: annihilation and opportunity. So, a crisis is a time to choose.

Our planet is also in crisis.   Perhaps the pressures we have put on our planet have been pointing out the way for us all along. We seem to be at least partly to blame for putting the planet into a time of profound crisis by not nurturing it and nearly ruining it. Similarly we have put ourselves into a time of profound crisis by forgetting to nurture our impulse to spend time seeking our sense of the Self/God. In order to turn our crisis away from a destructive path, maybe we have to turn to our planet and pay attention to it, rather than looking for ways to escape it and find an alternative home. Similarly, we might have to look inwards to seek our sense of a Self/ God. If we simply stop using and polluting the planet, to some extent it will start to recover on its own, but this recovery has to be actively managed and some things have to be sacrificed. Our habit of consumerism is central to this. In parallel, is our nurturing of the Self by stopping polluting it with an external view.

The state of our planet and our impulse to spend time seeking our sense of the Self/God have much in common. Whilst we get on with our daily routine, we are not particularly conscious of either of them. In fact most of the time we don't pay much attention to them, because we are usually not in the right state to see the bigger picture and see them in that context. We usually only become concerned about the state of the planet when we see or experience a change in our own weather system or see it on the news. But all the while there is an extremely thin layer of atmosphere around our blue planet.

Likewise, how often do we have the opportunity to be aware of our impulse to spend time seeking our sense of the Self/God. Usually we become aware of our impulse to seek our sense of the Self/God at a time of crisis, such as the death of a loved one. It is then that we see the true bigger picture, and our impulse to seek our sense of the Self/God becomes important for a while.

In the past, probably because there were fewer distractions, people spent a lot more time following the impulse to seek a sense of the Self/God. These days just taking time out seems so difficult. So, just how can we seek our sense of the Self/God? However you approach it, there are only two ways. There is the path of outward devotion to an exterior idea of the Self/God or there is looking inwards. Because outward devotion is focused on a projection of what is inside us, the results have to be the same as looking inwards, provided we recognise it as such. It makes no difference whether it is the sun, a mountain, a guru or a saint which is the externalised projection of the Self/God.

Another aspect of practice is constantly going inwards, or practicing devotion at various times throughout the day. In the past this was most evident in the strictly regulated lifestyle of monks. Glastonbury Abbey in the west of England, which has its origins in the early seventh century and closed in 1539, was, like most ancient Christian sites, almost certainly built on the site of a pre-Christian place of worship. The daily life of the monks was divided into seven Offices, or periods of prayer and worship. In his rule St Benedict said, 'Seven times a day I will give thee praise.'

The day at the Abbey was very rigid in its division.

2.00 am Rise for the Night Office followed by work and study.

5.00 am (Daybreak) Matins. This took place at daybreak and consisted of a series of services throughout the morning, designated by Latin numerals.

6.00 am (Third hour of daybreak) Terce Office followed by work and study.

9.00 am (Sixth hour of daybreak) Sext Office followed by work and study.

12.00 (Noon - the ninth hour) Nones Office. Nones was the central Mass of the day and was timed to be performed at midday, which gives us the word 'noon' (nones) for 12.00 midday. This was followed by lunch which was eaten in silence while the monks were read to from the Bible or other book of instruction. This was followed by a period of work.

6.00 pm Vespers as the working day draws to a close.

9.00 pm Compline, the evening office, after which the

monks retired to bed.

This harsh daily routine was probably developed to heighten the monks' concentration on the spiritual and enable them to experience man's impulse to spend time seeking his sense of the Self/God. The only constant in their fragmented days and nights, with probably a maximum of three to four hours sleep, was the awareness of the Self/God.

Laymen were also frequently reminded of man's impulse to spend time seeking his sense of the Self/God. In some monastic and contemplative communities there is an ancient custom known as The Angelus, which is a good example of how monks and priests expected lay people to follow their practice of regular devotion. The ringing of the Angelus—the triple stroke repeated three times, with a pause between each set of three (a total of nine strokes), is performed three times a day – at six in the morning, at noon and at six in the evening – to remind people to stop their work and to say a devotional prayer. I remember it as a child in the west of Ireland. In Ireland the Angelus bells can still be heard three times a day in some Catholic churches, and it is still broadcast on the national radio and television channel. This early Franciscan monastic tradition was first described in 1263 and is still practiced three times every day in churches in Mexico, the Philippines, the USA, Canada and Germany. The point was to regularly and repeatedly remind people and emphasise the importance of the impulse to spend time seeking a sense of the Self/God.

The common man cannot spend all day engaged in spiritual exercise; he has tasks and daily routines he has to perform, and it is because of his busyness that he needs frequent reminders to seek his sense of the Self/God.

If modern man wants to revitalise his undernourished impulse to seek out his sense of the Self/God, he will need to be reminded to look inwards, or practice devotion several times a day. Although some people practice daily devotion or meditation, a more spontaneous and irregular practice is just as likely to be effective in our daily lives.

Lastly, a retreat to a quiet place of solitude might prompt us to see that we have something that is deeper than just our mind or our ego. In order to see this, we can perform a ritual, visit a sacred place or even watch a solstice. But visits to sacred places and observing wonders are there only to inspire us to look inwards to experience the Self/God and not to turn us into festival or spiritual tourists; although, that might be someone's own particular way of being more in touch with their sense of the Self/God.

By observing nature we gain insight into a presence of something in our selves other than the mind, a sense of the sacred Self/God. It may be the sight of stars, the sound of the wind, the presence of a new baby, experiencing the threat of our own death, or the actual death and disappearance of a child, a friend or a wise person. We wonder in awe, transfixed, at nature and life's events.

When we ask about the origins of our sense of the sacred Self/God, if the question comes from the mind, then the answer comes from the mind and can only consist of thinking, which is limited by the capacity of the mind for logical reasoning. It seems the mind cannot understand certain insights which we experience, because the mind simply lacks the capacity to do so. Frustrating though it is to become conscious of the limitation of thinking, this also shows us our dependency on thinking. Try as we may to answer the question of our sense of something greater than just our thinking, using the disciplines of philosophy, religion, psychology, physics and mathematics, they all lack the competence to answer the question. They fail, because they use thinking to try and explain a consciousness of something which is not governed by thought.

Whilst the mind fails in this, art seems to be a better form of expression of the Self/God. Most artists know that all art is plagiarism, but maybe what is really being plagiarized is the sense of being transfixed in consciousness, where our sense of the sacred Self/God actually originates.

In evolutionary terms, there is probably nothing new about standing transfixed by natural wonders or phenomena and, thereby, taking one further step in our search for the sacred, just like in the Stone Age. Today we are still confronted with our sense of being, consciousness and happiness. What is different now is that few go to that place of silence.

It seems man has left the inner place of the origin of the sacred Self/God, preferring instead to think intellectually about it at the expense of being able to get back there. The use of myth and symbol have helped stem the tide of intellectualism, but the answer we are looking for isn't in merely thinking or reading about it.

Orkney is a sacred place of extraordinary stillness which enables us to see our inner silence. Maybe the answer to the secret is in going to that place of silence and just being our true self ... being still.

13616430R00172

Printed in Poland
by Amazon Fulfillment
Poland Sp. z o.o., Wrocław